Defending God

Defending God

Biblical Responses to the Problem of Evil

JAMES L. CRENSHAW

OXFORD
UNIVERSITY PRESS

2005

OXFORD
UNIVERSITY PRESS

Oxford University Press, Inc., publishes works that further
Oxford University's objective of excellence
in research, scholarship, and education.

Oxford   New York
Auckland   Cape Town   Dar es Salaam   Hong Kong   Karachi
Kuala Lumpur   Madrid   Melbourne   Mexico City   Nairobi
New Delhi   Shanghai   Taipei   Toronto

With offices in
Argentina   Austria   Brazil   Chile   Czech Republic   France   Greece
Guatemala   Hungary   Italy   Japan   Poland   Portugal   Singapore
South Korea   Switzerland   Thailand   Turkey   Ukraine   Vietnam

Published by Oxford University Press, Inc.
198 Madison Avenue, New York, New York 10016

www.oup.com

Oxford is a registered trademark of Oxford University Press

Library of Congress Cataloging-in-Publication Data
Crenshaw, James L.
Defending God: biblical responses to the problem of evil / James L. Crenshaw.
    p. cm.
Includes bibliographical references and index.
ISBN-13 978-0-19-514002-6
ISBN 0-19-514002-8
1. Theodicy—Biblical teaching.   2. Good and evil—Biblical teaching.   3. Bible. O.T.—
Criticism, interpretation, etc.   I. Title.
BS1199 .T44C74 2004
231'.8—dc22   2004011803

9 8 7 6 5 4 3

Printed in the United States of America
on acid-free paper

To my students

Estrangement
(Genesis 22:1–19)

The familiar voice that bids me
 go to an unknown mountain
pierces my heart but stays the knife
 in a trembling hand.

The deed's undone,
 yet the unspeakable lingers
between me and Sarah,
 Isaac and his dad,
the three of us and that voice,
 suddenly alien.

James L. Crenshaw
29 March 2000

Preface

You do not find the Grail, the Grail finds you.
Vous ne trouvez pas le Saint Graal, c'est le Saint Graal qui vous
trouve.

—Sir Leigh Teabing in *The Da Vinci Code*

I did not find theodicy. It found me as a child of four when my father died, leaving a widow with four small children in rural South Carolina in the wake of the Great Depression. My mother found comfort in Rom 8:28, Paul's promise that God works in all things to bring about good for those who love him. From that day in 1939 until today, she has continued to trust those words. That early encounter with one of life's anomalies sensitized me to similar enigmas in society at large and inaugurated an agenda that has lasted throughout my professional career.

My 1964 Ph.D. dissertation was published in revised form eleven years later under the title *Hymnic Affirmation of Divine Justice: The Doxologies of Amos and Related Texts in the Old Testament* (1975). Various articles dealing with theodicy followed, as well as an edited book, *Theodicy in the Old Testament* (1983), with an introduction on the shift from theodicy to anthropodicy. A year later came *A Whirlpool of Torment: Israelite Traditions of God as an Oppressive Presence* (1984). In 1994 when Walter Brueggemann wrote an article for *Religious Studies Review* assessing my contribution to the study of the Old Testament ("James L. Crenshaw: Faith Lingering at the Edge,"

29:103–10), he stressed theodicy as my primary interest. A recent Festschrift concurred: *Shall Not the Judge of All the Earth Do What Is Right? Studies on the Nature of God in Tribute to James L. Crenshaw*, ed. David Penchansky and Paul L. Redditt (2000).

The present volume is therefore the fruit of a lifetime of research. Several discrete units in the book have been presented at professional meetings. For example, the material on theodicy in the psalms of Asaph was a plenary address at the national meeting of the Catholic Biblical Association in Los Angeles. It was also presented in New Haven, Connecticut, at a meeting of the Colloquium for Biblical Research. Portions of the material on theodicy in prophetic literature were published in *Theodicy in the World of the Bible*, ed. Antti Laato and Johannes C. de Moor (2003), 236–55. The first part of the analysis of the story of Abraham's intercession for Sodom and Gomorrah appeared in *God in the Fray: A Tribute to Walter Brueggemann*, ed. Tod Linafelt and Timothy K. Beal (1998), and two sections in the final chapter appeared in journals: "The Reification of Divine Evil," *Perspectives in Religious Studies* 28 (2001): 327–32 and "Some Reflections on the Book of Job," *Review and Expositor* 99 (2002): 589–95. I am grateful to the publishers for granting permission to reprint this material in revised form.

Four people have given valuable assistance in the preparation of the manuscript for publication. Above all, Carol Shoun has turned my prose into a more reader-friendly discussion of complex topics. Her remarkable eye for felicitous expression, painstaking checking of details, and generosity are a source of admiration. Matthew R. Schlimm checked the Hebrew transliterations for accuracy and prepared the index. As usual, Gail Chappell entered my handwritten text into the computer, saving me much time and energy. My colleague Ellen Davis read the introduction and the first three chapters, offering helpful suggestions in a number of places. I wish to thank them for making this book better than it would otherwise have been.

Over the years I have learned much from my students, who have enriched my life beyond words. By dedicating this book to them I wish to acknowledge my debt and my appreciation.

Contents

Defending God

Introduction

How can you say that the glass is half full when I can clearly see
that it is half empty?

—Popular saying

In Bertolt Brecht's play *The Good Woman of Setzuan*, the generosity
of the female shop owner threatens to impoverish her, necessitating
a stern male presence to secure the tiny shop from bankruptcy. The
woman's compassion toward needy customers—and greedy ones as
well—eventually depletes the store's entire stock, whereas the man's
severity puts the business back in the black. Readers do not have to
endorse Brecht's identification of the qualities of justice and mercy
as male and female, respectively, to appreciate his dramatization of
the near impossibility of keeping them in harmonious relationship.

Every civilized society endeavors to honor these competing demands to treat individuals justly and to act mercifully toward those
in need. And when this desideratum is projected on the heavens, as
the German philosopher Ludwig Feuerbach insisted was true of religion, God (or the gods) is expected to present a perfect balance.[1] Yet
each quality, by its very nature, violates the other. Strict justice requires that I get what I deserve, no more and no less. Mercy allows
my just deserts to be set aside, my transgressions overlooked or forgiven. How can the deity perfectly embody both?

In the Bible the classic text that expresses the tension between

justice and mercy within God is Exod 34:6–7, which has the deity proclaim the
various divine attributes to Moses:

> YHWH, YHWH, a God merciful and gracious,
>   slow to anger, and abounding in steadfast love
>   and faithfulness,
>   keeping steadfast love for the thousandth generation,
>   forgiving iniquity, transgression, and sin,
>   yet by no means clearing the guilty,
>   but visiting the iniquity of the parents
>   upon the children
>   and the children's children,
>   to the third and fourth generation.[2]

By virtue of the initial position and the number of attributes related to
compassion, the emphasis of this early confession seems to fall on mercy. One
could argue, however, that the larger context and the lingering repercussions
of the final attribute—an exacting punishment for every offense—shift the
emphasis to the side of justice. The struggle to balance these qualities of justice
and mercy in describing God's interaction with a covenanted people permeates
much of the Bible—indeed, exposing a conflict within the soul of Israel. This
book tells the story of that difficult struggle.

Opposing Views of Reality

We begin by considering two psalms that highlight the sharp differences in
Israel's descriptions of the deity's conduct, differences that reflect the dissonance within the covenant people's understanding—and experience—of reality itself.

Divine Benevolence: Psalm 104

> Bless YHWH, O my soul.
>   YHWH my God, you are exceedingly great.
> You are clothed in honor and majesty.
> He is the one wrapping himself in light as a garment,
>   spreading out the heavens as a tent,
>   laying the beams of his chambers in the waters,
>   making clouds his chariot,

> riding on the wings of the wind,
> making the winds messengers,
> fire and flame his ministers. (Ps 104:1–4)

Psalm 104 is a hymn of exuberant praise, a relative anomaly within the Psalter, where complaint rises to YHWH far more often than praise.[3] We see in this psalm a reflection of the author's deep embeddedness in the larger cultural environment, particularly Egyptian ways of thinking—again, a relative anomaly. The psalm shares with the Egyptian Hymn to the Aten[4] an exhilaration over the beauty of the universe and an appreciation for the order of nature that approaches Leibniz's frequently parodied formulation, "the best of all possible worlds."

The author of Psalm 104 looks beyond the tiny space occupied by humans. His[5] sweeping survey extends to all creatures and, more importantly, to their creator. Indeed, his sole point in mentioning a variety of animals and their thumb-endowed rival is to laud divine benevolence and wisdom. The graphic depiction of YHWH combines imagery from the worship of Baal, the Canaanite deity of the storm ("the rider of the clouds"),[6] and solar worship, widespread in the ancient Near East ("clothed in light," "messengers of fire").[7]

Readers who are familiar with ancient stories of creation from Egypt, Canaan, and Mesopotamia may be surprised by the near absence in Psalm 104 of the myth of a cosmic battle between the creator and personified chaos.[8] Israelites were certainly aware of this way of describing the establishment of the viable order that is essential to human existence and a national state, as is abundantly evident in other biblical texts (Ps 89:10–11; Isa 25:6–8, 27:1, 45:5–7, 51:9–16; Job 38:8–11, 40:25–32). In any event, the transformation of the monster Leviathan into a playful creature of the sea (v 26) and the comment about restricting the ravenous appetite of the sea's waves (vv 6–9) fit smoothly into the mythic tradition. The muted language about the sea can easily be understood as a faint echo of the old story of the flood.

Just as the priestly story of creation in Gen 1:1–2:4a speaks of a creator's sense of satisfaction—indeed, pride—over the result of divine speech ("Let there be"), Ps 104:13 has the earth mirror that contentment. All creatures who live on this good earth enjoy its bounty: water for quenching thirst, food for assuaging hunger, places of refuge for resting securely. Although the psalmist acknowledges the predatory action of lions during the night, the consequence of this behavior is construed as divine gift. Birds sing in the branches of trees and build their nests there, wild goats leap on the sides of mountains, rabbits hide among the rocks, and all of these creatures measure their actions by the divine markers of time: sun and moon, day and night.

In two ways the psalm singles out human beings: first, to concede that they do not live by bread alone, if that is what the reference to happiness implies; second, to acknowledge that, unlike other animals, they must imitate YHWH in transforming a fixed state into something more beneficial—seed into grain and grain into bread.[9] In this brief vignette (vv 14–15), three foods are mentioned: wine for happiness, oil for a luminous countenance, and bread for strength.[10]

If the psalmist has stood open-mouthed while observing the ordered creation within easy reach, he seems almost overwhelmed at the thought of the marvelous array of underwater creatures far below passing ships. Small wonder that this section begins with an exclamation of praise for YHWH's wisdom (v 24), a point that eases somewhat the angst aroused by utter dependence on YHWH's sustaining care and the sober reminder of finitude in v 29: "Take back their breath and they die; to dust they return." The suggestion that the deity may hide his face and take back the breath of life elicits no utterance of protest. Death may come, but life persists as YHWH continues to renew creation.

Such a litany of praise has as its primary purpose to foster in YHWH a strong inclination to rejoice in a finely tuned universe. Here we come upon an audacious concept: *imitatio dei* has given rise to the idea of God's imitation of a human being, the psalmist functioning as an example for the deity. The summons to praise YHWH serves that end, for Israel's God was thought to be enthroned on praises (Ps 22:4). In this context of spontaneous praise, however, the first half of the final verse sounds a note of discord. Suddenly there arises an urgent request for the extirpation of the wicked, who naturally do not belong in the idyllic world just described. The poet refuses to speculate about the manner in which these evil ones have surfaced or to blame YHWH for their disturbing presence. True, they are an annoyance, but their activity in no way negates what has gone before. Their removal is conveniently placed in the capable hands of the creator. No more need be said, save a final "Bless YHWH, O my soul. Praise YHWH!"

A kindred feeling of adoration for the solar deity fills the Egyptian Hymn to the Aten:

> Splendid you rise in heaven's lightland,
> O living Aten, creator of life! . . .
> You fill every land with your beauty.
> You are beauteous, great, radiant,
> High over every land;
> Your rays embrace the lands . . .

Though one sees you, your strides are unseen . . .
Earth brightens when you dawn in lightland . . .
The entire land sets out to work,
All beasts browse on their herbs;
Trees, herbs are sprouting,
Birds fly from their nests . . .
Ships fare north, fare south as well,
Roads lie open when you rise;
The fish in the river dart before you,
Your rays are in the midst of the sea . . .
When the chick in the egg speaks in the shell
you give him breath within to sustain him . . .
O sole God beside whom there is none! . . .
All peoples . . . you supply their needs . . .
You set every man in his place,
You supply their needs;
Everyone has his food,
His lifetime is counted. . . .

Lichtheim, *Ancient Egyptian Literature*

Here we find an aesthetic appreciation for the beauty that unfolds everywhere as the sun emerges each morning but also a warm testimonial to an indwelling by the deity, a felt presence within the heart. The cognitive dimension is not excluded, for the poet looks upon the god as a mentor giving instruction in the divine ways. Nor is the mysterious dimension of reality overlooked, here illustrated by a fetus in the womb and a chick in its shell, each growing beyond human ken and in due time emerging from its place of gestation. The observant poet makes sociological and anthropological distinctions, noting that the creator has given life to different ethnic groups and languages.

The deep piety that infuses this Egyptian hymn is little diminished by the use to which it was originally put: royal worship. In time, the poem came to be recited by a courtier in the ruler's behalf, but even then the sentiment was probably widely felt among the pharaoh's subjects. Like Psalm 104, the Hymn to the Aten views the universe through a lens of sheer adoration. The creator has prepared a well-ordered place for all living creatures, one that makes life both possible and pleasant. In such a world, the proper human response is wonder and praise. Anything short of that marks one as an ingrate.

Divine Betrayal: Psalm 77

We turn now to another psalm, 77, and to one verse in particular:

> I think of God, and I moan;
> I meditate, and my spirit faints. (Ps 77:4)[11]

The contrast between this expression of intense agony at the very thought of God and Psalm 104's exuberant praise could hardly be sharper. What makes the difference? To answer this question, it is necessary to examine the mournful sentiment in context.

The first thing to note is the topic being brought to God's attention in this prayerful lament: a perceived sense of divine betrayal. Echoes of Exod 34:6–7 resound in the second of four brief stanzas (vv 5–10).[12] The psalmist poses a fundamental question about YHWH's trustworthiness, which has come under close scrutiny because of present circumstances.

That interrogative stance is bold and unrelenting, as one query after another emphasizes the gaping disparity between divine promises and reality here and now. The psalmist inquires about the fragility of God's memory and the permanence of divine affections. Instead of experiencing God's steadfast love and compassion, he can think only of having been rejected and forgotten. More importantly, he wonders how long this rejection will last. A single conclusion presses itself on the poet: "And I say, 'It is my grief that the right hand of the Most High has changed'" (v 11).

Deep reflection on the divine attributes has brought nothing but distress in this instance. Cognitive dissonance has suddenly arisen in the absence of convincing proof that a cherished creed corresponds to reality. The psalmist feels trapped, caught in the hiatus between times of old and the immediate present. He cannot forget, something YHWH appears ready to do. Worse still, the troubled poet believes that God prevents sleep, permanently propping his eyelids open (v 5). Counting sheep will bring no rest for this troubled soul.

Such a radical change in the deity would elicit little surprise if the poet had betrayed YHWH, but this has not happened. His prayer is pure or, at the very least, has been carefully examined. Moreover, that prayer is both sincere and constant, according to his testimony in the first stanza (vv 2–4). The syntax suggests something approaching inarticulate groaning, a true match for the content. If praying without ceasing counts in the heavenly domain, the psalmist has earned a positive hearing. Still, no comfort arrives for the dejected worshiper.

The poet has left no clues that would assist in solving the mystery that triggered his distress. Had he done so, the usefulness of the psalm in public worship would have been seriously impaired. Its present form invites other Israelites to join in the prayer for relief regardless of the specific occasion for religious doubt. The possibilities are limitless: sickness, drought, invasion by enemies, humiliation, bereavement, and so on—anything that renders an individual vulnerable. The poet, in his precarious situation, believed that God would bring comfort as promised in revered tradition. But instead of the expected comfort, more grief has arrived, and the injustice of his suffering has issued in a variant of the most poignant cry of all: "My God, my God, why have you forsaken me?" Sadly, the psalmist is bathed in neither justice nor mercy.

Like virtually all laments in the book of Psalms, this one does not end on such a dismal note. Somehow the psalmist climbs out of the pit and thanks God for delivering him from Sheol's clutches. The third stanza (vv 11–16) reflects on YHWH's wonders, echoing the appellative used by the mysterious angel when appearing to Samson's mother and father (Judg 13:18).[13] This epithet, "one who does wonders," becomes a fixture in hymnic praise of YHWH. Stanza four (vv 17–21) combines the myth of the conflict between a creator deity and chaos with the story of the exodus, which was also furnished with elaborate mythic features. A single statement stands out—"yet your footprints were unseen" (v 20b)—recalling an observation in the Hymn to the Aten that the solar deity's strides were invisible to the naked eye.[14]

The structure of this psalm—two stanzas that describe the poet's agony followed by two stanzas that extol YHWH for gracious activity in history and in nature—accentuates its complex narrative style.[15] The initial stanza consists entirely of a self-referential account; this reporting of the poet's deepest feelings continues in stanza 2 except for the introductory accusation hurled at God ("You keep my eyelids from closing; I am so troubled that I cannot speak," v 5). Direct address returns in the last two stanzas, which weave together narrative and prayer, third person and second, resulting in an intricate verbal tapestry that traces the contours of the psalmist's soul.[16]

The hymnic resolution of the poet's disquiet is not without ambiguity. First, the appeal to YHWH's wondrous feats succeeds only by comparison with alternative gods, who, although unmentioned, lurk in the shadows. In contrast to them, YHWH works wonders; the signal event, the freeing of slaves from bondage in Egypt, attests to the deity's greatness and holiness.[17] Second, the majestic display of meteorological might seems remote from what is required at the moment: comfort in the form of fidelity to creedal assurances. The final verse, which refers to YHWH's leadership of a flock, assisted by Moses and

Aaron, is often thought to be a later addition to provide this need.[18] The verse occupies a wholly different semantic realm than the description of storms and earthquakes that precedes.[19]

Like Tevye in *Fiddler on the Roof*, the psalmist has difficulty comprehending God's conduct but goes directly to the source of the problem, speaking *to* the troubler of Israel, not just about him. The biblical poet is caught in the tension that arises from deferred justice. His pain is exacerbated by memory, which must struggle to come to grips with events that have become inflated through repeated telling. His experience resembles that of Gideon, the warrior-judge, who exclaims when greeted by an angel with the assurance that YHWH is with him: "But sir, if YHWH is with us, why then has all this happened to us? And where are all his wonderful deeds that our ancestors recounted to us, saying, 'Did not YHWH bring us up from Egypt?' But now YHWH has cast us off, and given us into the hand of Midian" (Judg 6:13).

Ceremonial celebrations of a deity's uniqueness and mighty acts function like a two-edged sword, cutting both ways. People who have experienced what they understand to be a miracle naturally tell that story, which takes on larger dimensions with each telling. In this way they demonstrate true devotion; they cannot be faulted, for love often exaggerates, and through the eyes of love, the statement may even be perceived as true. When caught up in rhetorical flourish, prophets such as the great exilic poet who composed Isaiah 40–55 often make extreme promises that cannot possibly accord with reality: "I will open streams on the hillside and fountains in the middle of valleys; I will transform the desert into ponds, the parched land into springs" (Isa 41:18). When such expectations are taken with a degree of literalness, the resulting anguish is neither surprising nor easily expunged.[20]

The psalmist has given intellectual assent to the divine attributes as heralded in Exod 34:6–7. Now his world has begun to founder because present circumstances belie such a description of the one at the helm. Frantically, the poet begins to search—the text does not specify the object of this investigation—and he goes directly to the vocabulary of compassion. Instead of lovingkindness, favor, grace extending for generations, he contemplates being spurned by YHWH, who has closed the portals of blessing.

At issue here is change. God has shown a different face from that lovingly painted in the old creed. The benevolent smile, dominant in that portrait, has been replaced by a forbidding frown. This is the age-old dilemma. What have I done to deserve such harsh treatment? The psalmist wastes little time on such a self-centered response.[21] Instead, he proceeds to the problem without delay. God has changed for some unknown reason. That much is certain. What is not known concerns him most. How long will this new countenance prevail?

The poignancy of the psalm is deepened by contrasting emotions: voiced complaints and inarticulate moans, sleepless agitation and anguished silence, accusatory questions and self-reproach. Such display of human emotion fails to move the deity to pity. God remains in hiding,[22] even when the poet reaffirms traditional belief. In light of the penetrating questions about YHWH's constancy, one wonders how much comfort can be found in singing hymns that either contradict reality or have little if any relevance to the problem that is bringing so much pain.

Modern readers can readily sympathize with the psalmist, for religious people place considerable value on stability. They cherish traditions, which link the past with the present—and, they fervently hope, the future. Change, in any form, is purchased at a high price. Yet however disconcerting change in liturgy or praxis in general may be, theological innovation is even more vexing, as we saw with the furor over the death of God in the 1960s. The modern controversies over issues such as historical criticism and creationism suggest that believers across the millennia, when faced with a perceived threat to cherished tenets, are much the same. The psalmist has committed himself to tradition as passed along by those he trusts. Now he discovers the inadequacy of the teaching that has shaped his view of YHWH. He can either reject the tradition or reaffirm it in the face of all available evidence. He chooses the latter.

Perhaps an analogy with twentieth-century theology will enable modern readers to grasp the depth of the poet's consternation. During the nineteenth century and the first decade and a half of the twentieth, three fundamental assumptions came to define the religious scene in Germany and, through the influence of German theologians, the United States. The first assumption, belief in progress, arose from discoveries in science, geology, and anthropology, all of which seemed to suggest that European society was advancing toward establishing God's kingdom on earth. The second assumption, optimism, joined forces with this philosophy of history that celebrated human intellectual and moral achievement, seemingly so obvious when Europe was compared with "primitive" societies. The third assumption, continuity, elevated human beings to a position just below God, with whom they managed direct contact through music, art, and poetry. This classic liberalism came crashing down as a result of two world wars and the Holocaust,[23] leaving a void that was soon filled by two opposing views: a reaffirmation of evangelical themes that came to be known as neo-orthodoxy and the rise of militant atheism, at least in language.

The collapse of worldviews produces a crisis of confidence,[24] placing enormous strain on the sustaining power of memory. How can memory continue to nurture the faith and praxis of a religious community when the things that replenish it cease? Like a well that runs dry when the water table falls, memory no longer sustains when its connection with truth—which alone can nurture it—fails.

In certain circumstances, memory actually acts in a negative manner to exacerbate inner turmoil. The psalmist's perplexity increases precisely because he recalls former days when God's smile brought peace. A vivid recollection of a harmonious relationship with YHWH forces the psalmist to consider a radically new understanding of the divine character, an understanding that entails an element of betrayal.[25]

What intrigues me most about this psalm is the thought that meditating on God can cause extreme anguish, like the dark night of the soul experienced by St. John of the Cross and other Christian mystics. Many modern readers share this anguish as a result of zealots' egregious conduct but, regrettably, do not share the mystics' deep trust in God's benevolence. For good reason, a lively debate rages on the subject of religion's inherent worth: has religion done more harm to the human race than good? Almost everyone can cite a litany of woes inflicted on innocents by religious zealots, agreeing with Blaise Pascal that "men never do evil so completely and cheerfully as they do from religious conviction." This excess arises, of course, from the belief that the conduct is pleasing to God. Christianity's hands have been bloodied through the centuries by the "holy" oppression of witches, Jews, gays, heretics, and victims of religious wars. Other religions have their own list of shames—which are better left to their consciences.

It stands to reason that evildoers would extract precious little comfort from thinking about God, for after all they persist in flouting directives for living that entail both gratitude and compassion. They might be expected to laugh in the face of an irrelevant concept or to scorn the prospect of judgment if they even took the time to nod toward a deity. Similarly, atheists would hardly experience chagrin when letting the mind entertain thoughts about a nonbeing, except possibly to become angry over human stupidity, as they might consider theism to be an example. This psalm deals with neither evildoers nor atheists, however. Instead, it treats the innermost reasoning of a person who claims to love YHWH passionately but thinks of that ardor as unreciprocated.[26] This unexpected turn is what makes Psalm 77 so troubling.

A Hermeneutical Dilemma

What contributes to the way an individual looks at the world? Confucius was not far off in locating the answer within the sensory perception itself. Two people may observe the same objects but view them as entirely different, depending on the experiences that have formed their individual outlooks on life. This is particularly apparent when dealing with abstractions like justice and mercy. As in the case of pain, levels of tolerance vary with respect to what may be considered an injustice. Moreover, differing levels of altruism predispose individuals to resist injustice or not and to blame others or self, even if that other is sublime. Dire circumstances at the present moment, therefore, do not always explain one's interpretation of reality. The sum total of past experience, hidden to all but the one involved, shapes what is imagined, spoken, and written.

This concession places readers squarely in a hermeneutical dilemma over which a bitter controversy swirls today: To what extent can one move from text to historical reconstruction?[27] I concur with those who see every text as a fictive construction, the product of imagination. The degree to which what is written corresponds to observable phenomena varies with each written work. Readers are seduced into the world of the imagination by the text's credibility. What takes place in the act of reading? Do we learn more about ourselves than the subject in the text? This fundamental question takes on added significance when we consider rhetorical devices like irony and fantasy. Evolving reading strategies that take cognizance of a given text's polyvalence, its multiple meanings, show much promise, although no single one currently enjoys wide favor. The interpretive approach in the present volume relies heavily on "close reading"[28] but incorporates features of newer forms of literary theory as well.

The preceding interpretation of these two psalms is the result of straight reading, a voluntary suspension of disbelief. This approach may be the most natural, but if we ask questions different from those posed thus far, a more disturbing picture emerges. Less generous readers—or less gullible ones— may be inclined to suspect the poets of manipulation, originally of the deity, but eventually of the human audience as well. The author of Psalm 104 may have been creating a fantasy world, seeking to bolster trust when societal chaos threatened the status quo that had brought him both prestige and wealth. Viewed suspiciously, the composer of Psalm 77 may have been a rogue, presenting an innocent demeanor in an attempt to use the deity for personal gain. By shifting responsibility for the failed relationship from himself to YHWH, this poet sought to avoid popular scorn. Such readings, which imply irony at the very least, and fantasy as well, rely on utilitarian assumptions about the texts.

According to this latter approach to the psalms, the high point of Psalm 104, the hymn about the orderly universe, comes when the presence of the wicked makes a mockery of everything that has gone before. The astute reader knows that evildoers wreak such havoc as to negate all the benefits that accrue from a finely tuned universe. The psalm derives its power from silence and understatement; the wicked make such a clamor that nothing more need be said, particularly when an allusion to death hovers in the immediate background. Similarly, Psalm 77 reaches its height of irony when extolling an inactive deity as one who works wonders and conceding that no one can discern any trace of God's presence during the mythic battle with the seas. Readers who have never known a providential deity—a performer of mighty deeds in their behalf—may find the two hymnic fragments wholly unrealistic, just as those beset on every side by rapacious villains may consider the sunny portrait of divinely instituted harmony an insult to their intelligence.

In this latter reading, the psalmist who complains because the familiar patron deity has suddenly presented a hostile or an indifferent face is guilty of a kind of entitlement thinking. He reasons that virtue on his part entitles him to special treatment from the deity, who has become indebted to the worshiper. The rule of justice, he thinks, requires YHWH to reward a life of morality. Each psalmist considers the deity derelict in administering justice, for the wicked thrive in both environments, ordered and chaotic.

On either reading of the two psalms, a concern for divine justice looms large, as does a longing for the deity to show mercy to the downtrodden. Basking in an extraordinary display of divine benevolence, the initial psalmist invokes God to add a healthy dose of justice for evildoers—or, beset by the wicked, he ridicules the Pollyannas of his day who choose not to see rampant wrongdoing. The author of the second psalm appeals to a pure heart as the basis for YHWH's coming in justice, or he seeks to conceal his own duplicity while praising the deity for manifold deliverances, all the while hoping to benefit from God's mercy.

The qualities of justice and mercy run through the Bible like a red thread. They are intricately woven into the various literary forms that enliven its pages from beginning to end. Because of their significance, they have been attributed to the Israelite God—with painful consequences. Indeed, the unanticipated results of attempting to define the deity with abstract qualities continue to this day.

The Problem

The struggle to comprehend how a supposedly benevolent deity could allow injustice to flourish on earth has taxed the human intellect at least since the beginning of recorded history.[29] The existence of a just and merciful deity should, it seems, preclude evil and suffering, at least horrendous evil and innocent suffering.[30] Belief in God thus requires a convincing explanation for the problem of evil.

The effort to deny evil is just as futile as the effort to deny death.[31] Evil insists on making its unwelcome appearance, bringing in its wake suffering and death. These three basic entities—evil, suffering, and death—are tightly interwoven. The myth of the fall in Genesis 3 brings them into close connection,[32] as does human finitude itself, for creatures of flesh and blood are by nature subject to pain and eventual decay.

Evil is manifested in at least three forms: moral evil, natural evil, and religious evil. Perhaps the simplest definition of moral evil is "doing harm without a redeeming purpose." The qualification "without a redeeming purpose" is necessary, for it takes into consideration instances where temporary harm is done with the goal of bringing healing, as in surgical procedures. Whereas moral evil operates on the horizontal plane, involving fellow human beings, the other two forms of evil, natural and religious, play out in the vertical dimension. Natural evil consists of such things as earthquakes, tornadoes, floods, plagues, and genetic flaws—phenomena attributable to nature or God alone. Although powerless to suppress this form of evil, humans can make it worse through foolish decisions (such as building tall structures over a seismic fault) or unwise choices (such as entering procreative relationships that will pass along genetic flaws).

The third form of evil, more difficult to recognize because of its beguiling features, involves the relationship between individuals and God. Religious evil resides in an inner disposition that has the capacity to pervert authentic response to the holy. Such perversion may take the form of idolatry, which implies worship directed away from God to a pale reflection of the Ultimate. Deceit and pride play major roles in this form of evil. Precisely because of its hidden character, it may do grievous injury to humans who are misled by its apparent goodness. Religious evil is all the more pernicious because it thrives in the human imagination. When unchecked, for whatever cause, it stretches a cloak of secrecy over the heavens, presuming indifference, remoteness, or blindness on the part of God.

Each manifestation of evil achieves its sharpest focus in suffering,[33] which, like prosperity, confronts individuals with a test. The experience of undeserved suffering shapes character—a point the Apostle Paul makes in Rom 5:3–5— disclosing hidden flaws in some and unknown strengths in a few. Its potential for good notwithstanding, such suffering presents a particular challenge for people who believe in a loving creator. Unjust suffering raises serious questions about a deity who is assumed to embody both justice and mercy.

There is another aspect of suffering, however, a divine aspect, that perhaps hints at an answer. The high view of God in Judaism and Christianity generates a daring concept: divine pathos.[34] The biblical God, capable of strong feelings, both positive and negative, understands human suffering firsthand, through his own experience. God himself suffers. Moreover, the deity's suffering is a direct by-product of divine choice—a decision to become involved in the human experiment. Thus suffering, while profoundly human, is rooted in divine mystery.

The Responses

In the ancient world, the mystery of suffering evoked various responses among those who struggled to understand it: suffering was viewed as retributive, disciplinary, revelational, probative, illusory, transitory, or simply incomprehensible.[35] The varying sources of these concepts—jurisprudence, the family, the cult, metallurgy—to mention only the first four, indicate the scope of the problem and the near universal awareness of the existential struggle. First, jurisprudence: the demand for punishment that matches the crime underlies the idea of retribution, a court-enforced measure-for-measure exaction from offenders. Second, the family: parental wielding of the cane, which associates suffering with unpleasant but necessary reinforcement for learning, provides the model for discipline. Third, the cult: religious ritual and liturgical narration draw their extraordinarily evocative power from the assumption that both language and action to some degree reveal the mystery of divine will. Fourth, metallurgy: ore that is extracted from the depths of the earth at enormous risk is subjected to a refining process that separates pure metal from worthless dross. The activity of these courageous risk takers furnishes a useful perspective on a very different cavern, one equally dark and cold, in contrast to the bright fires that are associated with the refining process itself.

The undeniable presence of evil in the world necessitates different responses, depending on whether the universe is considered to be an accident or the product of intentionality. Belief that the vast planetary expanse owes its origin to a creator, together with the conviction that this transcendent being is favorably disposed toward all of creation, becomes problematic when confronted with evil in its various forms. The question asked by Epicurus (c. 300 BCE) expresses the dilemma succinctly: "Whence evil—if there be a God?" A conception of this divine source of life as all-knowing, all-powerful, and all-benevolent encounters difficulty in the face of evil. The presence of evil appears to require dropping at least one of the three attributes. If God lacks full knowledge, neither unlimited power nor a gracious disposition can exclude evil. Absent full power, neither good intentions nor complete knowledge can guarantee a perfect world. The lack of divine goodness opens the door for evil, rendering omniscience and omnipotence irrelevant to humans, except as oppressive awareness.[36]

The need to defend God's justice—that is, to produce a theodicy[37]—varies with individuals. For some, inequities suffered by the innocent constitute the sole justification for questioning the deity's performance at the helm. This variant of the battle cry raised by theologians of liberation, "preferential option for the poor,"[38] points to a generosity of spirit that transcends self-serving dispositions. The differing thresholds at which individuals perceive theodicy as a philosophical problem require an infinitely more complex explanation than is found in simply questioning the faith of those compelled to raise the issue. For some people, at least, theodicy constitutes "a weak link in the chain of a religious approach to life."[39]

Theodicy is also a hierarchical issue, its urgency mounting with each child's pain and reaching a climax with occurrences of mass atrocity. The Bible attends to both of these, although for obvious reasons it focuses on the collapse of the Davidic empire at the hands of Babylonian soldiers and the concomitant burning of the divine dwelling place in Jerusalem. For the earliest Christians, the question from Psalm 22 placed on Jesus' lips—"My God, my God, why have you forsaken me?"—expressed genuine puzzlement about the consequences of faithful obedience, the concern that gave rise to the psalm in the first place. The Apostle Paul shifted the emphasis by asking about the implications of election by God, of primary importance to a religious entity that considered itself newly chosen and grafted to the original vine, Israel. Confidence in a future resurrection empowered Paul to move beyond the psalmist's concern to ask about divine intention itself.

No single issue, however profound, exhausts the pressure points of theodicy in the Scriptures.[40] These explosive concerns include, among others, undeserved suffering, chaotic events that fail to demonstrate divine control, natural calamities, the prosperity of the wicked, anticipated eternal punishment, apparent divine malice, and intellectual bafflement. Such variety suggests that the issues are not peculiar to any single group within society. They command attention from prophet, priest, sage, apocalyptist, and ordinary citizen alike. They appear in prose and poetry, dialogue and monologue, prayer and harangue, oracle and inquiry.

The Approach

What is the best way to approach the study of biblical theodicies? Here, too, we face opposing viewpoints: diachronic and synchronic readings. The utility of tracing the development of different responses to perceived divine injustice has been brilliantly demonstrated, in the case of ancient Egyptian texts, by Antonio Loprieno. He notes a tendency "from the Old Kingdom to the Late Period to gradually shift the focus of theodicean discourse from the cosmic and political aspects of a dichotomy between good and evil ultimately rooted in the very act of divine creation to the problems of the individual experience of evil measured against the background of proper religious behaviour."[41] Such a diachronic approach requires reasonably accurate dating of texts, something lacking in biblical studies because of the accumulation of tradition over decades and centuries.

In studying biblical literature, the synchronic approach therefore seems more promising than its rival, inasmuch as it maps the many different responses to the problem of theodicy over the years, yet without hazarding an evolutionary timeline for their emergence. When the responses are set within a historical continuum with a calamity of almost cosmic proportions—the destruction of the temple in 587 BCE—as its center, we can conjecture the resulting cognitive dissonance among the populace and its leaders. Beyond that singular event, we can assume that the period of extreme persecution of the Judeans by Antiochus around 170 BCE and later Roman atrocities, especially in 70 CE, contributed to the emergence of new ways of dealing with theodicy. Attention to this historical reality will prevent an overemphasis on the individual, as opposed to sociological interests.

The typology that undergirds the following discussion is derived from biblical texts rather than speculative theology or philosophy, despite much overlap among the three areas of analysis. Literature on the problem of evil is extensive, but a comprehensive study of biblical theodicies has yet to appear. The recent monumental volume *Theodicy in the World of the Bible*[42] is a rich repository that in many specifics will supplement the contribution of this volume.

I propose to trace the biblical evidence of the search for a convincing response to the problem of evil and God's perceived injustice. I divide the exploration into three parts: "Spreading the Blame Around," "Redefining God," and "Shifting to the Human Scene." The unifying theme is the abiding tension between justice and mercy, evident in a biblical confession, Exod 34:6–7, and in a well-known midrash that has Abraham remark to God: "If you want a world you will not have justice; if it is justice you want, then there will be no world."[43]

Chapter 1, "The Atheistic Answer: Abandoning the Quest," examines a little-used response in the biblical world with its host of deities. The closest approximation to atheism, which modern interpreters call "practical atheism," crops up in a few psalms and is attributed to the fool's unarticulated thoughts. Similar views, proclaimed in a mocking context, have come to rest most unexpectedly in Prov 30:1–14, but safely placed in the mouth of a foreigner.

Chapter 2, "Alternative Gods: Falling Back on a Convenient Worldview," focuses on a single psalm, the eighty-second. It looks at the polytheistic environment's influence on the biblical poet, who concedes the existence of rival deities to Israel's God but accuses them of being derelict in their responsibility to administer justice among nations other than Israel and Judah. Because of this failure, the deities are condemned by God to die, a sentence that carries a degree of irony, for God, too, has neglected his charge. Nevertheless, this psalm marks a truly revolutionary concept: the death of the gods.

Chapter 3, "A Demon at Work: Letting Benevolence Slip," already begins a redefinition of God but places the emphasis on a lesser subject, Satan. The late emergence of this figure, despite interesting antecedent role players, lifts the onus from God's shoulders only slightly, for God has ultimate control over Satan. Later fascination with this figure and its increasing power to introduce evil offers an important lens through which to view the postbiblical Jewish and early Christian temptation to find a convenient scapegoat to which to transfer guilt. A positive feature of such speculation about an inferior heavenly being is the anticipation of its subjection or eradication, which keeps eschatology at the forefront of discussion.

Chapter 4, "Limited Power and Knowledge: Accentuating Human Freedom," continues the redefinition of God, emphasizing now the deity's self-limitation for the sake of human freedom. This way of salvaging divine honor may come at the expense of men and women, who now bear ultimate responsibility for their own suffering, but at least it recognizes that they are not automatons. Possessing freedom of choice, they bring upon themselves a full range of evil consequences of wrongful decisions, which the deity neither knows in advance nor controls. The self-imposed circumscription of divine power and knowledge endows human beings with dignity.

Chapter 5, "Split Personality: Reconciling Justice with Mercy," concentrates on biblical texts in which the deity is described as conflicted precisely because of an inner desire to retain a balance between strict justice and gracious mercy. Because God takes evil seriously, wrath wells up and strains to be let loose on the wicked, but, the prophet Ezekiel insists, YHWH does not desire the death of sinners. Torn between wrath and forgiveness, the deity seeks a means of allowing the latter to prevail.

Chapter 6, "A Disciplinary Procedure: Stimulating Growth in Virtue," attends to the significant body of sacred literature that depicts God as a parent or teacher who must apply the stick to the backs of lazy or unruly children for their own good. From the disciplinary perspective, a little adversity is a good thing because it brings strength of character. This approach to evil found a champion in Irenaeus, an early Christian theologian, and continues in modern process theology. Such soul-building with an eschatological component turns evil into a catalyst for something positive: growth in moral and spiritual discernment.

Chapter 7, "Punishment for Sin: Blaming the Victim," deals with the most widespread explanation for evil, one that when pressed too far brings extreme distress. The book of Job illustrates the downside of this approach to the problem: a tendency to consider anyone in dire straits a sinner on whom just punishment has fallen. Israelite historiography applies this principle to the twin histories of Israel and Judah, thereby imputing to divine intention a dubious account of sin and retribution.

Chapter 8, "Suffering as Atonement: Making the Most of a Bad Thing," shifts the attention from God to humans and suggests that the righteous might redeem evil by the supreme gift of love. The unjust death of a prophetic servant, reported in Isa 52:13–53:12, is construed as so pleasing to God that it actually results in forgiveness for others. The idea of substitution, borrowed from ritual, takes center stage in the Passion Narrative and in Pauline thought.

Chapter 9, "Justice Deferred: Banking on Life beyond the Grave," traces the second revolutionary concept in the Bible, the death of death—that is, belief in the resurrection of the righteous. From early beginnings in legend concerning Enoch and Elijah, who were "taken by God," to similar language about devout people like the unknown author of Psalm 73, this conviction that exceptionally good people belong with God was broadened, especially in the face of martyrdom brought on during the Maccabean revolt in 165 BCE. Confident that heaven awaits faithful servants of God, pious people put up with evil as a temporary burden.

Chapter 10, "Mystery: Appealing to Human Ignorance," follows the trail of biblical sentiment about the dark veil that conceals the divine realm from human scrutiny, especially in the book of Ecclesiastes. This response to evil has two sides: one with respect to the divine essence, another pertaining to the nature of the human intellect. From the divine side, God's hiddenness derives primarily from the intentional hiding of his face as a result of human disobedience. This idea becomes especially prominent in intertestamental and rabbinic literature. From the human side, God cannot be fully known because the human mind can only know the observable world and from that, by analogy, make educated guesses about the divine realm.

Chapter 11, "Disinterested Righteousness: Questioning the Problem," asks whether the biblical search for a viable theodicy is a result of anthropocentricity. It does so from two directions. First, the possibility is raised that the biblical depiction of God as a literary construct shares the same limitations of human knowledge discussed in chapter 10. If so, then the postbiblical reification of this depiction has resulted in false attributions that represent human projections, with dreadful consequences. Second, the book of Job provides a clue for responding to what is perceived to be divine injustice. The author of this ancient text invites readers to serve God without thought of reward because God has already given them the greatest gift of all, life. For this reason, God owes them nothing, and everything comes as grace. In short, the conflict within God between justice and mercy has been resolved in favor of compassion, and the proper human response is disinterested righteousness in which, like God, we embody forgiveness.

PART I

Spreading the Blame Around

I

The Atheistic Answer

Abandoning the Quest

Seek simplicity and distrust it.

—A. N. Whitehead

For many Westerners today, the natural response to the evils that beset us is to deny the existence of God. This emptying of the universe has been aided by many factors, not the least of which are Copernican astronomy, Darwinian biology, Freudian metapsychology, Marxist ideology, higher biblical criticism, technocratic cultural biases, secularization, the unjust distribution of human resources, occurrences of mass atrocity, and calamitous natural events.[1] For the eighteenth century, the deciding moment came in 1755 with a devastating earthquake at Lisbon; for the twentieth century, catalysts included the gas chambers at Dachau and Treblinka and the atomic bombs dropped on Hiroshima and Nagasaki. After these horrors, any talk about a providential ruler of the universe rings hollow; indeed, praying to God as merciful seems to make a mockery of more than a million and a half innocent Jewish children who perished in the death camps and far more children who have died from hunger, disease, and oppression in third-world countries. If the divine eye that is said to rest on the sparrow extends to the human species as well, this inactive deity is at best an Epicurean god who does neither good nor evil. Such a deity cannot inspire men and women to render selfless service in behalf of the weak or to conquer their base inclinations.

The decisive issue concerns the deity's failure to do what he routinely did for Israel, according to the Bible: intervene to effect a good result. Why the difference between the past and the present? For a growing number of people, the easy answers of earlier times—divine discipline and patience, punishment for sin, eventual settling of the account—no longer suffice. Like the author of Psalm 77, they inquire about divine constancy: Has YHWH changed? Or, more radically, were the biblical writers mistaken about the existence of a transcendent being?[2]

Answering this question in the affirmative has become much easier with the failure of supporting arguments for theism based on ontology, cosmology, and teleology. Such reasoning from being to ultimate Being, cosmos to personal originator, purpose to providential ruler persuades only those already committed to theism. Changes in the nature of philosophical discourse have largely rendered former questions passé. At the same time, it is the nature of the enterprise that scientific investigation can neither demonstrate nor disprove the claim of a transcendent being. Both science and religion are left to ponder the same question: What sparked the universe? The two answers they reach—accident and intention—are worlds apart. Increasingly more people in the secular West choose the first of these two options, as many on the global scene, influenced by a resurgence of fundamentalism, champion the opposite.

Ancient thinkers, resembling the latter group, rarely ventured to question the existence of gods or a God. To them, the world made no sense apart from the presence of a creator who maintained continuous control of the universe. Only fools dared to question God's existence, they insisted, and even then those doubts turned more on divine compassion than on being. "There is no God" in their realm of discourse really meant "God does not care." Furthermore, such foolishness was believed to derive more from moral deficiency than from inadequate intellect.[3]

Two biblical psalms explore the topic of the practical atheist, who can discern no evidence of a heavenly judge before whom mortals must account for their deeds. Psalms 10 and 14 offer lively descriptions of such a person, although only the latter text (which is repeated, with minor changes, in Psalm 53) portrays direct denial of God's existence. Psalm 14 [53] calls the practical atheist a fool (nabal); Psalm 10 uses language that is similarly—and, for modern readers, more apparently—ethical: "the wicked one" (rasha'). Both psalms have the expression "says in his heart" ('amar belibbo),[4] by which they identify this person's objectionable remarks as imaginary—that is, unrelated to reality.

Psalm 10

The Septuagint translator of Psalms 9 and 10 understood them as a single unit. Some modern scholars concur in that assessment,[5] largely because of the partial acrostic that begins in the former and continues throughout the latter.[6] The absence of a superscription in Psalm 10 has also led some interpreters to join it to the previous psalm.[7] Within Book 1 (Psalms 1–41), only four psalms— 1, 2, 10, and 33—lack a heading.[8] Moreover, it has been suggested that Psalms 9 and 10 present a mirror image of Psalms 1 and 2.[9] That is, Psalm 1 treats individuals, both good and bad, while Psalm 2 focuses on nations. The reverse happens in Psalms 9 and 10, where the former emphasizes nations and the latter concentrates on individuals. Finally, several linguistic features in both psalms reinforce the conviction that the two form a single literary unit: the short form of the relative pronoun; the particular expression for "a long time"; the phrase *le'ittot batstsarah* (in times of trouble); the request that YHWH arise; the verb *'azab* (to forsake) with reference to the deity; the plural form of *'anawim*, one of the Hebrew words for the poor; the investigative sense of the verb *darash* (to seek); the reference to nations; and the use of the word *'enosh* for a human being.[10]

We must acknowledge, however, significant differences between the two. The dominant mood of Psalm 9 is praise; Psalm 10 is a petitionary lament. Although the exhilaration of the first diminishes momentarily at the thought of God's temporary forgetfulness of the poor, the poet is confident that the lapse will not endure. The nations—a major interest of Psalm 9—will be reminded that they are mere humans. In contrast, the uncertain destiny of the poor troubles the author of Psalm 10, who experiences God as continually distant and hiding. Nevertheless, the psalm concludes on a positive note, with a royal judge dispensing justice on behalf of the powerless. If written as a single unit, the psalm descends from the mountain to the gates of Sheol, dwelling at length in the valley of skepticism before daring to hope once again. Without asserting a definitive judgment on the matter, we shall draw on elements of Psalm 9 in the following discussion of Psalm 10.

Psalm 10 is of primary interest to us at the moment, for it speculates about the private thoughts of an unknown person (or persons) designated as wicked. It juxtaposes his imaginary musings against other sentiments more in line with those of the poet. The wicked one talks about the deity in a pejorative manner, while the psalmist addresses God personally—at first as distant and hidden, but eventually as helper of the fatherless.

The threefold occurrence of *'amar belibbo* (he thought; literally, he said in his heart) functions thematically, conveying the arrogance of powerful individuals who think that nothing stands in the way of their lawless conduct. In the end, however, the schemes of the wicked fail, and the hearts of the lowly are established when YHWH listens to them (v 17).

The initial use of this thematic expression indicates the extent to which the villain has embodied an attitude of practical atheism: "He thought ['amar belibbo], 'I shall never be moved'" (v 6). The rest of the boast is unclear, although it seems to state that the speaker will not fall into difficulty, possibly because protected by vast wealth. This feeling of stability echoes the religious sentiment of pious individuals in other psalms who think their feet have been firmly planted to prevent slipping into danger. Experiences of the sublime have produced an unshakable confidence: nothing can move me from the secure position that I now occupy. The Hebrew idiom here for "never" (ledor wador) refers to passing generations, thus pressing beyond the lifetime of the speaker.

The second use of the expression "he said in his heart" moves in a different direction. "He thought ['amar belibbo], 'God has forgotten; he has hidden his face; he never sees'" (v 11). A similar claim appears in Ps 94:7: "YHWH does not see; the God of Jacob does not understand." This comment is placed in the mouths of those who in the metaphorical language of the psalmist "murder the widow, the sojourner, and the fatherless." The psalmist identifies the murderers as fools who lack wisdom and asks rhetorically: "He who planted the ear, does he not hear? Or he who formed the eyes, does he not see? . . . YHWH knows the thoughts of humans, for they are breath" (Ps 94:9, 11 for the quote; 94:6–11 for the larger context described here). Later rabbinic interpreters used the phrase "he has hidden his face" to explain divine inaction during perilous times.[11] When confronted with the unspeakable—the Holocaust—some modern interpreters as well have turned to the concept of a hiding God. The idea that God is subject to forgetfulness and temporary blindness reinforces the notion of a hiding deity, which became a commonplace as a result of Deutero-Isaiah's powerful rhetoric: "Truly you are a God who hides, God of Israel, Savior" (Isa 45:15).

The thought that YHWH might forget the humble is too much for the psalmist, who urges immediate action that will silence the wicked. In this context, the third use of "he said in his heart" becomes a huge signpost for YHWH to observe, pointing to the dangerous consequence of divine aloofness:

> Arise, YHWH God; raise your hand;
> do not forget the humble.
> Why should an evildoer spurn God?
> He said in his heart, "You will not investigate." (vv 12–13)

In the poet's mind, only the exercise of divine authority will put to an end such feelings of invulnerability. Failing that, YHWH simply encourages dissidents to become a law unto themselves, the true meaning of rejection of God.

Divine inactivity puzzles the psalmist, who is convinced that YHWH takes note of the trouble brought on by the evildoer and watches closely with an eye to dispensing justice (v 14); only here does the emphatic pronoun *'attah* (you) occur in the psalm. The difference between the evildoer and the one who suffers abuse at his hand could not be sharper. Whereas the former condemns God, the latter abandons himself to YHWH.

In addition to providing these three references to the false assumptions of the wicked, the psalmist also mentions thoughts and schemes specifically. In doing so, he introduces the theme word *darash* (to investigate). This particular verb occurs three times in Psalm 10. Its initial appearance expresses a conviction on the part of the evildoer that God does not examine human thoughts and actions:

> Proudly the wicked snorts, "He does not investigate;
> there is no God."
> [Thus] all his thoughts. (v 4)

The move from a deity who does not seek out wrongs and avenge them to denial that God exists is wholly understandable. In essence, it announces that God does not care.

We have already encountered the second occurrence of *darash*, in the discussion of the other thematic expression. Surprisingly, the psalmist slips up in this instance, letting the evildoer address the deity in the second person: "You do not investigate!" (v 13). This direct address was removed by the translators of the Hebrew text into Greek and Syriac, which employ the third person: "He [God] does not investigate."

The final use of *darash* in Psalm 10 follows an imperative directed to God: "Break the arm of the wicked; you will investigate wrongdoing until you find none remaining" (v 15). Nothing less than an exhaustive search for every offense will satisfy the psalmist, who believes that YHWH will leave no stone unturned until every bit of evidence has been located. This verb also occurs twice in Psalm 9, affirming YHWH's attention to injustice ("For the one who seeks blood [*ki doresh damim*] remembers them; he does not forget the cry of the humble," v 13) and categorizing faithful worshipers as those who seek YHWH (v 11). The psalmist insists that YHWH will not abandon such loyal devotees.

Still another word, *satar* (to hide), comes close to functioning thematically in Psalm 10. This word is applied both to the deity and to the evildoer, functioning negatively in both cases. It is not enough that God hides his face (v 11); the evildoer conceals himself as well. His purpose is to surprise victims and pounce on them like a robber or a lion attacking prey (vv 8–9). The language emphasizes violence: lurking, hiding, slaying the innocent, pouncing on the afflicted, drawing a net. Repetition of this language (threefold use of the verb *yashab* [to lurk] and twofold use of *satar* [to hide] and *khatap* [to pounce]) reinforces the notion of violence. Likewise, the choice of nouns for identifying victims heightens the sense of atrocity, for only here is a victim called *kehelekah* (the innocent)—the only use of this noun in the Hebrew Bible.

Language of corporeality permeates Psalm 10. Comments about the evildoer concentrate on the organ of speech. Curses, fraud, and deceit fill his mouth; trouble and iniquity hide under his tongue (v 7). He boasts and curses while spurning God (v 3).[12] God is likewise described in physical terms: possessing eyes, ears, face, hands, and feet. God stands afar off, in contrast to the evildoer, who lies in wait nearby. As both king and helper, YHWH embodies royal ideology of the ancient Near East,[13] watching over powerless members of society.[14]

Who posed such a threat to the defenseless citizens for whom the poet raised a voice? Neither psalm provides a clear answer to this mystery. The frequent reference to nations in Psalm 9 places the spotlight on the dominant powers around the Jewish people, especially in postexilic times. In a judicial context, the poet states that YHWH, acting as judge, has rebuked the nations, extinguishing the wicked and eradicating their very memory (9:6–7). YHWH then sits on his throne as judge of the whole world and its occupants (vv 8–9). The last six verses of Psalm 9 describe the fate of the nations in graphic detail. They sink down into a self-made pit, their feet trapped in a net of their own devising (v 16). All nations that forget God will then return to Sheol (v 18). The psalmist pleads with YHWH to arise and let nations be judged "before [his] face," that is, in person (v 20). Having placed fear in front of the nations, YHWH makes known the fact that they are mere mortals (v 21). The shift in Psalm 10 from this concentration on nations to equally dense language about unnamed wicked individuals points away from foreigners to local adversaries (10:2, 3, 4, 13, 15). Such language implies deep divisions between the wealthy members of Judean society and others who would be easily victimized by those in positions of power.[15]

What have we learned from this brief venture into the mind of the composer of Psalm 10? Precisely this: Any delay in punishing the perpetrators of violence only encourages them to throw off all restraint. Seeing no evidence that a supernatural being watches over humankind and decisively punishes those who act wantonly, persons inclined to profit from others' weakness naturally conclude that no such deity exists. At least, they give that impression to external observers like the poet, who offers readers insight into his own tormented mind. Certainly, the psalmist thinks that delayed punishment promotes practical atheism. By openly articulating this view, he may hope to combat such thinking among weaker members of his own community. Above all, however, he directs his remarks to YHWH, whom he dares to hold culpable in the present circumstances.

Psalm 14 [= 53, with minor variations]

(1) The fool thinks [literally, says in his heart],
    "There is no God."
    They act corruptly, generating abomination;
    None does the good [thing].

(2) From heaven YHWH looks down
    on humankind
    to see if anyone is wise,
    seeking God.

(3) All have turned aside,
    they are entirely loathsome;
    none does the good [thing],
    not even a single one.

(4) Do they not know,
    all the workers of iniquity,
    who eat my people
    just as they consume bread?
    They don't even invoke YHWH.

(5) There they greatly dreaded;
    but God was with the devout generation.

(6) You brought the advice of the poor to shame,
    but YHWH was their refuge.

(7) O that Israel's salvation would come from Zion;
    when YHWH turns the captivity of his people,
    Jacob will exult, Israel will rejoice.

We turn now to another psalm introduced by the thematic expression "he said in his heart." This time the speaker is called a fool (*nabal*),[16] which, as mentioned above, represents a moral rather than an intellectual judgment in the Bible. In wisdom literature, where sharp contrasts between the wise and the foolish figure prominently, at least eight different Hebrew nouns are used to designate forms of folly.[17]

Psalm 14 uses the standard term for a knave who behaves with total disregard for the consequences of his actions—a term that is amply illustrated by an episode in David's life, recorded in 1 Samuel 25. The fleeing warrior comes into contact with a wealthy man from Carmel, appropriately but improbably named Nabal, this Hebrew word for fool. After protecting Nabal's sheepshearers from harm, David dispatches some men to ask him for material assistance. Nabal, however, denies the request and, for good measure, heaps insults on David and his men. Upon hearing of David's resulting fury, the terrified Nabal suffers an apparent heart attack. Within days, the "foolish" man is dead.

This term for fool is not gender specific, for the noun that Job uses in rebuking his wife when she proposes that he curse God and die is the feminine plural of the same Hebrew word. In context, the rebuke implies that such talk has become proverbial, suggesting frequency and openness. This audacious proposal places Job's wife among the ranks of women who lack moral fiber, at least in the eyes of her husband.[18]

On the other side, another biblical woman is known for warning against an action that belongs to the realm of folly. When David's son Amnon tries to seduce his half-sister Tamar, she characterizes his action as foolishness:

> No, my brother, do not force me, for such a thing is not done in Israel. Do not do this foolish thing. As for me, where could I carry my shame? And as for you, you would be like one of the fools [han-nebalim] in Israel. (2 Sam 13:12–13)

Tamar's objections are no match for Amnon's passionate desire, for he is in no mood to wait. Her suggestion that he speak to the king, requesting her hand in marriage, is wasted effort. Nothing can prevent the tragedy that unfolds, and by raping his sister, Amnon becomes a doomed fool.[19]

The fool in Psalm 14, however, has in mind something other than satisfying lust at the expense of family tranquility. By denying the existence of God, he undermines the moral fabric of society. That attack on the foundation of ancient morality unleashes conduct that can best be called total depravity, at least in the first three verses, where the negation 'en (there is not) occurs four times.

We know the speaker in the first half of the initial verse, but who makes the additional pronouncement about human sinfulness? There are at least three possibilities. First, the fool. Nothing indicates a change in speakers, and the fool is the last person identified as a speaking subject. Besides denying the reality of God, the fool goes on to indict the human race. His sweeping claim empties heaven and at the same time besmirches earth. Alternatively, the fool accuses the gods of not caring. His evidence for that extraordinary claim is that the gods are totally corrupt, behaving abominably and never doing good. We shall see in chapter 2 that this accusation is not entirely missing from the Psalter, for that is precisely what YHWH (or Elohim) accuses the gods of being and doing in Psalm 82.

Second, the psalmist. The fool is actually a figment of the poet's imagination; this bold figure illustrates the extreme to which rebels have taken the Israelite community. To them, nothing is sacred; everything is permitted. The poet presents the fool's creed and then comments on its depressing consequences. The number of fools has grown so rapidly that they have corrupted the entire human race. In the first instance, "they" refers to fools, but by extension, the word becomes universal. Does the psalmist exclude himself from this judgment?[20]

Third, God. The abrupt shift from the fool's assertion "there is no God" to an account of God's activity may be the poet's way of foregrounding a divine conclusion. The pronouncement of human waywardness would then be God's assessment of the human situation, akin to the divine verdict on humanity during the days of Noah in the story of beginnings: "When YHWH saw that the evil of humankind and every imagination of his thought was thoroughly wicked all the time, he repented that he had made humans on earth, and it vexed his thoughts" (Gen 6:5–6). The distress associated with such corruption on earth moved the deity to dire measures aimed at wiping out all living creatures.[21] The story states that one person, however, brought a divine smile: "Now Noah found favor in the eyes of YHWH" (Gen 6:8).

The second verse in Psalm 14 echoes another story from the mythic past—that concerning the tower of Babel. This sequel to the narrative of the flood reflects on the colossal ego of puny earthlings. Hoping to establish a permanent reputation for exceptional achievement and to avoid dispersion to the ends of the earth, the people in this story busy themselves with building a city and a tower to heaven. Their efforts engage YHWH's attention, and he decides to go down and look at their work. Noting the implications of continued success, the deity confuses their language, forcibly separating them into different linguistic groups. By chance, the Hebrew verb used for confusing the speech of the people (*wenablah*) contains the same three consonants as the noun "fool" (*nabal*). The famous temple towers of Babylonia thus provide the author's inspiration for explaining the existence of multiple languages, as well as mocking human efforts to achieve a lasting reputation. The biblical narrator views this communal bonding as defiant refusal to obey the divine command to repopulate the land.[22]

Unlike Genesis 11, which describes YHWH as descending from heaven to get a closer look at the imposing product of ambitious people, Psalm 14 attributes perfect sight to the resident of heaven. There is no necessity for YHWH to go down. In contrast to v 1, where the subject *nabal* stands in the normal position within the sentence, after the verb, v 2 places the verb after the subject. This variation from the usual sequence puts the emphasis on the deity.

The subject of divine scrutiny is nothing less than every male and female, the children of Adam in an inclusive sense. The object of this ocular exercise is to determine whether or not a wise person exists. The issue has shifted from the disputed existence of God to that of a *maskil*. The precise meaning of this Hebrew word is not known, but the psalmist appears to define the predicate adjective form in the second half of the verse as a person who is "seeking God." The participle indicates constant activity, a habitual turning to God.

The verb *darash* (to seek) frequently indicates cultic worship, either at a high place or in the temple. We have already encountered it in Psalm 10, with the nuance of investigating the unknown. For the prophet Amos, this verb captures the essence of the moral imperative, for in a single chapter he uses it in several different formulations: "Seek me and live" (Amos 5:4b), "Seek YHWH and live" (5:6a), and "Seek good and not evil so that you may live" (5:14a). Just as Amos advises the people of Israel to seek YHWH, he warns them against seeking local sanctuaries.

Curiously, the *maskil* surfaces, at least hypothetically, in the immediate context of Amos's third admonition, to seek good rather than evil. Here the prophet lashes out at those who hate fair-minded adjudicators, oppress the poor, extract bribes, and divert the needy from legal redress. He pronounces a futility curse on them, warning that they will build houses but not dwell in them, plant vineyards but not drink wine from them (5:10–12). The wrenching oracle ends abruptly with this obscure comment: "Therefore the *maskil* will remain silent at this time, for it is an evil time" (5:13).[23]

The term obviously has something to do with prudent, intelligent action. In short, an astute individual knows better than to speak when utter lawlessness breaks loose in society. In Amos's mouth, the remark reeks of irony. If the comment originated as an editorial gloss on a prophetic word, it may be an oblique reference to the dark fate of the prophet, only hinted at in the brief narrative about the conflict between Amos and the priest Amaziah (Amos 7:10–17). That anecdote may be the basis for the fuller legend in 1 Kings 13 about a man of God who paid the ultimate price while trying to faithfully serve his deity.[24]

God's search for a single wise person who longs for the deity the way the thirsty crave water has ended in vain. That is the import of the declaration in

v 3. The repetition of the assertion from v 1 that none does the good turns it
into a sort of refrain. The second occurrence does not stand alone, however; it
is reinforced by the comprehensive *'en gam-'ekhad* (not one). This time, there
is no room for exceptions. The pronouncement paints a dark picture of humanity. No one walks the straight and narrow path, and filth clings to everyone's hands. The words in vv 1 and 3 for corrupt conduct (*hishkhitu*) and departing from the way (*sar*) echo those in the old account about the fashioning
of the golden calf. The idolatrous people turned away from YHWH (*saru*) and
became corrupt (*shikhet*) as a result of their rebellious act (Exod 32:7–8). In the
first colon of v 3, two Hebrew words out of four underscore the all-inclusive
nature of this judgment. The second colon uses four out of a total of six words
to rule out any exceptions to the assertion of universal wickedness.

The Hebrew word for good (*tob*) is the exact opposite of evil,[25] here understood as departing from the right path. Seldom do biblical writers define
the good, but the prophet Micah reminds the residents of Judah that YHWH
has told them what is good: "to do justice, to love kindness, and to walk humbly
with God" (Mic 6:8). Not only does Micah indicate the richness of this concept,
but he also uses the Hebrew verb for seeking, here with reference to YHWH:
"He has told you, mortal, what is good [*tob*]; and what does YHWH seek [*doresh*]
from you but doing the just thing, loving compassionate deeds, and conducting
a life characterized by humility in God's presence?" (6:8). The first two requirements concern horizontal relationships, those with other humans, who
are to be treated fairly and compassionately. The third refers to the vertical
relationship, indicating a way of life characterized by a deep awareness of utter
dependence on God.

In the context of Psalm 14, we need to determine who pronounces such a
depressing judgment on humankind. The psalmist has just stated that YHWH
has made a global survey with a single purpose in mind: to see whether there
is anyone, like Noah, who can bring a smile to the divine countenance. It
therefore seems natural to view v 3 as the deity's conclusion that the search
has turned up no one worthy to bear the adjective *maskil* (wise).

The pronominal suffix *i* (my) attached to the word *'am* (people) in the next
verse supports this reading of the pessimistic assessment of humankind, even
without a formula designating it as an oracle. The problem seems to be one
of ignorance, as well as malice. The psalm proceeds to make that point tellingly:
"Do they lack understanding, all these workers of iniquity who devour my
people as if eating bread?" These nine words in Hebrew are then balanced by
just three: *YHWH lo' qara'u* ("YHWH they do not invoke!").[26]

The graphic image of cannibalism seems like something from another
world, although modern instances of such extreme behavior under dire cir-

cumstances have been attested. Within the Bible, extreme hunger reportedly produced the unthinkable act of eating children to stay alive. The book of Lamentations describes such conditions following the Babylonian siege of Jerusalem.[27] The metaphoric use of this horrible image struck Micah as an apt portrayal of the abuse heaped upon the weak by rulers who butcher people as they would cut up a wicked beast (Mic 3:1–3).

The psalmist, too, presses this metaphoric sense of devouring the defenseless. The precise nature of the attack on helpless victims is not clear—and the victims are not called innocent. 'Ammi (my people) may be simply a word for mortals, not a small group of the righteous as is the case in so many psalms. The sweeping generalization of total perfidy eliminates such separating of the good from the bad. Or perhaps the universal indictment is an overstatement,[28] and the qualification of kol (all) acknowledges that fact. Only workers of iniquity fall into the unflattering category described in the preceding verse. In that case, maskil can specify the devout, who are so often under duress in the psalms.

As a matter of fact, the following verse actually recognizes a separate group that deserves the distinction "righteous."[29] Here we suddenly have two opposing types, one hitherto unacknowledged. The wicked are still present, although no longer wreaking havoc. Instead, they have become the object of divine attention, which engenders dread—the scope of which is implied by the cognate accusative construction,[30] which yields the emphatic "they dreaded a dread."

Nothing is said about the nature of their anxiety. Its reality is underlined by an adverb: "there" (sham) they experienced dread. This lone adverb sheds no light on the exact location, and nothing in the context helps clarify its reference. Does the allusion to invoking YHWH imply a cultic setting, perhaps Zion? If so, the adverb would locate God's vindication of the righteous in Jerusalem. Psalm 48:7 uses this adverb with reference to the holy city, where kings are said to be overcome by fear like the pain associated with giving birth. Similarly, Ps 76:4 states that "there" (in Zion) YHWH broke the weapons of the enemy. Not every psalm uses the adverb sham in this sense. Some psalms use it without indicating a specific place (Pss 36:13, 122:4–5, 132:17). In one instance it occurs with reference to the river Jordan, where Israelites are said to have crossed on dry land (Ps 66:6). In Ps 139:10 the adverb refers to heaven, and in Ps 104:26 it is exclamatory: "There [sham] go the ships." This exclamation recalls the unexpected allusion in Ps 48:8 to YHWH's destruction of the ships of Tarshish by means of an east wind.

The adverb sham rarely occurs in wisdom literature. The prose narrative in the book of Job has the well-known observation "Naked I came from my mother's womb and naked shall I return there [shamah] (1:21)." The word is either a euphemism for Sheol or an allusion to mother earth.[31] Job's initial lament uses the adverb with reference to Sheol, where, he muses, all are at rest and free of taskmasters (Job 3:17). The divine speeches in Job refer to a place afar off from which a bird of prey begins its attack and at which her young suck up the blood of the slain (Job 39:29, 30). Within the book of Proverbs, this adverb refers to Sheol (Prov 9:18) and to heaven (8:27). The four uses of the adverb *sham* in Ecclesiastes indicate where a fallen tree lies, the final destination of rivers, wrongly placed evil, and the place of judgment (Eccl 11: 3, 1:7, 3:17, 3:16).

The lack of a specific location for the adverb *sham* in Ps 14:7 may suggest that rectification can occur at any place. Wherever evildoers succumb to fright, God has become present to the righteous. The predicate adjective *tsaddiq* (righteous) often has a juridical sense.[32] In this context, the word means "innocent in a court of law"; to be pronounced righteous is to hear the verdict "not guilty." Its opposite, *rasha'* (wicked), carries the connotation "guilty."

The psalmist now addresses those workers of iniquity, accusing them of turning the counsel of the poor into something shameful. This perverted advice may have originated with the lowly or it may have been directed to them, depending on whether the genitive is subjective or objective. In any case, the effort to derail good advice is doomed to failure, or so the poet believes, because YHWH is the refuge of the humble.[33]

This image of the deity as a safe asylum during times of danger permeates the book of Psalms. Given a culture where anyone who had been wronged felt it necessary to avenge the offense and where a kinsman was obligated to restore honor to the family, the necessity for places of refuge is obvious. The Bible mentions cities of refuge (Exod 21:13; Num 35:9–15; Deut 4:41–43, 19:1–13; Josh 20:1–9), as well as sacred places like the altar, where persons could reasonably count on being safe. The fact that not everyone respected the sanctity of those places did not prevent the idea from being transferred to the deity (1 Kgs 2: 28–34). The longing for safe harbor was deeply embedded in the followers of Israel's God.

The last verse in Psalm 14 is petitionary. It expresses a desire for a display of deliverance on Israel's behalf that will reverse its destiny and generate jubilation. That the victorious intervention will originate in Jerusalem suggests that the psalmist subscribes to the ideology of Zion as the divine residence. The extent of this belief among those who composed the Hebrew Bible can be recognized by its presence in prophetic, priestly, and apocalyptic texts.

The curious phrase "when YHWH turns the captivity of his people"[34] is usually taken to be of postexilic provenance. It is used by the author of the book of Job to indicate the reversal of Job's fortunes once he has interceded for his friends (Job 42:10). Likewise, the expression occurs in Joel 4:1 with reference to the restoration of Judah and Israel in the last days (see also Deut 30:3; Jer 29:14, 30:3, 30: 18, 31:23, 32:44, 33:7, 33:11). Elsewhere in the Psalter this phrase refers to Jacob (Ps 85:2) and Zion (Ps 126:1); each of these psalms associates the restoration of fortunes with joyous shouts, as in Ps 14:7. In Psalm 14 the old names for the national entity, Jacob and Israel, elaborate on the earlier term *'ammo* (his people). The identity of the two is explained by the legendary story about Jacob's encounter with a mysterious adversary in the night (Gen 32:29, "You will no longer be called Jacob, but Israel").

For an unknown reason, this psalm has been duplicated in the Psalter, appearing also, with slight changes, as Psalm 53. Was the issue with which it wrestles, practical atheism, of such pressing concern that those who compiled Books 1 and 2 chose to include the same psalm twice? If the collection of psalms that have substituted the name Elohim for YHWH contains an earlier group that originated in the northern kingdom, as some interpreters think, Psalm 53 may actually be older than Psalm 14.

Even Psalm 14 does not use the divine name YHWH exclusively. In v 1 the generic Elohim occurs after the particle of negation, but v 2 has YHWH looking down from heaven and Elohim as the object of the participle for seeking. Verse 4 uses YHWH as the object of the missing invocation, while v 5 reverts to the generic Elohim in the clause that affirms divine presence in the company of the righteous. The last two verses employ YHWH when connoting a refuge and the one who returns an exiled people to their homeland.

Apart from the different divine names, the variations in the two psalms occur in vv 1 [53:2], 3 [53:4], and 5 [53:6]. The noun for objectionable conduct in v 1 [53:2] differs, but with little change in meaning. Whereas Ps 14:1 uses a neutral word for deeds (*'alilah*, in the singular here and in Ps 66:5; elsewhere it appears only in the plural), Ps 53:2 has a word that indicates unrighteousness. Neither noun is necessary, for their associated verbs communicate wanton behavior. The word used in Ps 14:1 designates divine works in several instances (Pss 9:12, 66:5, 77:13, 78:11, 103:7, 105:1), the mood of which is illustrated by the second one: "Come and see God's works; awesome is his work concerning humankind" (Ps 66:5).

The verb *sur* (to turn aside) in Ps 14:3 does not appear in Psalm 53, which has the verb *sug* (to become dross). In Hebrew the difference is slight, a single consonant. This change introduces the image of smelting, the process by which pure metal is separated from impure. The image was popular among moralists, who viewed hardship as a refining fire that produced pure gold. The psalmist imagines just the opposite result; everyone has emerged from the refining process as worthless dross.

The biggest change in the psalm takes place in v 5 [53:6]. Instead of assuring the righteous of God's presence as in Ps 14:5, Ps 53:6 states that there is no dread, having just asserted that the people will dread a dread there. The implication is that a sudden sensation of terror will overcome people who think they are immune from danger. The psalm continues: "For God has scattered the bones of those who encamped against you; you have brought shame, for God has rejected them."[35] Psalm 141 also mentions a divine scattering of bones, this time at Sheol (v 7). This context, like Ps 53:6, seems somewhat convoluted.

Interestingly, a text from Ezekiel (29:13–16) combines the language of scattering [bones], the adverb *shammah*, and the expression for restoring fortunes. Here the purpose of restoring Egypt to its former place is to render it insignificant and to make Egyptians know that YHWH is Lord. Is this the missing object of the verb *yade'u* (know) in Ps 14:4 [53:5]? Do the workers of evil not know that YHWH is supreme? Another text from Ezekiel uses both the verb for scattering and the adverb *sham* when talking about YHWH's shepherding activity[36] on behalf of the elect (Ezek 34:2–14). The prophet Jeremiah speaks of scattered Jacob and Israel, whose fortunes will be restored (Jer 30:3, 10–11, 18).

Thus far we have restricted ourselves to the Hebrew text of the psalm under discussion. Two Greek manuscripts—Vaticanus and Sinaiticus—include a fuller ascription of universal sinfulness after Ps 14:3, one that also appears as a scriptural citation in Rom 3:10–18:

(10) As it is written,
     "None is righteous, no, not one;
(11) no one understands, no one seeks for God.
(12) All have turned aside, together they have gone wrong;
        no one does good, not even one."
(13) "Their throat is an open grave,
        they use their tongues to deceive."
     "The venom of asps is under their lips."
(14) "Their mouth is full of curses and bitterness."
(15) "Their feet are swift to shed blood,
(16)   in their paths are ruin and misery,
(17)   and the way of peace they do not know."
(18) "There is no fear of God before their eyes." (RSV)

This litany of human failure is drawn from various scriptural texts: Pss 14: 1–2 [53:2–3], 5:10, 140:4, 10:7; Isa 59:7–8; Ps 36:2.[37] With the exception of two verses, the Greek of this addition follows the Hebrew texts closely. Verse 15 of Romans 3 shortens the reference to quick feet and omits a comment about iniquitous thoughts; v 18 substitutes "fear of God" for "justice" and "before their eyes" for "in their paths." Because there is no similarity between the Hebrew words involved, the change appears to be intentional.

The clear association of practical atheism with gross immorality has thus imbued Pauline theology. The psalmist's concept of moral bankruptcy has become an instrument that Paul wields to undercut the dominance of the law in the minds of his readers. Belief that salvation comes through obedience to the law of Moses is far removed from belief that righteousness comes through acknowledgment of the existence of God.

Proverbs 30:1–14

One other text, Prov 30:1–14, may fall into the category of practical atheism; indeed, it may advance beyond practical to theoretical atheism. The pertinent verse, v 1, has multiple textual problems and has plausibly been taken to contain some Aramaic words in addition to the more extensive Hebrew. This interpretation is less striking than it might appear at first glance, for long sections of Aramaic are preserved in other texts of the Writings (Ezra 4:8–6:18, 7:12–26; Dan 2:4b–7:28; see also Gen 31:47a and Jer 10:11). Moreover, the sage who is identified in Prov 30:1 probably hails from an Aramaic-speaking region of Transjordan called Massa.[38]

Like the other two proverbial collections that derive from a foreign teacher (Prov 22:17–24:22 and 31:1–9),[39] this one begins with a common prophetic formula: the noun *dibre* (the words of) followed by the identity of the instructor or prophet. Thus we have "the words of [unnamed] sages" in Prov 22:17 and "the words of Lemuel's mother" in Prov 31:1; similarly, the book of Amos begins "the words of Amos, who was among the shepherds from Tekoa," and the book of Jeremiah has "the words of Jeremiah son of Hilkiah."

An additional word in Prov 30:1 goes beyond identifying the speaker: "The words of Agur the son of Jakeh, an *oracle* [or the Massaite; *hammassaʾ*]." The present Masoretic pointing of the word "Massa" strengthens the suspicion that these words are presented as oracular, hence prophetic rather than merely human. That interpretation is further supported by the next word, *neʾum*, one of the oracular terms that often accompany prophetic sayings. The word is usually translated as simply "oracle" and is typically paired with the Tetragrammaton YHWH. Here, however, the author substitutes the word *haggeber* (man); hence, we have "the oracle of the man." The attribution of an oracle to a man is extraordinary, for the deity is usually given credit for such words. The story about the foreign diviner, Balaam, uses similar language in reporting his third and fourth oracles, but each time Balaam goes on to attribute the message to God (Num 24:3–4, 15–16). David, too, states that the oracle he utters is actually divine speech, making him merely a medium through whom the spirit works (2 Sam 23:1–2). The juxtaposition of human against otherwise prophetic indicators in Prov 30:1 commands our attention as the sarcasm slowly sinks in: the expected oracle of YHWH has been replaced by human speech.

What new insight merits such an opening line? If what follows, *le'iti'el le'iti'el we'ukal*, actually means "There is no God, there is no God, and I am exhausted," the message lives up to its stunning introduction. Other interpretations of the difficult text have been proposed: "I have no God, I have no God, but I can endure"; "I am weary, God, I am weary, God, and exhausted"; "I am tired of God"; "I am not God"; "Would that there were a God"; and "To Ithiel, to Ithiel and Ukal."[40]

The last of these readings has the least to commend it, inasmuch as it turns the language into gibberish. Why would anyone address two persons in this manner, mentioning one of them twice? Who are these individuals, and why would Agur single them out as worthy of attention? Equally unpersuasive is the reading that has Agur make a self-evident concession that he is not God. Who would have thought that he was? Besides, this interpretation requires major emendation—in particular, the addition of the personal pronoun "I."

The other interpretations are plausible and require only vocalic changes, always more probable than consonantal alteration, since the vowels were not added until the Masoretic period (fifth through tenth centuries CE). One of these readings actually depicts Agur as an atheist who utters a wish that has no possibility of being true. This is the function of the particle that, in this reading, precedes the particle of existence: "Would that there were a God!"

To some extent, the most rewarding interpretation of this verse depends on the way one breaks up the rest of the unit under consideration. How much of the chapter derives from Agur? Scholars often limit his words to the first four verses, largely because of the seemingly contrasting piety reflected in vv 5–9. However, the brief section that follows, vv 10–14, has nothing to preclude its coming from Agur. It presents a commendable ethic, one that lacks any explicit theological underpinning.

In my view, the unit extends to v 14, with vv 5–9 coming from an interloper and constituting a dialogue in which, as it were, a pious defender of orthodoxy beats Agur over the head with a scroll. The combination of pious orthodoxy and harsh treatment of those with different views has a long history, it seems. Even so, the exquisite prayer in vv 7–9 rises to a remarkable level of theological sophistication. One could even say that the prayer alone[41] justifies the presence of the threat posed to the believing community by atheism, which seems to have given birth to exceptional resistance. That prayer recognizes the effect of personal circumstances on religious life:

> Two things I ask of you,
>> Do not withhold them from me before I die.
> Keep vanity and a deceitful word far from me.
>> Give me neither poverty nor wealth,
>>> break off for me my portion of bread,
> Lest being sated I lie
>> and say, "Who is YHWH?"
> Or lest being poor I steal
>> and sully the name of my God. (vv 7–9)

The distance between this prayer and Agur's opening remarks is vast.

Agur moves from a position of practical atheism and its accompanying ennui to bitter irony. At first he denies having a place among humans, confessing brutish stupidity and a lack of ordinary understanding. Then he insists that he has neither acquired wisdom nor learned anything about holy ones. Indeed, he knows of no one who has attained such lofty insights. He asks:

> Who has gone up to heaven and come down,[42]
>> who has gathered the wind in his hands?
> Who has wrapped the waters in a blanket;
>> who has established all the limits of earth?
> What is his name, and what is his son's name?
>> Surely you know! (v 4)

With biting sarcasm Agur attacks the popular myth that extols a creator who displays mastery over the rebellious waters, here swaddled like an infant, and sets boundaries for those who inhabit the earth. The final words, "Surely you know!" recall YHWH's mockery of Job, who was reminded of his abysmal ignorance about the universe (Job 38:5). The comment about extraterrestrial travel may have arisen as a response to stories about certain privileged people, like Enoch, whose journey into the heavens and back to earth is celebrated in intertestamental literature.[43]

An alternative reading of Agur's remarks is certainly possible. A humble but weary man confesses his limited knowledge but claims to know about the holy.[44] He then praises the creator by mentioning a few familiar features of the standard myth, ending with the assertion "For you know [this]" (v 4). To identify the name of the one being extolled, Agur cites scripture: "Every word of Eloah is reliable; he is a shield to those who trust him" (v 5, citing Ps 18:31 [= 2 Sam

22:31]). What, then, does one make of v 6: "Do not add to his words lest he rebuke you and you be made to lie"?

On my reading, an editor tones down Agur's stringent remarks (v 5) and, in turn, is attacked (v 6). The addition of two editorial comments is not unprecedented, as is demonstrated by the ending to the book of Ecclesiastes (Eccl 12:9–12, 13–14).[45] On this interpretation, Agur's voice resonates with the imaginary speeches that the person who composed Psalms 10 and 14 found so troubling. Whether the product of a fertile imagination or the genuine thoughts of religious dissidents in the ancient world, this expression of doubt about the existence of God represents one response to the problem of theodicy. If there is no God, the need to defend the way the universe is run has vanished.

Most Israelites, however, thought this path too hazardous to be lured into its uncharted terrain. As they saw things, the universe was filled with deities. In such a belief system, alternative gods provided a ready solution to the presence of radical evil that threatened a just order. The particular deity that one wished to honor was thought to have nothing to do with evil, which was attributed to another god or many gods. The next chapter will consider this answer to the problem of theodicy.

2

Alternative Gods

Falling Back on a Convenient Worldview

Man is the Cosmic Orphan. He is the only creature in the universe who asks, "Why?"

—Loren Eiseley

Historians of intellectual development in the ancient Near East would do well to record two revolutionary events within the Psalter. The first sees the author of Psalm 82 deconstruct the notion of a host of deities comprised in a heavenly assembly, analogous to royal courts below. An utter failure to protect the rights of marginalized citizens, to ensure social and ethical justice, has convinced the psalmist that the divine assembly has forfeited its claim on terrestrial devotees. In the psalmist's view, a single deity remains, one who judges the divine assembly and condemns it to mortal status.[1] On this remaining god's integrity and commitment to justice the psalmist rests all hope for rectitude among humans.[2]

The second revolution within the Psalter sees the author of Psalm 73 break out of the causal nexus between deed and consequence and voice a complete spiritualization of the relationship between worshipers and God, one that renders death powerless to break its immortal bond. This remarkable author has endured a severe test of faith, the inevitable disparity between belief and reality, but has emerged from that wrenching experience with even stronger, although completely different, conviction. The resulting internalization of religious experience approaches—if it does not actually reach—an assurance that death has no sting for believers, who through divine mystery cross the threshold into the eternal realm.[3]

A striking irony attends these decisive revolutions in human thought. Whereas the condemned gods lose their coveted status as eternal beings, mortals gain that status, joining favored men of old like Enoch and Elijah in being taken by YHWH. The possibility of being grasped by the divine hand and ushered into glory, whatever that may mean, now lies open to everyone. The secret resides in the cognitive perspective—in getting the heart right, to use the thematic language of the psalmist.

A glance at comparable (though converse) revolutions in modern thought may help us appreciate the changes wrought in the ancient world by such iconoclastic ideas. The collapse of the notion of progress has been called the end of religion,[4] and the death of God[5] is said to have ushered in an age of self-reliance, a maturing of humankind, who needs no religious crutch.[6] The loss of teleology implies the nonexistence of a benevolent creator, as well as the absence of eschatological hope. The scientific prediction that the universe will eventually end with a whimper only emphasizes the utter futility of all life, as the author of Ecclesiastes perceived with such clarity. These modern revolutions—or, perhaps better, devolutions—if true, nullify the ancient ones achieved in Psalms 73 and 82.

This chapter focuses on the first revolutionary moment in the Psalter, the death of the gods. The other decisive breakthrough, which may be called the death of death,[7] will be taken up in chapter 9. Both revolutions occur in the collection of psalms attributed to Asaph,[8] to which we now turn.

The Psalms of Asaph

The initial psalm in this group of twelve, Psalm 50, asserts that the heavens proclaim divine justice, while the remaining ones, Psalms 73–83, reflect on the accuracy of this claim in light of evidence to the contrary. That evidence is of two kinds: the ruined state of Jerusalem, YHWH's sacred abode, and the prosperity of the wicked. Thematic consistency within the collection is reinforced by the language of divine silence. Psalm 50 promises YHWH's coming to break his troubling silence and justifies divine speech. Psalm 76 announces the deity's reduction of the earth to silence, and Psalm 83 pleads with God to keep the promise not to remain silent.

Northern interests are apparent in several of the psalms of Asaph.[9] The brutal attack on YHWH's sanctuary, conveyed in Ps 74:5 by a picture of woodsmen hacking down a forest, leaves a haunting memory intensified by mystification over how the deity could have sat idly by while the divine residence went up in flames. Present humiliation contrasts with ancestral belief, here reiterated, that YHWH conquered the mythic beasts that spawned chaos and established an orderly universe (vv 12–17). The enemy's taunts being hurled at YHWH do not alter the Napoleonic pose with concealed hand. Psalm 50 offers a rationale for a templeless Jerusalem: YHWH has no need for sacrifice, for he owns the cattle on a thousand hills. The sacrifice the deity does require—which cannot be bound by temple walls—is obedience to the covenant and praise.

Psalm 80 addresses the problematic situation in the northern kingdom when the divine shepherd abandons the flock. A threefold refrain, "Restore us, O God; let your face shine on us that we may be saved," varies only in the progressive intensity of the object of address: God in v 4, God of Hosts in v 8, and YHWH the God of Hosts in v 20. The perplexity of the situation is underscored by the contrast between YHWH's exposure of his transplanted vine to trampling by wild beasts and the divine gardener's earlier solicitous care. Joseph's descendants now drink their own tears instead of the anticipated wine, surely a play on the exquisite song of the vineyard in Isaiah 5, another song of disappointed expectation:

> I will sing for my beloved
>   a love song concerning his vineyard.
> My beloved had a vineyard
>   in a fertile location.
> He prepared the soil, cleared the stones away,
>   and planted select cuttings.
> He built a tower in it,
>   a wine vat too.
> Then he waited for grapes,
>   but it produced stinking grapes. (Isa 5:1–2)

The minstrel goes on to identify the vintner as YHWH and the vineyard as his people, once more reinforcing the fact that the much-awaited grapes are foul. "What more could I have done?" asks the disappointed vintner, who threatens to annihilate the garden plot:[10]

> For the vineyard of YHWH of Hosts is the house of Israel,
>   and the people of Judah are his precious planting.
> He looked for justice, and lo! Bloodletting;
>   for righteousness, and lo! Outcry. (Isa 5:7)[11]

Psalm 77 looks closely at divine constancy as preserved in active memory and finds it wanting. It seems that divine forgetfulness has replaced remembrance, and this sense of abandonment gives no hint of being assuaged. Is the present lack of compassion a temporary lapse, or does Elyon now suffer from a weak hand? A remembered majestic theophany only serves to increase consternation over the deity's inactivity.

To the author of Psalm 82, divine justice is a matter of life and death. Against the backdrop of squandered immortality by divine beings, God's failure to take a stand against vicious foreign soldiers and wicked neighbors within the elect community evokes the most tortured of all questions: Why? How long?[12]

The psalms of Asaph offer various responses to the vexing question of divine justice, all of which will be examined in subsequent chapters: suffering is a test of loyalty (73); adversity is brought on by waywardness (78:10, 37); God controls the clock, choosing precisely the moment to make a move (75:3); YHWH remains true to the divine nature revealed to Moses in Exod 3:13–14 (78:38);[13] and divine presence compensates for perceived injustice (73). Only one of these responses exonerates the deity by placing blame on humans. The other four offer hope by appealing to the character of YHWH.

In these psalms of the Elohistic collection,[14] the progression from the first-person plural suffix with Elohim, 'elohenu (our God, Ps 50:3), to first-person singular, 'elohay (my God, Ps 83:14), contrasts with the cool distance of the Tetragrammaton. The name YHWH is absent altogether in one psalm in the Asaph collection, and a remarkable psalm it is.[15]

Psalm 82

(1) Elohim has stood up in the divine assembly;
       in the midst of the gods he judges.
(2) How long will you judge perversely
       and show favor to the wicked? (selah)
(3) Execute justice for the weak and the orphan,
       guarantee the right of the oppressed and dispossessed.
(4) Rescue the weak and needy;
       from the hand of the wicked deliver them.
(5) Without knowledge, without understanding,
       they walk in darkness;
       all the foundations of the earth totter.
(6) I said, "You are gods,
       all of you, children of Elyon.
(7) Truly, like Adam you will die;
       and fall like one of the Princes."

(8) Arise, Elohim, judge the earth;
     for you own all the nations.

The first and last verses of Psalm 82 can be understood as the words of the psalmist: a prophetic vision, like Amos 9:1–4 or Isa 6:1–13, and a prayerful plea for divine action, to which is affixed a reason.[16] The beautifully crafted chiastic vv 2–4 and the formally balanced vv 6–7 describe events in the divine assembly, with God (Elohim) as speaker and the other gods (*'elohim*) as the ones being addressed.

The text of the psalm is largely unproblematic. An early demythologization of v 1 occurs in the Greek texts Aquila and Symmachus and in the Latin Vulgate, where we find "in the midst, God judges." Although the Hebrew *beqereb* (in the midst) is not elsewhere used absolutely, this reading avoids the use of the generic name for God in two different ways within the same verse. The uncommon repetition of the word *dal* (weak) in v 3 and 4 troubles some modern interpreters, who suggest that the similar *dak* (crushed) may have dropped out in v 3. Such an emendation lacks versional support but gains credence from the fact that *dal* is ordinarily paired with the word for the needy, not the orphan, as in v 3, and Ps 10:18 has the pair orphan/crushed (*dak*), similarly preceded by a form of the verb *shiptu* (to judge).[17]

The literary unity of the psalm has been challenged, with vv 2–4 being extracted and labeled a later indictment of Jewish judges.[18] One interpreter, Oswald Loretz, identifies vv 1–4 and 6–7 as a Canaanite short story,[19] but those who view the entire psalm as Israelite are probably right.[20] None would contest the Canaanite parallel in the Keret episode, although differences certainly exist. According to this Ugaritic text, Yassib, a young prince and heir apparent, demands that his father, Keret, relinquish the throne for failing to attend to the needs of the widows and orphans in his kingdom. The son pays dearly for his temerity: his father pronounces a curse on his head. The expectation that rulers would protect the powerless was widespread in the ancient world; indeed, every society seems to have idealized its rulers, although few lived up to such lofty standards.

In biblical ideology, kings rarely attained the noble ideal and were rebuked accordingly by historiographers and prophets. The significance of that ideal permeates the Queen Mother's advice to her son in Prov 31:1–9. After warning him against squandering his energy on wine and women, she urges him to raise a voice on behalf of those whose extreme poverty has rendered them silent. His energy, she insists, ought to be devoted to adjudicating the cause of the poor and needy.

A Heavenly Court

The peoples of the ancient Near East conceived of the gods as forming a heavenly assembly, a kind of divine council. Indeed, the compelling evidence of this understanding effectively sets aside the ongoing discussion about an extended meaning in Psalm 82 of *'elohim* as human judges. Even in the early versions, debate raged over the precise meaning of *'elohim*, primarily in the interest of refuting the psalmist's polytheistic understanding of the world.[21] An interpretation as human judges is found already in the Aramaic Targum Jonathan, which also seeks to defuse the troublesome implication in v 6 that the existence of other deities was acknowledged by God himself—a telling sign that the polytheistic world of the Bible was understood to be more than simply a literary construct.[22]

Students of the Bible will have little difficulty finding evidence of belief in a heaven populated by numerous divine beings, often called *bene 'elohim* (literally, sons of God). Because all language about the supraterrestrial world is by necessity inferential, the convenient analogy of earthly courts became the model for descriptions of the heavenly realm. As king, God naturally had subjects who did the divine bidding. These lesser beings were believed to possess wills of their own, even rebellious spirits. The very thought of divine rebels led to enormous speculation about the most notorious rebel of all, the satan, in the Judaism of the Second Temple period and within Christian circles.[23] Similar flights of fancy surrounded the exploits of angels, increasingly filling a void created by the portrayal of the deity as transcendent.

Allusions to this heavenly court can be found in texts of various genres, beginning in Genesis and continuing through much of the Bible. The creator in Gen 1:26 invites the heavenly court to participate in making humans after their likeness,[24] and divine beings become overly fond of female members of the human race in Gen 6:1–4. A fearless prophet named Micaiah ben Imlah has a vision in which YHWH converses with members of the heavenly court (1 Kgs 22:19–22), and the prologue to the book of Job describes an assemblage of divine beings, two of whom evaluate Job's character and wreck his life. A heavenly court provides the imagined setting of the divine speeches that flow from the mouth of the lyrical poet who composed Isaiah 40–55. Such an assembly also inspired several psalmists, who celebrate YHWH's majesty in elevated language (Pss 29:1–2, 89:6, 97:7, 103:20–21, 148:1–2).

This manner of speaking was by no means unique to Israel. Among Israel's neighbors, polytheism was the norm, and within a panoply of deities, one god would claim supreme authority. Ever changing on the basis of the fluctuating fortunes of city-states, this claimant to dominance would rule over the lesser gods. The literature from Egypt, Mesopotamia, and Ugarit names a host of deities. The heavens were thought to suffer from overpopulation just as the earth does; measures thus had to be taken to reduce the numbers. The ensuing combat among the gods gives an all too realistic commentary on the biblical concept of humans being made in the divine image.

Belief in multiple gods pervaded the ancient world. Indeed, a growing body of evidence supports the view that the Israelite commitment to polytheism survived much longer than earlier scholars believed to be the case.[25] The emergence of monotheism after an undetermined period of henotheism—the veneration of one deity while others are conceded to exist—was a gradual process. Old theological ideas have a way of lingering among the masses long after the official cult has pronounced them inadequate.

A striking contrast to Psalm 82 is found in Isa 41:21–24: "Declare the future to us so that we may know that you are gods" (v 23). In these verses YHWH challenges the gods to bring convincing proofs that they are deities, either by predicting the future or by performing frightening works. Their inability to do so leads YHWH to dismiss the gods as nothing. Although the language is the same—"You are gods"—one text, Ps 82:6, recognizes that they actually exist,[26] whereas the other, Isa 41:21–24, denies their reality.[27]

YHWH as Prosecutor and Judge

The basic problem in understanding Psalm 82 arises from an inability to ascertain the speakers and those spoken to and about in vv 3–5. If the initial Elohim replaces YHWH, as elsewhere in the Elohistic collection of psalms (42–83), a credible but by no means proven hypothesis, the text conveys a vision in which YHWH stands up in the divine council and accuses the patron deities of the nations with dereliction of duty. According to the Greek text and the Qumran fragment of Deut 32:8–9, Elyon assigned to the gods all the nations but reserved Israel for his own inheritance. The gods' responsibility, therefore, entailed the maintenance of justice within society.

YHWH's assuming a standing position has troubled some interpreters, largely because they apply the analogy of human judges, who ordinarily sit during judicial proceedings. When YHWH executes judgment, however, he stands, the sole exception being Dan 7:9–10, which bears Persian influence:[28] "As I observed, thrones were placed and the ancient of days took his seat . . . ; the court convened and the ledgers were opened." The argument that YHWH stands because of inferior status in Elyon's court is not plausible unless one assumes that the author is non-Israelite.[29]

The dramatic scene in Isa 3:13–15, which depicts YHWH standing to judge the oppressors of the poor, is typical:

> YHWH has stood up to adjudicate,
>   he is standing to judge his people.
> YHWH enters into judgment
>   with the elders and princes of his people.
> "You have devoured the vineyard;
>   the spoil of the poor is in your houses.
> Your words crush my people
>   and grind the face of the poor,"
>   says the Lord YHWH of Hosts.

The two verbs in synonymous parallelism emphasize both the initial moment in which YHWH rises to contend with powerful offenders and his maintenance of that commanding posture. The participle form of the second verb for standing emphasizes an ongoing process. YHWH charges the leaders of society with ruthless disregard for the well-being of the weak. By storing the full harvest in their granaries and wine cellars, they have in effect brought starvation upon those who depend on gleaning in the fields. The image is forceful, whether literal or metaphoric.

In Psalm 82, as both prosecutor and judge, YHWH first admonishes and then sentences the deities. Because they have permitted their charges to develop a corrupt legal system that favors the powerful and oppresses the marginalized, these gods are divested of their immortality. For failing to distinguish between good and evil, they lose the quality that Adam forfeited for the same reason. YHWH acknowledges an earlier assessment of them as divine beings—indeed, as Elyon's offspring (an expression that occurs only here in the Bible)—but sentences them to mortal status.

The precise reference in v 7 is unclear. Does "like Adam/man" allude to the first man who lost status and was driven from Eden or to humans generally, and does "like one of the princes" refer to ordinary princes or to a mythic Prince like the fallen ones in Isa 14:3–21 and Ezek 28:1–19?[30] The affinities between Psalm 82 and these derogations of powerful kings in neighboring territories commend close examination. In both prophetic texts, a ruler who thought himself worthy of deification has fallen to lowly status, becoming weak like the shades in Sheol (Isa 14:9–10) or ashes, like all mortals (Ezek 28:18). In Isaiah, Babylon's mighty one, who considered himself like the Most High, has fallen to the depths of Sheol. The Day Star, son of Dawn, has become like a loathed infant, tossed out to perish. In Ezekiel, Tyre's chieftain, who boasted that he was a god, has been sentenced to die the death of the uncircumcised. His narcissian self-admiration has brought expulsion from the garden of Eden.

Ezekiel acknowledges this ruler's exceptional wisdom, which has turned entrepreneurial efforts into vast riches, ranking him above the Canaanite notable Daniel. At the same time, however, he rejects the ruler's divine status: He may claim to sit among the gods, "But you are a man and not god, although you have made your heart like that of God" (28:2). Ezekiel asks him sarcastically, "Will you still insist that you are a deity to your executioners?" (28:9a). For a second time, he stresses the ruler's mortality: "But you are a man and not god" (28:9b).

The variants of fallen heavenly beings and of the story of the first human in the garden of Eden are converted in these texts into a stinging reminder that self-aggrandizement is no more than an exercise in futility. Even kings are brought low, despite their delusions of grandeur. Violence against their own people, fueled by greed and pride, serves only to seal their doom.

Knowledge plays the decisive role in the ascendancy of Tyre's ruler, presenting a notable contrast with the condemned gods in Psalm 82. In the opinion of the psalmist, these gods have shown an utter lack of wisdom:

> Without knowledge, without understanding,
>> they walk in darkness;
>> all the foundations of the earth totter. (v 5)

Like the oracles against the foreign nations in Amos 1:3–2:3, Psalm 82 indicts the gods for failing to ensure justice among non-Israelites.[31] The offense is sufficiently grievous to threaten the earth's foundations, which—in Isaiah's image of Jerusalem as the center of the earth—are laid out by justice and righteousness, instruments that do not lie (Isa 28:16–17). In such a city, Isaiah insists, special covenants with death carry no force. Nothing can protect the wicked from God's wrath.

The language seems clear enough, but what exactly does Psalm 82 mean? The poet envisions the dramatic transition from polytheism to monotheism and interprets that shift in terms of an ethical system that gives priority to the weak and defenseless members of society. The six (or five) words for this disenfranchised group amplify that point. Moreover, the poet passes judgment on the nations and fervently urges Elohim (or YHWH) to replace the fallen deities—that is, to assume responsibility for the whole earth. Thus, in the psalmist's eyes, monotheism is accompanied by universalism.

Such is the revolution in Psalm 82, and its impetus rests in theodicy. Deferred justice calls for a different deity! The eschatological urgency of the final prayer does not hide the irony. YHWH has judged the divine beings in a heavenly assembly but must be implored to stand up and render a similar verdict on earth. Proceedings in that upper sphere do not necessarily unfold below, it appears, but must be influenced by ardent voices.

The brevity and beauty of this psalm conceal its profundity. It strikes us as surreal, for we do not believe in a world filled with deities, corrupt or otherwise. To appreciate its grandeur, however, we must enter into its worldview. Doing that must have been terribly difficult for readers soon after the psalm was incorporated into the collection of sacred texts. Sophisticated worshipers of YHWH must have found its content as dubious as numerous modern thinkers find the belief in a deity at all. That reaction explains the early efforts to replace the obvious meaning of the text with more palatable theology by substituting human judges for divine beings. With such a move, however, theodicy dissolves into anthropodicy—the gods being let off the hook and humans taking their place—and a monumental insight into cosmic reality recedes from view.

The move away from many gods to a single deity came at a high price. A convenient answer to the presence of evil in the world was sacrificed for ethical monotheism. As long as there were multiple deities, evil could readily be attributed to one or several of them with little harm to the total worldview. The emergence of belief in only one god who is both good and powerful brought an attendant problem: explaining evil. An early attempt to resolve this difficulty was to retreat, as it were, into semipolytheism. That is what happened when a semidivine being of demonic nature was introduced. In chapter 3, we examine that approach to explaining the problem of evil, which has become even more perplexing than before.

3

A Demon at Work

Letting Benevolence Slip

Moral atheism, the denial of the moral predicates, and not subject
atheism is the real threat to religious faith.

—Harold M. Schulweis

Until now, the primary examples of theodicy that I have discussed
have been taken from the book of Psalms. In this chapter, I draw on
texts from the Torah[1] and the book of Job. Within the first five books
of the Bible, we encounter various attempts to justify God's conduct[2]
almost from the very beginning. When Eve weakly defends the deity
against charges of tyranny leveled by the serpent, she launches a
movement that gains momentum in book after book. Its initial high
point occurs in the account of God's placing a rainbow in the sky as
a permanent sign that from this moment forward his mercy will triumph over wrath.[3] The next significant effort at exonerating the deity from acting unjustly involves a compassionate Abraham who
pleads with God for the sparing of two condemned cities, Sodom
and Gomorrah. After that comes the monstrous test in which the
patriarch is commanded to bind his son on an altar as a burnt offering to God. Here an angel appears, presumably at God's bidding,
and to some extent salvages the deity's reputation.

Within the book of Exodus, the author ponders the destructive
nature of Israel's God, who is described as both warrior and healer
(Exod 15:3, 26). In a divine self-revelation that has come to occupy a
prominent place in Jewish liturgy, specifically at Passover, YHWH

identifies justice and mercy as the two controlling characteristics of the divine nature (Exod 34:6–7). The rest of the story of YHWH's interaction with the chosen people in the Pentateuch shows how mercy trumps justice as an exiled people is finally poised to enter the land of promise. That privileged position has entailed considerable bloodshed, leaving absolutely no place for the idea of cheap grace.

This point is made in a face-to-face confrontation between Moses and YHWH, who is determined to wipe out the chosen people for an infraction of the deity's demand for singular devotion. Their leader intercedes for them, placing his own life at risk in their behalf. "If you will not forgive them," he pleads, "blot me out of the book you have written" (Exod 32:32).[4] The narrator credits Moses with demonstrating greater love for his people than does the deity, at least when overcome by anger. In the end Moses prevails, and YHWH opens a tiny crack in the door of hope—yet withholds access for the present generation.

In contrast to divine law in the Torah or to oracle in the Prophets, much of the literature in the third division of the Hebrew Bible, the Writings, is written "from below."[5] The book of Psalms, for example, consists of prayers, laments, and hymns directed to God. The books of wisdom—Job, Proverbs, and Ecclesiastes—comprise human observations about coping with life's anomalies. In addressing the problem of theodicy, the book of Job uses a didactic story to frame a lively debate that involves the hero and initially three friends, then a fourth, and finally the deity. In this chapter, I restrict comments about the book of Job to the framing story.

Besides denying the existence of God for any practical purposes (chapter 1 of this volume) and acknowledging a pantheon of deities (chapter 2), ancient Israelites also believed that their God had a dark side, one that eventually manifested itself as an independent being, at first as a servant of the deity but ultimately as a powerful opponent. This elusive figure appears only three times in the Hebrew Bible, and on two of these occasions an article is attached to its descriptor, *satan* (the adversary), which should not be translated as a proper name (Job 1–2; Zech 3:1–2). Only 1 Chr 21:1 understands the word as a name, Satan. This figure replaces the troubling anger of YHWH from a parallel text in 2 Samuel, as noted below. The emergence of the adversary, called Satan in later literature, corresponds to Persian influence that began in the late sixth century BCE and extended into the second half of the fourth century.[6] The antecedents of this figure, however, are genuinely Hebraic.

The Bible has preserved several glimpses of the deity's shadow side, the most disturbing of which is found in the story about the near sacrifice of Isaac. Echoes of this narrative can be heard in the related folktale about tests put to an innocent Job. These incidents tower over other enigmatic reports of divine conduct that is neither appropriate nor ethical by human standards. How can any reader make sense of the many inconsistencies in the divine character portrayed in the Bible?[7] To name but a few: the brief anecdote about God's trying to kill Moses after having commissioned him to rescue an afflicted people in Egypt (Exod 4:24–26); the instances in which YHWH is said to have hardened an opponent's will to prevent him from repenting of wayward behavior (Exod 10:1; Isa 6:9–13); an inexplicable reversal when the deity commands a specific act and subsequently punishes an obedient servant (2 Sam 24:1–15); an arbitrary slaying of a certain Uzzah for trying to prevent the ark, a palladium of war, from falling to the ground (2 Sam 6:6–7). Such examples are numerous enough to project a huge question mark over the biblical image of God.

In this chapter, I examine the paradigmatic stories in Gen 22:1–19 and Job 1–2 and 42:7–17[8] that describe a dark side of the biblical deity. The first of these, usually called the Akedah in Jewish literature and the binding of Isaac in Christian theology,[9] simply attributes the test to the deity, whereas the second story introduces another heavenly being and places on it the primary blame for the ordeal through which the innocent victim must pass. This difference between the two stories has a parallel in the historiography that celebrates the exploits of chieftains in Israel and Judah. In 2 Sam 24:1–25, the deity commands David to take a census of the people, ostensibly for military purposes, but subsequently exacts a heavy price for David's very obedience to the divine decree. The revisionist historian responsible for 1 Chr 21:1 finds it necessary to exonerate YHWH by introducing Satan as the one who gives the original order to number the people. For a biblical writer, it is unseemly that the deity could behave in such a contradictory manner. In his telling of the story, then, an antagonist assumes responsibility for inciting David to act contrary to the divine will.

The Testing of Abraham (Genesis 22:1–19)

[1]Afterward God tested Abraham. He [God] said to him, "Abraham," and he answered, "Yes." [2]God said, "Take, I beg of you, your only son, whom you love, Isaac, and go to the land of the Amorites and sacrifice him there as a burnt offering on one of the mountains of which I will tell you." [3]Arising early in the morning Abraham saddled his ass and took two of his lads with him, together with Isaac his son. Having split wood for the sacrificial fire, he arose and journeyed to the place of which God spoke. [4]On the third day Abraham

lifted up his eyes and saw the place from afar. ⁵Then Abraham said to his lads: "Stay here with the ass; I and the lad will go yonder. We shall worship and return to you."

⁶Abraham took the wood for the burnt offering and laid it on Isaac his son, but he took in his own hand the fire and the knife, and the two of them journeyed together. ⁷Now Isaac said to Abraham his father, "Dad?" He answered, "Yes, my son." And Isaac said, "Look, here are the fire and the wood, but where is the sacrificial victim?" ⁸Abraham said, "God will see to the sacrificial animal, my son." The two of them journeyed together.

⁹When they arrived at the place of which God told him, Abraham built an altar there, arranged the wood, bound Isaac his son, and put him on top of the wood on the altar. ¹⁰Reaching out his hand, Abraham took the knife to slay his son. ¹¹An angel of YHWH called to him from heaven, "Abraham, Abraham." "Yes," Abraham answered. ¹²He said, "Do not stretch forth your hand against the lad or do anything to him, for now I know that you fear God since you did not withhold your son—your only one—from me." ¹³Lifting up his eyes, Abraham spied a ram caught by its horns in a thicket. He went (there), took the ram, and offered it as a burnt offering instead of his son. ¹⁴Abraham called the name of that place "YHWH sees," for it is said (even) today, "On the mountain YHWH is seen."

¹⁵Now the angel of YHWH called from heaven a second time, ¹⁶"By myself I swear, it is a whisper of YHWH, that because you have done this thing and have not withheld your son—your only one—¹⁷I will surely bless you and multiply your progeny like the stars of heaven and like the sand on the seashore; your descendants shall possess the gates of their enemies. ¹⁸All nations of the earth shall bless themselves by your descendants because you obeyed my voice." ¹⁹Then Abraham returned to his lads; they arose and journeyed together to Beersheba, where Abraham dwelt.

How are we to understand this troubling story, one that surely strikes terror in children and besmirches the character of the deity?[10] Above all, we must acknowledge the text as one that narrates a crisis in the relationship between humans and God—a God who, according to this text, cannot really be known. Beyond that, some readers may see it as a hideous display of tyranny by an egotistical but insecure God; others, as an ethical breakthrough in which an old practice is put to rest.[11] Still others may see it as a monumental Yahwistic theology of exodus.[12] Christian readers, who see an obvious association with the Passion narrative,[13] may even view the account as a parallel to Jesus' temptation in the wilderness (Matthew 4; Luke 4). However we understand the story, we cannot deny its linguistic beauty and anthropological constant. After all, the only death in the present form of the story is nonhuman and indeed largely ignored. The thought of actually slaying a child in response to a divine voice is alien to modern readers, who must be reminded that for the author, such a thing represented a real possibility.

The artistic subtlety of the narrative, often noted by its admirers, partially compensates for its shocking content. The narrator relates only the bare essentials of the story, leaving it "fraught with background," in the language of the literary critic Erich Auerbach.[14] Even the dialogue between father and son during the journey, set off by a refrain in vv 6 and 8 that has been called "perhaps the most poignant and eloquent silence in all literature"[15]—"the two of them journeyed together"—consists of only fifteen words in Hebrew: "Dad? . . . Yes, my son. . . . Look, here are the fire and the wood, but where is the sacrificial victim? . . . God will see to the sacrificial animal, my son."

The only apposition in the narrative ("your only son, whom you love, Isaac") emphasizes the depth of a father's affection for his son, just as the extraordinary Hebrew particle of entreaty, attached to the initial divine imperative ("Take, I beg of you, your only son") indicates God's awareness of the burden imposed on a faithful servant.[16] Finally, the disappearance of Isaac in the last verse, together with total silence about Sarah from beginning to end, sets fertile imaginations to work in an effort to fill in the gaps.[17]

Listen to some of the ways later readers have attempted to supply missing data:[18]

How old was the beloved son when he was subjected to this awful ordeal? Twenty-five—rather, thirty-seven.[19]

Did he resist, considering life more important than the commandment to honor father and mother? No, he freely offered himself as a sacrifice to God.

How did Sarah react when hearing the story of her husband's secretive behavior? She let out a frightening shriek and died.

Where did the actual sacrifice take place? At Moriah, the sacred mountain that later came to be known as Zion.

Did the episode permanently alter the relationship between father and son? Yes.

The relationship between Abraham and God? Yes.[20]

The skillful narrator creates an unforgettable scene that sustains readers' interest throughout.[21] Some features of the story require a knowledge of Hebrew to appreciate, especially the puns. The rare word for an only son, *yekhideka*, is echoed in the word *yakhdaw* (together) in the refrain ("the two of them journeyed together"), an association that is broken in the latter's final use, at the end of the account, for Isaac is no longer present. Moreover, the word for seeing (yir'eh) occurs also in the sense of providing and resembles the verb for fearing (yere'), both echoed in God's name for the place (hammoriyah). The only redundancy in the story comes from a voluble angel, who twice names Abraham and gives equal reference to his only son. To reinforce his promise that good things will spring from what has happened in this place, the messenger swears by himself and adds an oracular formula, "whisper of YHWH."

We do not know the exact date of composition, for the usual indications of different authors in the Pentateuch—specifically, the choice of divine names—suggest composite authorship or layers of tradition. The story balances the names YHWH and Elohim evenly, referring to each five times. The role of the angel and the theme "fear of God" in vv 1–14 and 19 are elsewhere attributed to the Elohist. The repetition in vv 15–18 of the promised blessings from Gen 12:2–3 belongs to the traditions associated with the Yahwist. The three uses of YHWH in vv 11 and 14 point to established idiom ("the angel of YHWH") and an ancient etiology associated with a sacred site. Obviously, this exquisite narrative represents a combining of earlier traditions, probably in the exilic period.[22]

The opening statement accomplishes two important things: (1) it places the story in a larger context, and (2) it provides vital information to readers that is withheld from Abraham—namely, that this horrible ordeal is a test. The actual events referred to by the word 'akhar (afterward) are not specified, but strong linguistic affinities with the preceding chapter and with Genesis 12 suggest that the narrative has been leading up to this episode from the outset. Indeed, it has been argued that key expressions also link this story with the holocaust offering in Exodus 19–24.[23]

In its present form, the account in Genesis 12 of the departure of Abram (the narrator's earlier name for the patriarch) from Ur of the Chaldees anticipates a costly sacrifice, for a man reputed to be already 75 years old is commanded to leave family and homeland in search of an unknown future. He sacrifices, as it were, the security of the familiar. Abandoning his parents, Abram sets out on a hazardous journey, accompanied by Sarah and a nephew, Lot. Both of these companions will later complicate that journey, but neither will bring the anguish brought by the son of promise. This child, long delayed but finally born to aged parents, has been preceded by an adoptive son, Eliezer, and another son, Ishmael, born to a rival wife who was given to Abraham by Sarah in the hope of having children through a surrogate. The narrator of Genesis 22 seems to have no knowledge of either Eliezer or Ishmael, and the same apparent ignorance applies to the deity and the angel as well. In Genesis 21, however we see that Sarah is very much aware of the existence of Ishmael, and in due time her jealousy boils over in a demand that Abraham drive the rival wife, Hagar, and her small son into the desolate wilderness. This virtual sentence of death does not generate sufficient compassion in the spineless (or placating) Abraham to resist Sarah's wishes. Consequently, mother and son are sent away to die, and Abraham is never informed that a watchful heavenly protector has frustrated Sarah's scheme. Thus, as far as Abraham knows, Isaac is his only remaining son by birth.

The emphatic position of the divine subject in verse 1 ("God tested Abraham") excludes any secondary cause for the ordeal that follows. From the standpoint of the narrator, God alone is responsible for the test of Abraham's obedience. Together with v 12b, "for now I know that you fear God since you did not withhold your son—your only one—from me,"[24] this opening declaration informs readers that a vulnerable deity searches for an answer to the question, Can I depend on Abraham to obey me without reservation?[25]

Behind the deity's uncertainty where human choice is concerned lies an extensive account of frustrated efforts to relate to humankind. The Yahwist has placed the story of Abraham at the culmination of a long series of rebellious acts that have incurred divine wrath again and again, finally bringing down a devastating flood. With the subsequent dispersal of humans after their attempt to reach heaven's gate, YHWH tries something entirely new. He chooses a single family and through them hopes to bestow blessing on all peoples. He cannot accomplish that goal, however, without total obedience by the chosen few. This story seeks to discover whether or not Abraham as head of that special family trusts YHWH completely. At stake is the first commandment: the demand of absolute loyalty.

Modern scholars have amassed considerable evidence of human sacrifice in the ancient Near East,[26] which supplements scattered indications of this practice in the Bible. The most explicit corroboration of the ultimate gift to the deity comes from the Covenant Code (Exod 20:22–23:33), generally considered to be the oldest legislation in the Bible: "Your firstborn son you shall give to me. So also you shall do with respect to your oxen and sheep. It shall be with its dam seven days; on the eighth day you shall give it to me" (Exod 22:28b–29). According to a more humane Exod 13:2, the firstborn is to be consecrated and a lamb substituted for him.

The notion of human sacrifice persisted in Israelite thinking as late as the eighth century BCE, for Micah ponders whether the fruit of the body will atone for one's sin (Mic 6:7). Even in the sixth century the divine command to sacrifice infants was remembered by Ezekiel, and Jeremiah notes the persistence of this practice. The prophet Ezekiel offers a shocking justification for the statute that requires the burning of the firstborn: YHWH was seeking to horrify the Israelites and to teach them his identity (Ezek 20:26). Jeremiah, in contrast, argues that YHWH had nothing to do with this abominable practice, which, the prophet insists, was their own doing and contrary to divine will (Jer 7:31). In all probability, extreme circumstances brought on by war, pestilence, drought, and plague drove some desperate people to revert to earlier practice in the fervent hope that YHWH would be moved to act in their behalf.

Abraham's reaction to the divine word in this story lacks any sense of surprise, unlike the earlier story about the intended destruction of Sodom and Gomorrah. The patriarch does not question the propriety of the command to immolate his beloved son, nor does he feel obligated to explain his intentions to his wife. Moreover, his explanation to the young servants who accompany father and son part of the way comes perilously close to deception. The stated purpose of their journey—to worship—while technically accurate, conceals the horror from the lads, including Isaac. The promise that both father and son will return is not fulfilled in the narrative, for Isaac is absent from verse 19, which reports that Abraham returned to the servants and they accompanied him to Beersheba. This gap in the story gave rise to later Jewish speculation that Isaac was actually slain on the altar.[27] Indeed, his death is implied by claims that the Akedah atoned for the people's sins. Jewish ritual was ineffective apart from the shedding of blood, without which there could be no atonement. The Akedah, the binding of Isaac, was said to bring redemption to Israel at the start of each new year when the ram's horn was sounded.

In the discourse of the narrator, Abraham's response to Isaac's puzzled question about the absence of a lamb may be intended to hide the true nature of their journey. "God will see to the sacrificial animal, my son" may be read in two ways, with "my son" understood as direct address or as apposition. If we choose the latter reading, Abraham really means to identify Isaac as the lamb. If we opt for the former, Abraham is calling Isaac "my son" rather than "the lad" as earlier, in v 5, which put Isaac and the servants on the same level and perhaps signaled Abraham's feeling that his beloved son was lost to him. His initial response to Isaac's address, "Dad," in v 7 shows Abraham's preference for the affectionate term "my son."

The missing element of surprise over the actual content of the divine word and the patriarch's readiness to obey suggest that Abraham considers the command, although extreme, totally in keeping with YHWH's character. Nowhere does Abraham raise the philosopher's objection or protest that morality requires that the voice be demonic. He experiences neither Søren Kierkegaard's incredulity nor Emmanuel Kant's moral outrage.[28] For the biblical hero, the voice is familiar and the command apt. Indeed, the command's threefold nature recalls the deity's earlier threefold command to depart from Ur of the

Chaldees, and Abraham's unquestioning obedience links the consequent blessing in Gen 22:15–18 with Gen 12:1–3. Even the openness of the instruction, its
failure to specify in advance the exact location for the sacrifice, recalls earlier
precedent. The original sending forth of the patriarch left ample room for trust,
for that journey's end would be made known only with the passing of time.
The present setting forth demands ultimate trust, for what Abraham already
knows about this journey's end can be faced only with the assurance of divine
accompaniment.

Abraham behaves as if the divine command is thinkable. Is the story then
intended to pass negative judgment on the ancient practice of devoting the
firstborn to the deity? Many interpreters have thought so, despite the lack of
any explicit renunciation of the rite. The substitution of a lamb for Isaac, with
divine approval, means that Abraham's willingness to slay his son is tantamount to performing the deed itself. This new understanding of sacrifice
presses beyond external conduct to the inner condition of the worshiper. It is
the disposition of the mind, not the outer display, that means most to YHWH!

The great prophets frequently make the same point, arguing that the right
condition of the mind is more pleasing to the deity than abundant gifts on the
altar. One function of the story, therefore, is to signal a shift in cultic practice,
making it acceptable to substitute an animal for a firstborn son. For the story
to accomplish that end, it need not have an explicit directive. The narrator is
far too subtle for that. Still, this understanding of the story as a shift from
human to animal sacrifice faces objections: (1) the loss of historical information
about the specific location of the incident; (2) the absence of any indication
that Abraham understands the event as involving a new ethic; and (3) the lack
of divine repudiation of human sacrifice.[29] The first argument loses force when
we recall that a similar loss of historical information surrounds other important
sacred places (Shiloh, Shechem, Gilgal). The second argument applies only if
we assume that the narrator identifies with the time of the narrative. The
difference between narrated time and the date of composition is crucial. The
narrator may be addressing readers in an era when human sacrifice is no
longer practiced. As for the missing divine repudiation—that is implicit in the
story itself. Once divine approval for the principle of substitution has been
voiced, what need is there for explicit comment?

From Abraham's perspective, the story is about obedience. Will he do what
Elohim commands him to do, even if it means placing the divine promise in
jeopardy? The narrator portrays Abraham as a loyal servant who acts without
questioning the deity. He demonstrates total allegiance, rising early in the
morning and preparing for the journey. Arriving at his destination, he goes
about his work with deliberate speed. The verbs at this point in the story have

a staccato effect, conveying determination and singleness of purpose. Even after the angel's announcement of reprieve, Abraham looks, goes, takes, and offers the substitute. Nothing more.

Through it all, the narrator refrains from conveying the slightest emotion on Abraham's part. Hermann Gunkel has detected a hint of parental concern in the allocation of the burden for the journey.[30] Abraham lays the wood for the fire on Isaac's shoulder while carrying the more dangerous items himself, specifically, the flint stone or hot embers and the knife.[31]

Although the narrator offers no glimpse into Abraham's thoughts, interpreters have been less restrained. Their reading between the lines takes several forms. The rabbis imagined the following dialogue between Abraham and God:

God	Abraham
"Take your son."	"I have two sons."
"Your only one."	"This one is the only son of his mother, and this (other) one is the only son of his mother."
"The one you love."	"I love them both."
"Isaac."	

Kierkegaard offers several different scenarios, culminating in Abraham's pretending to be a monster in order to protect God's reputation.[32] Rembrandt completed several renderings of the episode, most notably in an expansive painting when he was a young man and in a small etching many years later. These widely different depictions attest the profundity of the biblical story and its capacity to inspire awe and wonder. The initial painting shows a zealous father with knife in hand, eager to slay his son, whom he has roughly stretched out on an altar. Beside him stands a curly-haired youth with wings barely visible. The later etching pictures the agony on Abraham's face as the angel lovingly cradles him and stays the hand that grips the knife. Staring ahead, Abraham cannot see the angel, and "his face has the ravaged expression of someone who has survived something unspeakable."[33]

The narrator likewise reveals nothing of Isaac's thoughts beyond the mere expression of puzzlement over the missing victim. Jewish interpreters have calculated the boy's age as 37, thus emphasizing his voluntary surrender. Furthermore, they have credited him with a deep desire to assure the acceptability of his death. To this end, he requests to be bound so that he will not flinch before the knife and thus render the sacrifice unworthy. Comparisons between Isaac and Jesus are natural, even to the use of the servant poem in Isa 52:13–53:12 (which I discuss in chapter 8) as an interpretive clue. The deaths of both

Isaac and Jesus are viewed as atoning sacrifices willingly offered for the benefit of others. The different communities of faith probably arrived independently at this vicarious understanding of the Akedah and the cross.

A poignant comment addressed to Abraham by the mother of the seven martyred sons from the story in 2 Maccabees 7 implies that for some Jews, the comparison of Isaac and Jesus comes at the former's expense. She remarks: "Yours was the trial; mine, the performances."[34] That is, you and Isaac merely endured a test. My sons went far beyond enduring a test; they gave their lives for their faith. The midrash on the Akedah provides a powerful answer to this cry of a distraught mother. Isaac, too, it announces, gave his all on that fateful day. That was not the final word, for angels are said to have transported his body to paradise, nursing it for three years in the dew of heaven. Alternatively, the ashes were transformed when God resurrected an obedient son. In this manner, the justice of God is protected from a serious infraction.

The Testing of Job (Job 1–2; 42:7–17)

The other horrendous test in the Hebrew Bible is recorded in the book of Job.[35] The plot of the story that frames the philosophical dialogue of the central chapters is relatively simple. Job, a wealthy and deeply pious man, becomes the focus of a disagreement between YHWH and a heavenly subordinate, "the adversary" (*satan*), over the real basis for human loyalty.[36] The question at issue: Does Job serve the deity for the rewards freely bestowed on him? The two agree to subject him to a test to see if he will curse YHWH when the blessings are revoked. With the deity's permission, the adversary destroys all of Job's possessions, including his seven sons and three daughters, but Job responds as YHWH has predicted: "Naked I came from my mother's womb and naked I shall return there; YHWH has given and YHWH has taken. Blessed be the name of YHWH" (Job 1:21). A second heavenly assembly results in a discussion similar to the first, as well as another test, this time affecting Job's physical health. Again Job remains loyal to YHWH, even when pressed by his wife to curse God and die. Comparing her advice to that of foolish women, Job asks an incisive question: "Shall we receive good from YHWH and not receive evil?" (2:10).

Twice the narrator commends Job for retaining his integrity, stating that he did not sin and adding, the second time, "with his lips." The rectitude of Job's speech is further underscored in the epilogue, where Job's friends are censured by YHWH for having spoken falsely about the deity in their accusatory pronouncements against Job. They stand in need of Job's prayers in their behalf, YHWH says, and Job's intercession indeed brings pardon for them—and renewed blessing for Job. His relationships are reestablished, his possessions are restored twofold, and he and his wife have new children. Contrary to custom, his beautiful daughters receive an inheritance along with their brothers. What is more, the hero lives to see four generations of descendants and dies at a ripe old age.

The author of Gen 22:1 does not hesitate to attribute the monstrous test of Abraham to God, but the compiler of the didactic story in the book of Job resists such a harsh depiction of Israel's deity, preferring rather to blame a lesser heavenly being for the trial that turns Job's life upside down. The difference is minor, for YHWH grants permission to an underling and places limits on what the adversary may do: others may be killed in the course of the trial, but Job's life must be spared precisely for the sake of the test. Moreover, the text itself has the deity concede his role as the actual source of calamity ("although you enticed me against him to swallow him without cause," Job 2: 3b). The adversary is merely the catalyst that propels a menacing force to draw Job and all that he has into its maw. In the end, the attempt to let the deity off the hook has failed.

Echoes of Genesis 22 are easily detected in the story of Job's test. In both accounts, the verb *nsh* in the Piel identifies the incident as a test, and in both this vital information is concealed from the persons involved. Each story culminates in divine blessing, including a lengthy life. Other similarities include vast riches, the descriptive term "fear of God" for religious devotion, others' receiving divine blessing as a direct result of the protagonist's enduring the test, burnt offerings, and puns on the place names (Moriah and Uz).[37] Linguistic affinities include lifted eyes, rising early in the morning, the shift from son(s) to lad(s), reverse syntax for emphasis in Job 1:1 and Gen 22:1, the phrase "stretch forth your hand," and the word *yakhdaw* (together) as an indication of solidarity (Gen 22:6, 8, 19; Job 2:11).[38]

These similarities between the two narratives are negated to some extent by distinct differences, especially the presence of the secondary figure in the Joban prologue. Its role hardly corresponds to the angel who surprises a determined Abraham with a command to stay his hand. Another significant difference is the absence of any choice on Job's part about the ordeal to which he is subjected. A third distinction is the nature of each test: Abraham's test involves the impending loss of his son—at his own hand—as an explicit condition of obedience; Job's involves the actual loss of his children, together with his fortune and his health, in utter ignorance of divine intention or presence.

Honor is a major concern in the Job narrative, both for Job, who is surrounded by charges of base conduct, and for the deity, whose judgment has been called into question. YHWH believes that Job's devotion is disinterested and has nothing to do with reward or punishment. The adversary disagrees, charging Job with making an astute assessment of reality and using religion for his own benefit. The adversary articulates a cynical claim: "All that he has he will give for his life" (Job 2:4).

Behind this dialogue is a long religious history that can be summed up in three Latin words: *do ut des* (I give so that you may give). In short, an individual expects to gain something by serving the gods. In its crassest form, this belief constitutes the magical approach to religion: by acting in a given manner, one gains control over the gods, who, in a mechanistic universe, are obligated to reward goodness and punish evil.[39] Obviously, this conviction rests on the unfounded assumption that the universe is ruled by a principle of justice. Even the gods are subject to it and must reward faithful service.[40] The adversary's primary role in the book of Job is to determine whether Job's religious devotion transcends such a measure-for-measure calculation. Job's conduct in the prologue indeed challenges the magical conception of religion. That the happy ending in the epilogue reasserts this notion is considered a major flaw by many interpreters.[41]

Does the portrayal of the divine character remain constant within each story, or are there indications of change in either narrative? YHWH remains the same within the prose of the book of Job, but what about Genesis 22? Clearly, the description of the deity in Genesis 1–11 indicates frequent change as a result of trial and error, YHWH's chosen method of relating to rebellious humans. The subjection of Abraham and Isaac to this unthinkable test, however, brings no acknowledgment of divine error or remorse. Even the last-minute reprieve comes from an angel rather than the deity, who directly issued the initial command.

Like the test in Genesis 22, the story of Job's loss and subsequent restoration seems to have a complex compositional history.[42] The heavenly adversary may not have belonged to the earliest account, where relatives or friends probably played the role of antagonist. The revisions of the story, which occurred in the process of its interpretation over the years, continued long after its fixation in the canon, especially in the Testament of Job. Here Job's virtues are nearly unlimited, especially his charitable acts, and his wife is depicted much more favorably. Moreover, his struggle with the heavenly adversary is amplified, with Job recognizing the unwelcome intruder and successfully resisting its feigned favors.

The biblical story about Job consists of eight scenes, beginning on earth and subsequently alternating between heaven and earth, then returning to earth for the final three.[43] This shift from earth to heaven and back again is mirrored in the agents of destruction that deprive Job of his possessions. Marauding Sabeans are followed by "God's fire," and Chaldean soldiers give way to a devastating wind. The plot unfolds as human beings and nature itself conspire against Job's flocks and children, with slaves caught in the middle.

Extravagant use of repetition, especially refrains, gives the language of the narrative a ring of familiarity. The narrator credits Job with four attributes: integrity, justice, piety, and innocence (1:1), implying wholeness, fair treatment of others, proper reverence, and sufficient strength to turn away from temptation. On encountering the adversary for the first time, YHWH uses all four terms in boasting of Job's exceptional goodness, then hurls them in the adversary's face a second time after the first test (1:8, 2:3). When the messengers report a series of calamities to Job, they each use the same words: "I alone escaped to tell you" (1:15, 16, 17, 19), and the presence of the last three messengers is announced this way: "While one was speaking, another came and said . . ." (1:16, 17, 18). A single statement introduces and concludes this litany of horrors: "His/Your sons and daughters were eating bread and drinking wine in their older brother's house" (1:13, 18). Both YHWH and the adversary repeat themselves on their second meeting, as does the narrator:

> Another day the sons of God presented themselves before YHWH, and the adversary also took a stand in their midst. YHWH said to the adversary, "Where have you come from?" Answering, the adversary said, "From wandering on earth and walking about in it." YHWH said to the adversary, "Have you thought about my servant Job, for there is no one like him on earth, a man of integrity, just, religious, and turning away from evil . . . ?" (2:1–3)

In both encounters, the adversary uses the words "Stretch forth your hand" and YHWH grants permission for him to do so, repeating the words "Look, he is in your hand," as well as, in the first encounter, the adversary's phrase (1:11–12, 2:5–6). An appreciable difference occurs, however, when YHWH uses the phrase, for a restrictive element appears ("only do *not* touch him [literally, stretch forth your hand]"), and the phrase is replaced altogether in YHWH's second response ("Look, he is in your power [literally, hand]; only preserve his life"). By using the normal Hebrew word for providential care, *shamar* (to watch over), this admonition shimmers with irony.[44] The adversary's departure from the heavenly assembly is described in both instances in a single phrase, the only difference being the preposition: "The adversary went out from YHWH's presence" (1:12, 2:7).

The prose includes poetic lines with the usual parallelism ("Naked I came from my mother's womb and naked I shall return there; YHWH has given and YHWH has taken"). Hardly a Freudian allusion, this terse reference to "there" implies either Sheol or mother earth, as discussed in chapter 2. The narrative also employs elevated phrases that suggest frequent oral performance. The numbers point to completeness: seven sons and three daughters, seven thousand sheep and three thousand camels, five hundred cattle and five hundred she-asses (1:2–3); seven bulls and seven rams (42:8); seven uses of the verb "bless/curse"; seven days and seven nights. Even unrelated items add up to seven: three Chaldean company leaders (or columns) plus four corners of the house; Job's three friends plus four virtues.

In this narrative, two words form the spokes that radiate outward as from the hub of a wheel. The first, *khinnam* (for nothing),[45] encapsulates the gist of the entire story. Its initial appearance amounts to a stinging assault on the deity: "For nothing does Job fear God?" (1:9). Its emphatic position signifies the importance assigned to it. The adversary suspects that the protective hedge around Job and all that he owns guarantees his loyalty. Remove that, he insists, and Job will curse you to your face. In its second occurrence, this word comes at the end of a long statement by YHWH in which he praises Job once more and accuses the adversary of enticing him to swallow Job "for nothing" (2:3). Both the protection and the assault against Job fall into the category of "gratuitous" and thus magnify the irony of life itself. So much that comes our way is without cause, the story seems to say.

The second thematic word is the verb *barak* (to bless),[46] which is also used in the opposite sense of "to curse." Readers must decide on the basis of context which meaning to apply in each instance. Job fears that his sons may have cursed God in their thoughts (1:5), and his wife urges him to curse God and die (2:9). The adversary suggests that once Job has been rendered vulnerable he will curse God to his face (1:11; 2:5). Instead, a smitten Job concludes his first reaction to grievous loss with the prayer "May the name of YHWH be blessed" (1:21). The final use of the verb is reserved for the narrator, who reports that YHWH blessed Job's later life even more than his early days (42:12). The adversary has used the verb in this sense earlier when accusing YHWH of blessing Job so that his property bursts forth, as if to free itself of the protective hedge (1:10).

If these two words are like the spokes in a wheel, a third word resembles the hub. The noun *tummah* (integrity; adjective *tam*)[47] rolls off the lips of Job's wife with such ease: "Do you still cling to your integrity? Curse God and die!" (2:9). Similarly, YHWH reminds the adversary that "he still clings to his integrity although you enticed me against him to swallow him without cause"

(2:3). Twice, too, YHWH brags about Job's admirable character, which includes, among other things, integrity (1:8, 2:3). Indeed, the opening verse has the narrator praise the hero's integrity, which will soon be put to the ultimate test.

Perhaps, too, the unusual word that appears to mean "unseemliness" (*ti-plah*)[48] signals an important concept: "In all this Job did not sin or attribute unseemliness to God" (1:22). The narrator knows full well that perceptive readers will do just that; they will consider the deity's conduct wholly inappropriate. After all, the narrative claims, Job first came to the adversary's attention through the loose lips of YHWH, who must therefore bear some responsibility for the events that transpired after this disclosure of a handy object for testing.[49]

Once we have come to appreciate the skill with which the author frames the problem to be addressed in the poetic dialogue, we still must search for a precise formulation of it. At least three possibilities commend themselves: (1) How should one speak about the deity? (2) How should one respond to suffering? and (3) Does disinterested righteousness exist?

The adversary poses the first and third questions, whereas the second question, although never explicit, is evoked by the story's existential effect on readers. The hero demonstrates the proper way to speak about God[50]—specifically, to address the deity directly and reverentially. Rather than responding as conjectured by the adversary in an oath—"By God, he will curse you to your face" (1:11)—Job acknowledges his complete dependence on YHWH, who both gives and takes. In so doing, Job answers the third question, the adversary's challenge concerning disinterested righteousness. Yes, rare individuals—after all, both the narrator and YHWH concede Job's exceptional goodness—will worship God gratuitously, never counting the cost to see whether their allegiance pays dividends.

The answer to the second question—How should one respond to suffering? receives no direct answer in the framing story but is explored at length in the poetry. The traditional response that Job models in the narrative stands out precisely because it contrasts with the answers he endorses in the poetic dialogue.

The story of the monstrous test imposed by God on the patriarch and his son reflects badly, in most readings, on the deity's character. When composing a related account of a horrendous test, a clever author devised a means of sheltering the deity from opprobrium. In this manner a rival figure emerges to take responsibility for the test, becoming an extension of the deity through personification of a doubting thought.[51] The move fails in its intention, for the adversary cannot act apart from the deity's permission. This dependence of the subordinate figure means that responsibility for its actions rests ultimately with

God. The later development of this figure into a formidable foe, Satan, continues to suffer from this flaw. Perhaps, then, God's honor can be salvaged by another means—by accentuating human freedom. This move, of course, would at the same time limit the deity's power. In the next chapter I examine this way of responding to the problem of evil.

PART II

Redefining God

4

Limited Power and Knowledge

Accentuating Human Freedom

One man's justice is another man's injustice.

—Ralph Waldo Emerson

Like their neighbors in Egypt, Syria, and Mesopotamia, the early Israelites believed that supreme power resided with the deity. As creator of everything that was, YHWH controlled the universe in every detail, from the rising of the sun to the nocturnal prowling of the lion and everything in between. Rains came, and harvest, at the creator's bidding, as did famine and pestilence. Nothing took place under the sun that was remotely contrary to the divine will. Even social and political events were thought to be dictated by the deity, so firm was the ancients' belief in divine sovereignty. This heightened sense of God's power left minimal responsibility to humans, turning individuals into mere puppets manipulated by divine hands.[1]

Such is the impression conveyed by many ancient texts. Nevertheless, the literature also implies that men and women make free choices that shape their character and determine the consequences of their actions.[2] The story of the first couple in the garden emphasizes human culpability for making the wrong choice, and YHWH's warning to the first murderer emphasizes the primacy of human choice. Adam and Eve were fully responsible for their decision to eat from the tree, and Cain was fully capable of mastering his murderous anger. Vulnerable though they were, each freely chose a course of action in defiance of the creator—which the deity, in turn, chose not to overrule. The very concept of Torah, pervasive in the Bible, implies the freedom to obey or not to obey, unconstrained by divine intervention. Furthermore, once a decision is made, human experience takes one road to the exclusion of others. Until that choice is final, God cannot know the course of an individual's life. Free will requires an open future that would be a sham if God were prescient. It follows that the deity lacks complete knowledge.

Like the qualities of justice and mercy, divine sovereignty and human freedom clash with one another. Their irreconcilability leaves an indelible mark on biblical literature, which bears deep and conflicting imprints of both. In an effort to preserve an illusion of control in the heavens—in short, to address the problem of theodicy—certain biblical writers stress the distinction between the potential and the actual with respect to the deity. While YHWH possesses full potentiality for absolute power and knowledge, the deity chooses in actuality to limit those qualities so that he might endow human beings with self-determination.[3] In this chapter I consider this approach to theodicy in the writings of the biblical prophets.

Human Freedom

Within the biblical canon, the Former Prophets constitute a monumental theodicy, an almost heroic attempt to exonerate the deity from permitting the defeat of Jerusalem and the exportation of a large number of Judeans to Babylonia. In the view of the authors of the Deuteronomistic History,[4] this core event resulted from repeated acts of disloyalty on the part of a covenanted people, not from inherent weakness on the part of YHWH.[5] The rebellious conduct is described as nothing less than a cycle of sin, punishment, repentance, and deliverance. The cumulative effect of such human willfulness brought on a final calamity, the unthinkable razing of the cultic site believed to be the residence of the deity YHWH.[6] The fault, insofar as one can assess blame in matters of this kind, did not lie with the deity but rested on human shoulders as the direct result of human freedom.[7]

Historical events, however, never as simple as biblical literature implies, frequently took perplexing turns that defied systematization.[8] The Deuteronomistic understanding of strict reward and retribution activated by human choice was difficult to reconcile with the real-life experience of YHWH's people. Josiah's early death must have rendered speechless all who thought they had discovered a definitive historiography grounded in religious conviction.[9] In the stark light of historical reality, how could the tradition be kept intact?

Corporate Freedom

One strategy for preserving the traditional beliefs was simply to exclude all evidence to the contrary. This approach occurs in Zeph 3:1–5, which declares unmitigated corporate guilt and denies any possibility of divine injustice:

> Ah, soiled, polluted, oppressing city!
> She has obeyed no one,
>   received no instruction.
> She has not trusted in YHWH,
>   nor drawn near to her God.
> Her officials within are roaring lions;
>   her judges are evening wolves
>   that have reserved nothing until the morning.
> Her prophets are wanton, treacherous individuals;
>   her priests have profaned the sacred,
>   they have done violence to the law.
> YHWH in her midst is righteous [*tsaddiq*];
>   he does no injustice [*'awlah*].
> Every morning he pronounces judgment,
>   each dawn without fail,
>   but the unjust [*'awwal*] knows no shame.

The wanton exercise of human freedom has set Jerusalem's course. A righteous deity—present in her midst, despite her faithlessness—administers the judgment that she brings upon herself.

For Zephaniah, the holy city's corruption contrasts with the deity's perfection. Human leaders, without exception, are judged to be guilty—officials, judges, prophets, and priests. The usual deterrent to ravenous conduct, a desire to avoid the slightest hint of shame, has lost its power, leaving them utterly bereft of honor. Over against this perfidy stands a divine incapacity to do wrong, at least in the view of the prophet. Others may berate YHWH for failing to execute judgment in a timely manner, but Zephaniah detects no such dereliction of duty.[10]

Zephaniah's exuberant confidence in YHWH's justice matches that exemplified in Psalm 92, which envisions a just society in which God unfailingly rewards the righteous and ultimately crushes the wicked. The psalmist acknowledges the mystery of momentary success on the part of evildoers but attributes its inexplicability to a combination of factors, primarily human laziness and divine profundity (Ps 92:6–7). In this deity who causes the righteous to flourish like a well-watered palm, the psalmist can detect no sign of injustice.

The gloss that concludes the book of Hosea also rules out the existence of divine injustice:

> Those who are wise understand these things;
>   those who are discerning know them.
> For the ways of YHWH are right [yesharim],
>   and the upright [tsaddiqim] walk in them,
>   but transgressors stumble on them. (Hos 14:10)

The difference between this affirmation and Zephaniah's is noteworthy. Whereas Zephaniah characterizes YHWH as not guilty—indeed, incapable of doing wrong—the gloss in Hosea refers to divine activity rather than the deity's nature, using the adjective yesharim, a word that indicates straight dealings, and reserving tsaddiqim (not guilty, righteous) for obedient people.

Individual Freedom

The principle of self-determination, the ability to shape one's own destiny for good or ill, was applied originally to all of Israel, the corporate entity. Choices carried consequences for the entire covenantal community, understood to extend both geographically and across time.[11] This conception of Israel enabled religious leaders to reckon with individual miscarriages of justice, which were dismissed as inevitable anomalies within the community. As long as the larger group remained healthy, these minor injustices were bearable. Once the corporate entity was threatened, however, such individual aberrances required a better explanation. The necessity for serious reflection on this issue was impressed upon the sixth-century prophet Ezekiel by a popular saying that stated the problem succinctly: "Fathers have eaten sour grapes, and children's teeth have become sensitive" (Ezek 18:2).

On a literal level, this proverb, which was circulating among Jews in Babylon (and also in Judah, if its presence in the book of Jeremiah is not an editorial gloss),[12] made no sense. Everyone knew that only the person who ate the grapes would taste their bitterness. In the improbable scenario of the proverb, the unpleasant consequences of foolish behavior extended across generations, with children suffering for what their parents had done. An impossibility in the natural world became the logic of a deep rift in corporate solidarity, the rebellion of youth against their progenitors. Alternatively, the popular saying revealed a situation of lethargy, where young people were throwing up their hands in despair over a hopeless fate brought upon them by the older generation. In either case, the point of the proverb was a protest against the unfairness of having to suffer the consequences of the actions of others.[13]

The exact origin of this proverb is not known,[14] for like all such popular expressions, it can be applied to multiple contexts.[15] Its application to the period immediately following the fall of Jerusalem and deportation of a large portion of the population can scarcely be denied, for in war the decisions of a few in authority embroil the entire citizenry. Foolish decisions to engage in conflict bring suffering and death to countless innocents who are powerless to prevent the bloodletting. In the case of Judah, the calculated move of the ruler and his administrative personnel to resist Babylonian hegemony brought disastrous consequences upon all the people.

In the book of Ezekiel, the suffering exiles quote the proverb about the debilitating effect of foolish decisions on innocent bystanders—even on persons not present or not yet conceived—to register their complaint. A developing sense of ego has given rise to the notion of individual rights irrespective of the larger entity. Lacking any hope of survival beyond death, save a weak, shadowy existence in Sheol, the exiles protest that they have gotten a raw deal: divine justice, they assert, does not exist except in the imaginations of religious leaders. Ezekiel's response is clear and strong. The prophet affirms God's justice even in the face of the exiles' desperate situation. The divine ways are just, he insists, and the people's ways are unjust. The language of his argument resembles priestly pronouncements of innocence and guilt in the Torah, but without the authority associated with rulings by priests in ancient Israel. As a prophetic mediator of the divine word, Ezekiel can only excoriate the defiant populace, leaving all punishment to heaven.[16]

The resulting exercise in casuistry may strike modern readers as peculiar, for it intermingles cultic and ethical norms as if they were equal.[17] Indeed, in the view of priestly authors, they are: both represent divine statutes, and therefore both must be scrupulously obeyed. Breaking the prohibition against adultery is no more wrong than having sexual relations with a wife during her menstrual flow. Participation in worship of an unapproved cult center is just as heinous as murder, for YHWH has prohibited both.

The world that Ezekiel envisions corresponds to Oscar Wilde's definition of fiction: "so-called moral universes in which evil is necessarily punishment, in which, therefore, the good are blessed and the wicked chastised." Such a fictional world has never existed, despite the prophet's insistence that a rational rule assures the appropriate reward or punishment for human action. Sensing the difficulty of his worldview, Ezekiel presses further and further in the direction of divine solicitude, all the while resolutely adhering to the notion that YHWH rewards and punishes with exact justice.

Ezekiel's observations in chapter 18, wordy in the extreme, reach three peaks of insight before culminating in a dramatic announcement of a new heart and a new spirit. The first peak concerns the issue of just punishment; the next two relate to the character of God and make an appeal to the defiant rebels who have subscribed to the sentiment expressed in the proverb about parents and children.[18] The initial insight, found in vv 4 and 20, takes dogmatic form, like the related articulation of the idea in Deut 24:16: "The one who sins, he will die." To reinforce the point, Ezekiel insists that there is no transfer of guilt or innocence from one person to another, neither from son to father nor from father to son. The innocent will remain above reproach, he maintains, and the guilty will bear his own guilt. The second insight comes in v 23 and takes interrogative form: "Do I really take pleasure in the death of the wicked, says YHWH, and not in his turning from his ways and living?" Finally, lest there be any doubt, v 32 declares and then invites in the name of YHWH: "For I take no pleasure in the death of the dead, says YHWH; so turn and live." This combination of declaration and invitation works to emphasize divine compassion. The door stands ajar, even for the wicked, who need only repent and enter.

In short, the three insights into YHWH's innermost desires and their significance for humankind address the mistaken assumption that the prior deeds of others have sealed everyone's fate. Not so, Ezekiel reasons, for divine compassion awaits anyone who turns from sin and practices righteousness. In the eyes of the prophet, YHWH's justice is certain, and so is divine compassion.

How does Ezekiel support his claim? He sets out three hypothetical cases that involve three successive generations: a father, his son, and his grandson (Ezek 18:5–18). The father conducts himself according to YHWH's teachings and earns a favorable judgment. This man, Ezekiel insists, will live. That cannot be said for the man's wicked son, who earns a guilty verdict and will die. That man's son, however, leads a virtuous life rather than following in his father's footsteps. The grandson will live, according to the prophet's reasoning. The three examples thus refute the claim expressed in the proverb: "Fathers have eaten sour grapes, and children's teeth have become sensitive."

The rather limited catalogue of sins in this passage moves quickly from offenses against the deity to violations of human relationships. Following the pattern of the Decalogue, the list first takes up acts directed against the deity—in this instance, sharing a meal on the mountains, presumably to a deity other than YHWH, and harboring reverence for an idol. Adultery is mentioned next, followed by another sexual offense involving a woman during her menstrual period. These sins fall into the category of secret breaches of the divine will, for both acts would be carried out in private. The list concludes with crimes against the weak: oppressing a debtor by retaining a pledge, robbing, lending at interest, usury, and doing abominable things.

These sins are particularly relevant to the exilic period.[19] In Judah, the collapse of the official cult in Jerusalem created a void insofar as worship was concerned. Rival cults sprang up, and those forced underground during the Josianic reform in 621 probably experienced a resurgence once the administration in Jerusalem became ineffective. After the fall of Jerusalem, the poor had no champion at a royal court. The situation was ripe for unscrupulous individuals to take advantage of the vulnerable[20]—lending at outrageous rates,[21] holding pledged garments until the debt was fully repaid, hoarding possessions rather than sharing them with the needy. The prophet Amos complained about the same abuses in the eighth century, when a powerful king sat on the throne in Samaria. Clearly, the royal ideology of ruler as champion of the poor was not always a guarantee that oppressors would be brought to justice. In Babylonia, where Ezekiel carried out his prophetic vocation, the absence of an authoritative figure among the exiled Jews left the poor exposed more than ever to ruthless predators. Their vulnerability may explain Ezekiel's choice of offenses directed against humans,[22] and the diversity of Babylonian religious worship would certainly account for his choice of sins directed against YHWH.[23]

Ezekiel's rhetorical strategy extends beyond the citation of a popular proverb and illustrative anecdotes. Twice he imagines a reactive audience,[24] one that objects to his line of reasoning. In vv 19 and 25 he lets the people speak: "Yet you say, 'Why shouldn't the son bear his father's guilt?'" and "Yet you say, 'YHWH's way is unfair.'" The first objection makes no sense in the mouths of those to whom transferred guilt is wholly unacceptable. Why would they want to defend the idea that children ought to pay for what their parents have done? But the second objection is entirely legitimate, for, indeed, something other than justice is at work here.

The matter is perfectly clear. A wicked person amends his ways and begins to practice good deeds, for which he receives divine favor. All his former misdeeds are forgotten. Conversely, a righteous person falls into sinful practices, and YHWH forgets his previous life of virtue. The repentant sinner lives, and the errant righteous person dies. The verb used in expressing the people's objection indicates a departure from a standard of measurement. The exiles' concept of fairness would seem to demand something similar to Egyptian views of judgment at the time of death, when all one's deeds are weighed against the standard of pure justice.[25] By way of contrast, Ezekiel envisions a divine decision before death that takes into consideration only present deeds.

An individual may have done abominable things all his life until just prior to the moment of judgment, when the equivalent of a deathbed conversion entitles him to live.[26]

To counter the objection that YHWH's ways are unfair, the prophet contrasts divine readiness to grant the repentant sinner life with the Israelites' sinful ways. He mentions no specifics but merely turns their words around: "The house of Israel says, 'The way of YHWH is unfair.' Are not my ways fair, house of Israel? Are not your ways unfair?" Ezekiel makes one final appeal, urging the hearers to turn from their wicked ways lest they stumble. In the process of turning, he says, in the process of discarding all rebellious acts, they will begin to effect a mental transformation, forming within themselves a new heart and a new spirit. Their futures are in their own hands. With this mighty crescendo, the argument comes to a close.

Ezekiel is wholly convinced that the divine judge will render a just verdict based on an individual's present behavior—that is, on an individual's free choice. The sordid history of failure that has resulted in the exile, according to the standard biblical narrative, does not condemn the present generation. On the contrary, God's very nature as merciful offers a strong incentive to reform. All who respond to this open invitation can count on survival; all who reject it can count on death.

Divine Vulnerability

In choosing to endow humans with self-determination, the deity has relinquished full exercise of power and knowledge: human freedom entails divine constraint. Moreover, by entering into covenant relationship with particular human beings, he has made himself vulnerable, subject to the uncertainty of human choice. Vulnerability belongs to the essence of any intimate relationship, which must be grounded in mutual freedom. God's relationship with the creatures made in his own image bears the painful scars of this freely chosen vulnerability. As we saw in chapter 3, the poignant statement attributed to the deity at the conclusion of Abraham's horrible test—"Now I know that you fear God"—may be read as a telling display of God's vulnerability, a divine dependence on reciprocal love that cannot be ascertained unless submitted to radical choice.

YHWH's desire to love and be loved is evident in Isaiah 30, where the prophet denounces a rebellious people in YHWH's name, calling them a generation that has turned its back on the covenant in favor of alien gods. Deliverance was theirs for the asking:

For thus said Adonai YHWH,
   the Holy One of Israel,
"In turning and rest you will be saved,
   in calm and trust
will be your strength,"
   but you refused. (Isa 30:15)

Despite the people's open defiance, YHWH longs for their return:

Truly YHWH is waiting to show compassion to
   you,
   truly He will rise up to bestow mercy on you.
For YHWH is a God of justice;
   happy are all who wait for him. (v 18)

The sound of weeping will move the deity to immediate action, coming out of temporary hiding to replace harsh discipline with direct leadership along treacherous paths. Then at last, the prophet promises, the people will turn against the "relics" of foreign gods and embrace YHWH wholeheartedly. Nature itself will reflect this state of mutual love, from rain at the opportune time of sowing seed to bountiful harvest. Even such a cornucopia pales, however, before the image with which the prophet closes this unit: "The light of the moon will be like that of the sun, and the sun's light will be seven times, like that of seven days, the day YHWH binds up the wounds of his people and heals the injuries he inflicted" (v 26). Weeping has been transformed into laughter, the result of reciprocated love.

The depth of divine vulnerability is also echoed in the final chapters of the anthology attributed to Isaiah:

I let myself be sought by those who did not inquire,
   found by those who did not seek me.
I said, "Here I am, Here I am"
   to a nation that did not invoke my name.
I spread out my hand all day to a stubborn people
   who walk in the way that is not good,
      after their own thoughts. (Isa 65:1–2)

While the nation continues to rebel, a minority of faithful servants elicits from YHWH a promise of new heavens and a new earth, with the sound of mirth ringing throughout Jerusalem:

I will exult in Jerusalem,
   rejoice in my people;
never again will be heard in it

> a sound of weeping
> or a sound of distress. (65:19)

In this utopia, untimely death, the gravest issue of theodicy, will be no more. Infants will live out full lifetimes, far beyond the century mark. As for the rebels, YHWH's pronouncement is heavy with the language of choice:

> Just as they have chosen their ways
>   and delight in their shameful deeds,
> so I will choose their mockery,
>   and I will bring on them the thing they dread.
> For I called and none answered,
>   I spoke and none paid heed.
> They did evil in my eyes
>   and chose what I take no pleasure in. (66:3b–4)

The tone of intimacy then returns, this time in the imagery of maternal love:

> You will be carried on shoulders
>   and rocked on knees
> like a man whose mother comforts him;
>   thus I will comfort you,
>   and in Jerusalem you will be consoled. (66:12b–13)

In the book of Hosea, the theme of vulnerability to betrayal in an intimate relationship looms large. Here, YHWH is cast in the role of husband. The much-discussed narrative of a wife's infidelity and its painful consequences (Hosea 1–3), whether factual or symbolic, dramatizes both the deity's vulnerability and his all-too-human vindictive response, which prompts an alternative one, perhaps by a subsequent editor, that emphasizes YHWH's efforts at reconciliation:

> Therefore I will woo her,
>   lead her in the wilderness,
> and speak tenderly to her. (Hos 2:16)

This loving initiative will bring about a notable transformation, signaled by the manner of personal address:

> You will call me *'Ishi* [my husband];
>   no longer will you call me *Ba'li* [my master]. (2:18b)

The two conflicting responses to religious apostasy, viewed in the story as implying marital infidelity, permeate the rest of the book, with Hosea voicing

YHWH's divided reaction. "Compassion is hidden from my eyes" (13:14b) al-
ternates with "How can I give you up, Ephraim, how can I abandon you, Israel?" (11:8a). Heightened emotion yields textual uncertainty, and the interpreters' struggle to grasp the sense of the Hebrew text matches the intensity
of the original. So, too, does the knowledge that this people, so beloved of
YHWH, was marched off to Assyria and into oblivion, despite the promised
reconciliation.

Divine Order

In this context of the perils of intimacy associated with the exercise of free
choice, human and divine, the prominence of images from the realm of nature
is hardly accidental. After all, a definite rhythm is discernible in nature despite
its idiosyncrasies. The sun does rise predictably, and darkness inevitably follows. Like the farmers implied in Isa 28:21–29, people whose livelihood depends on such regularity arrange their activities accordingly.

Isaiah's brief depiction here of agricultural practice in the ancient Judean
hills is broadened at two significant junctures, each time pointing beyond the
routine to make a theological statement. The first claim concerns the source
of this knowledge about the optimum schedule for producing a desired harvest
("For they are taught accurately; their God instructs them," v 26). The second
removes all possibility of restricting such pedagogy to gods in general, identifying the earlier 'elohim with YHWH. This second claim is reinforced by a
reiteration of the first ("This also issues from YHWH of Hosts") and by the
introduction of traditional epithets ("Counselor of wonder, greatly perceptive").
In short, the text uses a fixed reality, encountered daily, to defend a view of
YHWH as both sagacious and powerful. This teacher, it asserts, does not apply
an arbitrary standard but follows the rule of law (lammishpat), even when executing a strange deed ("to carry out a work—strange is his work—and to do
a foreign deed—foreign is his deed," v 21b). Against the unpredictability of
human choice, the regularity of divine order stands firm.

Experience, of course, does not always bear that out. Nowhere within prophetic literature does a wounded spirit lash out at the natural order with the
intensity of Fourth Ezra,[27] but the prophets' sustained emphasis on human
perversity paves the way for this trenchant critique of reality and its creator.
The human propensity for evil throws into question the created order itself;
indeed, it would have been better, Ezra argues, if God had never made mortals.
Because they lack the will to reject sin, they become subject to a curse, thus
producing a condemned humanity, a massa damnationis. This grim prospect

presents a monstrous challenge to the deity. Will mercy triumph over justice? That issue, recognized earlier by the prophet Hosea, is never fully resolved, neither by traditionists responsible for the book by that name nor by others who preserved prophetic literature from the southern kingdom. One fact is certain: Israel fell to Assyria, and Judah to Babylon. Is the other possibility any less real—that justice in fact prevailed?

The prophets may not have turned against the natural order of things as completely as the author of Fourth Ezra, but they did understand something about divine pathos, the deity's pain at human perversity. The freedom bestowed by the deity on human beings became the very means of their rebellion against all external control, turning the potential for growth into an instrument of destruction. Is there anything within the divine character that corresponds to the conflict within humans between good and evil, which the prophets saw with such clarity? We have already seen a suggestion of divine conflict in the book of Hosea. In the next chapter I take up this notion of tension within the deity between justice and mercy.

5

Split Personality

Reconciling Justice with Mercy

If you want a world, you will not have justice; if it is justice you
want, then there will be no world. You are taking hold of the rope by
both ends—you desire both a world and justice—but if you do not
concede a little, the world cannot stand.

—Midrash Genesis Rabbah 49:9

The Sojourner Has Come to Play the Judge

The dramatic confrontation between Lot and the citizens of Sodom
takes a turn for the worse when the sojourner is accused of playing
the role of judge (Gen 19:9). Outraged at Lot's audacity[1]—indeed,
rejecting his presumption of comradeship[2]—the men of the city
threaten him with a fate worse than "sodomy."[3] The concept of judging lies also at the center of the episode that leads up to this story of
conflicting wills, Abraham's intercession for Sodom and Gomorrah.[4]
In that story, a sojourner par excellence utters the unimaginable,
daring to act as judge of God: "Shall not the Judge of all the earth
act justly?" (Gen 18:25).[5] No better paradigm exists for the indictment of—and the struggle to defend—divine justice, inasmuch as
human beings are quintessentially sojourners.[6]

At least two things make such "playing the judge" extraordinary.
First, a sojourner reckons from an alien ethos: the experiences and
relationships responsible for shaping his values are different from

those of the adopted environment. Second, a sojourner lacks any basis for authority. Anyone who has merely taken up residence among strangers but dares to pronounce judgment on their value system displays enormous audacity. When the audacity of the sojourner extends to its ultimate expression, the judging of the deity, there may be but one justification—the existential fact of life's brevity. This sobering reality, the death sentence proclaimed over the entire human race, may indeed issue in the boldness of desperation.

The patriarch's venture into this realm comes as a result of the deity's initiative. Reflecting on the special relationship with Abraham and his vocation with respect to the nations, YHWH ponders the expedience of informing him of the possibility, or probability, that the wickedness of the two cities signals their ruin. Like a true sojourner, Abraham meets the sovereign visitor with empty pockets, but the lack of a bargaining chip does not deter him from creating one and imposing it on the deity. Lying behind the poignant question, "Shall not the Judge of all the earth act justly?" is the notion that YHWH must abide by a moral code of human devising.[7] Abraham implies that the deity should aspire, at a minimum, to the same level of morality as that achieved on earth.[8]

The decisive issue concerns the indiscriminate sweeping away of the innocent with the guilty, as if virtue means nothing. An earlier sweeping away, with which this text has remarkable similarities, was less inclusive, for Noah and his extended family escaped the deluge. Hence Abraham's emphatic "indeed": "Will you indeed sweep away the righteous with the wicked?" Will the same principle not apply in this new irruption of divine judgment? Abraham's bold overture mixes an accusatory tone with self-effacing language: "Far be it from you," "I who am dust and ashes," "Let not YHWH be angry if I speak just once more."[9]

Stung—or pleased—by the sojourner's argument, YHWH accedes to his wishes. The principle of a minority functioning to save the majority is established through a combination of human and divine solicitousness. "For the sake of fifty, I will forgive the entire population" (Gen 18:26). Now it falls to Abraham to ascertain the limits of such forbearance, and he proceeds by gradations of five, then ten, until arriving at the point at which a group essentially dissolves into individuals.[10] With this the narrator concludes the episode, noting—with words that seem, from the perspective of this analysis, to carry double force—"and Abraham returned to his place."[11]

The principle of justice prevails in the destruction of Sodom and Gomorrah. None who hear the story of Abraham's intercession can accuse YHWH of sweeping away the innocent with the guilty. But Abraham's challenge of divine justice introduces a new issue: the saving of the guilty alongside the innocent. YHWH's willingness to spare the many for the sake of the few—if such can be found[12]—does not accord with the exact accounting spelled out by the prophets Ezekiel (14:12–20, 18:1–32) and Jeremiah (18:8–11). Moreover, the deity's readiness to apply the principle of mercy to a wholly faithless people,[13] yet not to his own inheritance, raises deeply troubling questions among the followers of this inscrutable God.

In the patriarch's intercession for the condemned cities, we encounter a rare feature within ancient Near Eastern theodicies.[14] The complaint of the human sojourner takes the form of direct address to the culpable(?) deity. In extrabiblical texts, such accusation commonly assumes a less confrontational mode, the speaker taking shelter in descriptive narrative. A pharaoh observes that the shepherd has neglected the sheep, demonstrating reckless disdain for life and social order;[15] an innocent sufferer accuses the creators of concealing their will;[16] another is told by a faithful friend that the gods are the source of human deception.[17] These critics of the gods acknowledge a measure of human fault, but they deny that it is met with commensurate punishment. Like Genesis 18 and 19, these ancient texts disclose a deep rift between human cognition and the conduct of deity.

The complaint of YHWH's critics is direct, as if face to face, sometimes in language just short of irreverent. Prophetic challengers confront the deity with sharp questions and thinly veiled rebukes. The judge Gideon reminds YHWH's messenger that the hardships of the moment create a cloud of disbelief over cherished stories about divine favor (Judg 6:13). Habakkuk impugns the deity's inaction with anguished cries of "How long?" and "Why?" (Hab 1: 1–17).[18] The prophet Jeremiah goes farthest of all, accusing YHWH of spiritual seduction and rape (Jer 20:7).[19]

Apparent contradictions in divine intention and conduct evoke in Jeremiah a maelstrom of troubled thoughts about the deity's justice.[20] Still, the traditional dogma maintains its power over him, forcing him to concede perhaps too much at the outset of his anguished accusation:

> You are "Not guilty," YHWH,
>   when I press charges against you;
>   nevertheless, I will read the indictment.[21]
> Why do evildoers prosper,
>   the treacherous thrive?
> You plant them, they take root,
>   flourish and bear fruit;

> You are near in their speech
>> but distant from their hearts. . . .
> For they say, "He [God] cannot see our ways." (Jer 12:1–2, 4b)

Jeremiah is torn between an intense desire to give YHWH the benefit of the doubt and the force of brutal reality, events that are challenging his worldview. Violent people succeed without the anticipated punishment from above, leading them to question the principle of reward and retribution that undergirds religion itself. The prophet's ambivalence is deepened by his own unanswered suffering as the deity's faithful messenger:

> Why is my pain constant,
>> my affliction terminal,
>>> rejecting a cure?
> Truly, you are like a deceitful stream to me,
>> like unreliable waters. (15:18)

The fountain of living waters, the One in whom Jeremiah has placed absolute trust, seems, in fact, to be a source of painful deception. From the prophet's perspective, the promised justice has been inexcusably delayed. Ambivalence gives way to outright repudiation:

> You have seduced me, YHWH, and I have been raped;
>> You have seized me and prevailed. (20:7a)

Significantly, the prophet is not alone in his distress. In the midst of his laments Jeremiah shows us a deity who is anguished as well, even as he pronounces judgment:

> But who will have compassion on you, O Jerusalem,
> Who will grieve over you?
> Who will turn aside to ask
>> about your well-being?
> You have forsaken me
>> —oracle of YHWH—
> You walk backwards.
> So I reached out to destroy you;
>> I cannot pardon.
> With a winnowing fork I will disperse them
>> through the gates of the land.
> I will make childless, I will destroy my people,
>> for they have not turned from their ways. (Jer 15:5–7)

The conflicting demands of justice and mercy are nowhere more evident than within the deity himself. The biblical writers struggle to depict a deity who is at once perfectly just and perfectly merciful. That is, some would say, they struggle without success, for even the deity cannot reconcile the irreconcilable. That approach to theodicy—the recognition of a split personality within the deity—is the focus of this chapter.

Who Knows What YHWH Will Do?

I consider two texts in which the split personality is highlighted in the question of divine turning, the divine impulse to allow compassion to prevail.

Jonah: Compassion Indicted

The apparent conflict within the divine character assumes center stage in the exchanges between the prophet Jonah and the deity, who has pressed him into service against his better judgment. Indeed, the angry prophet justifies his flight from the commissioned task precisely by appealing to YHWH's reputation for bountiful pardon, which seems to Jonah altogether inappropriate when applied universally. True, Jonah himself has experienced the divine long-suffering proclaimed again and again in Israel's liturgical tradition (Exod 34: 6–7), but he does not possess bloody hands like the people of Nineveh. It seems to him a gross miscarriage of justice for YHWH to turn away from the deafening cry of spilled blood and to pardon a guilty multitude of hated foreigners. Jonah's petulance is matched by divine forbearance, an eagerness to spare without limit. The irony of the exchange would not have been missed by readers familiar with Nineveh's actual overturn in 612 BCE.

Perhaps the very literary form of the book of Jonah—parody, or satire[22]—cloaks an effort to defuse a highly charged issue. The sharp question directed at the prophet by the deity, repeated for emphasis, specifies the problem: "Do you do well to be angry?" The issue goes beyond the likely discrediting of a prophet whose brief prophecy has turned out to be false.[23] Jonah has rightly detected the difference between his own understanding of the requirements of justice and God's eagerness to ignore human standards for fair treatment. As Ezekiel says, YHWH takes no pleasure in the death of the wicked, desiring only that they turn and repent. So many lives in Nineveh would have perished if strict justice had prevailed. Maybe, then, the time for mercy had come.

Jonah's stated reason for running away from the original divine commission, that he knew the deity's real nature to be merciful, strikes readers at first glance as ludicrous. Did not religious leaders frequently celebrate YHWH's compassion toward the downtrodden, his apparent attraction to losers—slaves, widows, orphans, strangers, the poor[24]—as opposed to those who wielded power? True, but a certain ambiguity has always clung to depictions of this deity.[25] The same Lord who cares for the lowly on earth has a stake in human structures of power, choosing kings and through them charting the course of history.

The object lesson employed by YHWH to persuade Jonah to take himself less seriously carries in itself a clear signal that even a piqued messenger does not dwell outside the circle of divine generosity. Still, the actions of the deity are ambiguous—allowing discomfort, then bringing relief, followed by worse discomfort. Jonah, like Job, does not question divine power, which is obvious to everyone. He does, however, wonder about justice, and the object lesson, however reassuring, leaves that issue unresolved—as does the divine question with which the book ends:

> As for me, should I not have compassion on Nineveh, that great city,
> in which there are over one hundred twenty thousand people who
> do not know their right hand from their left—and many animals?
> (Jonah 4:11)

A city with so many inhabitants devoid of moral discrimination needs divine pity, the text seems to say, whether you like it or not. We are left in the dark as to whether Jonah came around to the deity's way of thinking, perhaps because the fictional antihero correctly mirrors the perplexity of God's people.[26]

In Jonah's representation of YHWH as "gracious, compassionate, patient, abundantly loyal, and repentant concerning harm" (4:2), we come face to face with a powerful liturgical theme whose roots are in the Torah. In the earlier confession, however, the deity's compassion is placed in astonishing juxtaposition with judgment:

> YHWH, YHWH, a God merciful and gracious,
> slow to anger, and abounding in steadfast love
>   and faithfulness,
> keeping steadfast love for the thousandth generation,
> forgiving iniquity, transgression, and sin,
> yet by no means clearing the guilty,
> but visiting the iniquity of the parents
>   upon the children
>   and the children's children,
> to the third and fourth generation. (Exod 34:6–7)

This daring attempt to penetrate to the very heart of God's nature rather than resting content with descriptive accounts of his actions pushes aside the veil of darkness and discloses the split within the deity's being.

Justice or mercy? That is the eternal question. Judging from the sheer number of related attributes, the confessional formulation seems to be weighted on the side of mercy. But the last word, far from compassionate, acts as a mighty corrective on the side of justice. Placed in the mouth of the deity, this is a stunning admission, given our discussion in chapter 4. "Visiting the iniquity of the parents upon the children and the children's children, to the third and fourth generation"—whom are we to believe, the deity described in this confession or the one who assures the prophet Ezekiel (18:1–20) that such transgenerational punishment will not occur?

Joel: Compassion Implored

This same tension characterizes the book of Joel, which describes a dire situation in Judah brought on by a devastating plague of locusts and made worse by unprecedented drought.[27] A graphic description of that calamity, interpreted as a harbinger of the dreadful day of a vengeful YHWH, ends abruptly with an appeal to turn to a compassionate YHWH in prayer.

> But even now—a divine oracle—
> return to me with your whole mind,
>   with fasting, weeping, and mourning.
> Rend your inner disposition
>   and not just your clothes,
> then return to YHWH your God;
> for merciful and compassionate is he,
>   patient and abundantly loyal,
>   repenting about punishment.
> Who knows whether he may turn and relent,
>   leaving behind a blessing;
> a cereal offering and libation
>   for YHWH your God? (Joel 2:12–14)

Nothing that has gone before prepares readers for this radical shift. Suddenly, the prophet introduces traditional language taken from the old covenant formulary that lists YHWH's attributes. The specific traits cited in the present context emphasize mercy, compassion, patience, and loyalty. How can anyone who has experienced an infestation of locusts that has destroyed all vegetation, threatening the very survival of the population, give credence to the familiar confession? The most perplexing feature of the miserable Judeans' dilemma is their belief that the calamity has its source in the once-compassionate deity, now turned wrathful. What possible justification can the prophet find for petitioning the deity who has turned against the people of his own choosing? Moreover, is not Joel's identification of the consuming fire as a portent of the judgment to come (v 3) an indication that the time for adopting preventive measures has passed?

The invitation attributed to YHWH, "but even now" (v 12a), recognizes the lateness of the season at the same time that it indicates radical boldness, like an exasperated Job's "Look, even now my witness is in heaven" (Job 16:19a).[28] Both here and in Job's use of the expression, various signs point in a direction other than relief. Job is burdened by illness, together with unsubstantiated charges of misconduct; Judeans who have been buffeted by privation anticipate more to come. Each text shifts the point of view heavenward[29]—here, with the prophetic formula for an oracle.[30] In this way the appeal to turn to YHWH receives the highest possible legitimation,[31] one that originates in the deity who, for the moment, is bent on destruction.

The invitation to turn (*shub*) does not necessarily imply present guilt. In times of trouble, whether deserved or undeserved, turning to YHWH would be seen as the appropriate response, inasmuch as he alone can remove the adversity. Perhaps the prophet's silence on the matter of guilt registers his own inability to discern any offense on the part of the Judeans commensurate with the present misery. Modern interpreters, however, have been less hesitant to indict.[32] Naturally, any evidence to support a particular version of Judah's guilt is deduced from what Joel says—or refrains from saying. The arguments from silence run something like this: (1) Joel's formulation of the invitation—"return to me"—implies apostasy;[33] (2) the internalization of sorrow suggested by "rend your hearts" indicates pride not yet overcome by genuine remorse;[34] (3) the same expression in juxtaposition with ritualistic acts belies confidence in the efficacy of external behavior;[35] (4) the necessity of commanding priests to mourn and intercede points to a failed leadership;[36] (5) the calamity that has struck the community demonstrates breach of covenant, for the ancient treaty promised prosperity for faithfulness and adversity for breaking the conditions laid down at its ratification;[37] and (6) mockery of the Judeans by foreigners has issued in shame, which may even have driven YHWH's inheritance to another god.[38] Such charges say more about assumptions pertaining to a supposed moral universe than about the innocence or guilt of ancient Judeans.

Joel's invitation on YHWH's behalf lacks any sense of divine displeasure with public ritual. The precondition for divine favor, a resolute mind that finds embodiment in a devout life (v 12b), echoes the merging of cognitive and affective in Deut 4:30–31 and 30:2–3. There, too, the covenantal people are called in the midst of dire circumstances to return to YHWH with total mind and being. There, too, compassion is promised by the present wielder of harm.

The triple manifestation of wholehearted lament in Joel's appeal to the beleaguered people (fasting, weeping, and mourning, v 12c) can be found elsewhere in only one place, the book of Esther.[39] The situation described in that context (Esth 4:3) resembles that of Joel's time, for the Jewish people stand under threat of extinction. In both, the combination of a correct inner disposition and appropriate external expression has the potential to move YHWH in a favorable direction. Yet even a pious mind and pious actions do not guarantee divine repentance.[40] The story about David's remorse and intercession for the child of his illicit union with Bathsheba (2 Sam 12:15b–23) lingers as a cogent reminder of YHWH's freedom to act or not, which I take up below. Questions about the uncertainty of YHWH's favor despite presumed piety and regular cultic observance are answered elsewhere by charges that external ritual is being substituted for charitable works (Isa 58:3–9; Zech 7:3–14). The apparent ambiguity within the deity, however, is not always so easily explained, as is amply demonstrated in the disjunctive statements attributed to YHWH in Mal 3:6a and 7b: "For I YHWH have not changed" and "Return to me and I will return to you."

Verse 13 in Joel's appeal shifts to first-person address, employing the prophetic strategy of merging deity and human messenger. The use of symbolic language (weqir'u lebabkem, "and rend your heart") follows the ancient precedent recorded in Deut 10:16 and Jer 4:4 for urging the circumcision of the foreskin of the heart. The threefold expression of distress demands that Joel's further words be translated "and not *just* your garments." At this point a shift back to third person prepares the way for a doxological attribution based on Exod 34:6.

Joel's version of this confessional statement differs appreciably from the full expression of YHWH's nature in Exod 34:6–7. Joel does not mention faithfulness (we'emet) or a single attribute from v 7. Even the four attributes in common appear in entirely different syntax,[41] and the statement concludes with a new element, "and repents of evil" (wenikham 'al-hara'ah).[42] In this regard, Joel's formula resembles that of Jonah 4:2, the only difference being the direct address, "you, God." The similarity becomes even more striking when we compare the next verse in the book of Joel—"Who knows whether he may turn and relent?"—with Jonah 3:9, which is exactly the same, except for the addition of Elohim.

The rhetorical question that concludes Joel's invitation is altogether appropriate. The "Who knows?" leaves room for divine freedom, even in the face of sincere turning. "Who knows whether he may turn and relent, leaving behind a blessing, a cereal offering and libation for YHWH your God?" The fact is that no one knows what YHWH will do. That simple truth is underscored by the use of the rhetorical "Who knows?" which in all its occurrences has this same force (2 Sam 12:22; Joel 2:14; Jonah 3:9; Ps 90:11; Eccl 2:19, 3:21, 8:1; Esth 4:14).[43] Joel's use of the adverb *'akharayw* (behind) echoes his earlier reference to scarred fields left behind by locusts (Joel 2:3) and contrasts YHWH's previous actions with anticipated relief after the people's turning.

In the three verses of Joel's invitation, the verb *shub* (to turn) is used three times (vv 12, 13, 14),[44] spoken twice by Joel and once by YHWH, each with a different referent. In addition, there are two uses of the verb *nikham* (to repent, vv 13, 14), both with reference to divine turning. The essential meaning of the paired usage in v 14 is made explicit in Exod 32:12: "Turn [*shub*] from your intense fury and repent [*wehinnakhem*] concerning the harm [planned] for your people." Such divine turning brings well-being, which Joel signifies by cereal offering and libation. In his eyes, the people's prosperity redounds to YHWH's own well-being, as the linguistically awkward "for YHWH your God" concedes.[45]

Like most of the Hebrew Bible, Joel's typical discourse about YHWH emphasizes control of the world and its people through divine action. The prophet employed motifs from ancient theophanies, the day of YHWH, the enemy from the north, the sacred mountain, the outpouring of the deity's vital force, the formula of acknowledgment of YHWH, and mockery by foreigners. Moreover, beyond actions in history, Joel stressed YHWH's control of the rain and thus nature's productivity.[46] On this basis, Joel characterized YHWH's role as unique. Such grand theology, however, encountered an insurmountable challenge: experience did not bear it out.[47] Faced with the discontinuity between earlier confessional statements about YHWH's compassion and the harsh circumstances in which Judeans of his day found themselves, Joel struggled to retain both views of YHWH's nature. Integrity compelled him to remain silent when he could see no evidence that the disaster surrounding the holy city was deserved. Still, he placed his trust in YHWH's mercy as the only remedy for the present misery.

How differently the author of the book of Jonah viewed reality. Using the same statement about YHWH's compassionate nature, he condemned the deity for unprincipled conduct in sparing repentant foreigners. Even absent the ancient confession's emphasis on justice as a counterbalance to mercy, the confessional statement retains enough ambiguity to evoke both universalistic and particularistic readings.[48] Historical events inevitably complicated things for religious thinkers who believed that YHWH was both exacting and kind.

Justice and mercy make strange bedfellows, which explains traditionists' readiness to separate them.

What factors contributed to this apparent split within the deity in the perception of the authors who composed these texts? We may surmise that socioeconomic changes radically altered the people's understanding of their God.[49] A conviction in days of prosperity that the deity was eminently just could not survive the lean economic realities of empires on the move. Such difficult conditions fueled the conception of a merciful deity waiting in the shadows with outstretched arms. With that important change also came a shift in Israel's self-understanding. A heavy burden of sin began to pervade liturgical prayers and general descriptions of the nation. In the people's perception, to quote Goethe, "Two souls, alas, reside within the human breast."[50] Ancient Israel's God, like the covenant nation, was thought to struggle with the competing demands of justice and mercy. That tension notwithstanding, could a conflicted deity use adversity to build character? The following chapter treats that possibility.

6

A Disciplinary Procedure

Stimulating Growth in Virtue

I do not want to know why I suffer, but I do want to know that I
suffer for Your sake.

—Rabbi Levi Yitzhak of Berdichev

Chapter 5 focuses on competing impulses within the divine will.
This chapter examines divine pedagogy as a means of shaping human character. Whereas the dominant concept of the deity in chapter 5 is that of a ruler responsible for maintaining order in society,
the primary metaphor in chapter 6 is that of concerned teacher or
loving parent.[1] In this conception, the deity subjects mortals to rigorous training for the purpose of moral formation, or in the language of the Christian theologian Irenaeus, "soul building." The operative word is discipline, which often bears a negative connotation
because of its association with punishment. In the context of loving
discipline, however, the punishment serves a higher cause, spurring
its recipient on toward growth and maturity:

> Adonai will give you bread of adversity
>   and water of affliction,
> but your Teacher will no longer be hidden,
> for your eyes will behold your Teacher,
> and your ears will hear a word from behind:
>   "This is the path; walk in it,"
> when you veer either to the right or to the left. (Isa 30:20–21)

Among the many examples of this theme in the Bible, three stand out as worthy of special examination. The first comes from Jerusalem, the second from Alexandria, and the third from northern Israel.

We begin with Sir 4:11–19, appropriately, because it derives from a professional teacher who invites young students to lodge in his "house of instruction" and promises them a better life for doing so (Sir 51:23–30).[2] This instructor, Ben Sira, lived in the period just before the Maccabean revolt against Seleucid rule in 165 BCE and enjoyed privileged status as a conservative[3] who greatly favored priestly authority in Jerusalem. Steeped in biblical tradition, he represented the branch of knowledge peculiar to the books of Proverbs, Job, and Ecclesiastes. The wisdom literature, strangely devoid of reference to Israel's distinctive faith, had gradually fallen from prominence in some circles—not least because of the disjunction between the people's experience and this wisdom's extravagant claims. In the face of Hellenism's strong intellectual appeal, Ben Sira took a bold step, combining biblical wisdom with the religious heritage in the Torah and prophetic literature.[4] He addressed the vexing problem of theodicy directly by drawing on standard biblical and Greek arguments.[5] In addition, this innovative thinker introduced two new responses.

The first new response derives from philosophy. The created universe has twin principles, opposites that evenly balance things in a way that sustains life. Good and evil, light and darkness, truth and falsehood exist in even measure. Persons who habitually clothe themselves with virtue are protected by powerful forces in the universe that keep the negative ones at bay. Such an argument must depend on faith, for little in actual experience supports its claims.

The second response is from the realm of psychology. When lacking in virtue, the human psyche is plagued by inner dis-ease; anxiety thus functions as punishment for evil. This heavy burden imposed on mortals, this existential angst, can shatter psychological wholeness. Unfortunately, persons without a conscience are immune from soul-searching and its potential to heal. In this venture into the subconscious, the ancient instructor seems entirely modern.

Ben Sira peppers his teaching with avant-garde insights, frequently challenging students by means of technical tactics of debate. His favorite manner of combating dangerous views involves imaginary citation. By prefacing a quotation with "Do not say," he gives voice to heterodox opinions while simultaneously asserting their inadequacy. This particular rhetorical device occurs most often in contexts of theodicy, which must have been a popular topic in his day.

While his appeals to opposites within the universe and psychic stress emphasize the deity's role in fighting evil, Ben Sira recognizes human responsibility as well. Discipline involves both agent and object: it is applied by some external authority but must be used to good effect by its human recipient.[6] In Ben Sira's view, the agent varies from parent to teacher to personified wisdom to God.

Sirach 4:11–19

(11) Wisdom instructs her children[7]
     and exhorts all who understand her;
(12) Whoever loves her loves life,
     and whoever searches for her gains YHWH's approval.
(13) Whoever holds her fast discovers honor from YHWH
     and abides in YHWH's blessing.
(14) Whoever serves her is a minister of the holy one,
     and YHWH loves those who love her.[8]
(15) The one who listens to me[9] will judge nations,[10]
     and whoever pays heed to me will reside in the inner chambers of my house.
(16) If he remains loyal, he will inherit me;
     his descendants also will possess me.[11]
(17) Still I will secretly accompany him,
     initially testing him with trials,
     bringing fear and dread on him,
     and tormenting him with discipline
     until I trust him.[12]
(18) When his heart is filled with me
     I will place him on the straight path
     and disclose my secrets to him.[13]
(19) If he turns away, I will reject him
     and hand him over to spoilers.

This poem about wisdom, reminiscent of Prov 1:20–33 and 8:1–36, acknowledges the adversity with which humans are confronted but identifies it as benevolent rather than accidental or malicious. Such hardship, it claims, represents wisdom's pedagogy, an attempt to test both resolve and inner resources. A new feature in this poem is the linking of those who submit themselves to instruction with particular acts of devotion and service—to YHWH, in temple worship, and to society, in the capacity of judge.

Canonical texts in praise of wisdom had earlier drawn attention to her affinity with prophecy (Prov 1:20–33) and her association with the creator (Prov

8:22–36). In Proverbs 1, wisdom utters both invitation and threat, promising life to those who embrace her and destruction to those who turn away. In short, she determines the fate of human subjects on the basis of their response to her call. Moreover, according to the more developed concepts in Proverbs 8, she was a presence at creation—the first of God's creative acts—a confidante and a source of divine delight. In this privileged position, she observed the emergence of the universe and the divine restrictions placed upon it. Just as wisdom brought pleasure to the creator, the created world and its human inhabitants gave her reason to rejoice. In this extraordinary poem we look in vain for any sign of regret over the nature of the created world or humankind. Indeed, it insists, rulers decree what is just in this ideal world, for they are instructed by wisdom. Nevertheless, evil does exist in the form of pride, arrogance, and perverted speech.

The feminization of wisdom has its roots in Mesopotamia and Egypt, where the sustainer of justice and order was conceived as a goddess, variously named Isis or Maat. This concept was particularly apt in Israel, where the masculine imagery associated with the deity left little room for a feminine voice. The marital concept, so prevalent in certain prophetic speeches, reinforced the masculine understanding of YHWH, for Israel was described as the deity's bride. The figure of wisdom softened the deity's overt masculinity, placing a feminine presence alongside YHWH in a capacity that was important, if somewhat obscure.[14] In any event, Ben Sira reckons with this heavenly concept, enriching it almost beyond belief.

Several poems in praise of wisdom lead up to the climactic exposition of this concept in chapter 24.[15] Here wisdom lauds herself in the presence of God, boasting that she issued from the divine mouth and gently settled on earth like a mist. Traveling far and near, she sought a dwelling place in vain until the deity bade her settle in Jerusalem.[16] There she grew like a favored tree, yielding abundant fruit for all who desired nourishment. Then comes the crowning claim: all this is the Mosaic law, which overflows like the mythic rivers in the garden of Eden.

The interplay of imagery from the primeval history in Genesis 1–11, the story of the exodus, and descriptions of nature's bounty makes this rich poem a stunning celebration of the divine thought process, now given external form. From here it is a short step to reflections about the divine *logos* or *nous*, word or thought. Prophetic mediation gives way to a divine emissary, and once that step is taken, the skies soon teem with messengers, named and unnamed, angels communicating to eager humans the divine will.

How does this feminine expression of the deity's will function as disciplinarian? That is the topic of Ben Sira's observations in 4:11–19. Basically, wisdom holds out a carrot and a stick, offering promise as well as threat. Earlier writers had identified the deity as the one who puts humans to the test, as we have seen in the cases of Abraham and Job.[17] This idea grew out of an assumption that adversity builds character,[18] a constant theme in moral instruction both within the Bible and without. Or, understood as lacking omniscience, the deity used testing to ascertain the depth of an individual's loyalty.

The initial verse in this passage uses an unusual form for the word "wisdom," *khokmot*, replicating the spelling in Prov 1:20 and 9:1. The latter of these introduces a description of wisdom as hostess (Prov 9:1–6).[19] Having built a house with seven pillars, she prepares a meal consisting of meat, bread, and wine; sends servants to invite guests; and awaits their response. For these guests, she competes with a rival, conveniently called folly. Wisdom's rival also prepares a meal, far less lavish, and issues her invitation personally, using a seductive one-liner: "Stolen water is sweet, and bread eaten in secret is pleasant."[20] To his credit, the author highlights sin's strong allure. Folly spices her water with sexual favors. Wisdom, however, promises knowledge accompanied by an ever-increasing desire for more.

Ben Sira employs a pun in v 11 that recalls wisdom's activity as builder. Playing on the two consonants in the Hebrew verb *banah* (to build), which also form the noun *ben* (son), he alludes to wisdom's children and to their intellectual activity (understanding). Wisdom, like the deity, was believed to be hidden, manifesting herself only to deserving subjects. Both here and in Prov 8:35 the emphasis falls on human initiative, the necessity for active searching. For that aspect of intellectual inquiry,[21] the verse in Proverbs uses the verb *matsa'* (to find), together with a noun formed from the same root. Ben Sira, however, employs the more liturgical verb *baqash* (to seek).

In v 12, a love for wisdom is linked with a love for life—or, in the Hebrew text, *khayyim* (the living one), an epithet for YHWH. Viewed against the background of competing religions that celebrated certain deities' seasonal dying and rising and believed all gods to be mortal, this reference to a living YHWH can be understood as a corrective affirmation.[22] Israel's deity, according to the epithet, is alive and well. This belief merely heightened the difficulty when YHWH, to every appearance, was unresponsive. Still, a deity who transcends natural seasons would surely be able to establish justice by constant surveillance of human conduct and providential governance. The Hebrew text of v 12 follows Prov 8:35 in attributing the rewards of wisdom to YHWH, whereas the Greek text is more open, implying that they may come from one of three sources: YHWH, wisdom, or humans.

The loving and seeking by which the relationship with wisdom is established are not in themselves sufficient to sustain it. Hence, Ben Sira adds the notion of constancy in v 13. Together, these three ideas connote a person's prizing the life of the intellect, expending enormous energy to acquire it, and forming moral character that embodies it. The erotic language of *tomekeha* conveys a sense of fond embracing, but the object of love is remote from sensual pleasure. Ben Sira thinks of honor, a category often applied to YHWH with the meaning "glory." Here both the Hebrew and the Greek texts identify God as bestower of reward on the one fortunate enough to find wisdom. Here, too, the notion of blessing comes into play. At a minimum, it includes longevity, descendants, and prosperity. These rewards grant preferred status within the home and society at large.

To some extent, ancient peoples imagined blessing and curse as states of body and mind subject to outside control. Certain individuals were thought to exercise this control through positive or negative pronouncements, which, once uttered, could not be revoked. The story of one such practitioner, Balaam, demonstrates the ineffectiveness of pronouncements that are contrary to YHWH's will (Numbers 22–24). Still, the opinion was mixed in ancient Israel, for the blessing pronounced by Jacob in Gen 48:8–22 was thought to be binding, even in contravening the right of primogeniture. Similarly, Isaac's unintentional blessing of Jacob was viewed as irrevocable, much to the elder brother Esau's chagrin. Such stories indicate the complexity of ancient beliefs about blessings and curses. To some degree, they could be self-fulfilling, but they did not automatically work themselves out to bring weal or woe. As the biblical proverb states, men may make the plans for battle, but victory belongs to YHWH (Prov 21:31). Other peoples recognized the same thing: "Humans propose, but the gods dispose."[23]

The next verse moves beyond the images of seeking, loving, and holding to religious service. It links wisdom and YHWH, asserting that allegiance to one is tantamount to serving the other. The cultic language is unmistakable. The noun formed from the verb *sharat* (to serve) applies to priests in Joel 1:9 and 13 and 2:17, designating them as ministers of the altar and ministers of YHWH. Other verbs for seeking and inquiring, *baqash* and *darash*, also belong to the religious vocabulary for inquiring about YHWH at the cultic center, although they have wide secular use as well. The same is true of the verb used here in the sense of loving. It is evident that personal piety shapes Ben Sira's everyday language in distinct ways.

We must not overlook the significance of Ben Sira's equating intellectual inquiry with religious devotion. For him, the cultivation of the mind is identical with a life of piety. This differs appreciably from the older idea that religion both orients and makes knowledge possible, or that spiritual insight crowns all true knowledge. No longer does piety trump study, Ben Sira insists, for both priests and scholars minister to YHWH, each in their own way.

Whom do they serve? Ben Sira uses the divine epithet *qadosh* (Holy One), popularized by the prophet Isaiah in a longer form, *qadosh yisra'el* (Holy One of Israel). Ben Sira's short form soon gained popularity and in rabbinic times was usually followed by *baruk hu'* (blessed be he). The unpointed text of Ben Sira can be read as a divine epithet or as a place, presumably the temple. Like v 12, where a participle form of the verb *'aheb* (to love) occurs alongside the verb itself, this verse has a paired occurrence of the verb *sharat* (to serve): "Those who serve her also minister to [serve] the Holy One." Repetition was not frowned upon in Hebrew syntax, nor in the languages throughout the ancient Near East, possibly because the culture was essentially oral.

The Hebrew text of the second colon in v 14 lacks the reference to divine love, but the Greek rendering shows no reluctance in this regard, reading "and the Lord loves those who love her." Rarely does the verb *'aheb* (to love) appear with YHWH as subject and an individual or a people as object. Some late texts attest this use, especially Prov 3:12, Isa 48:14, and Mal 1:2, but even the deep piety in the book of Psalms never goes this far.[24] It speaks of YHWH's love for Torah, statutes, and the like but not for Israel or any specific individual.

With v 15, Ben Sira introduces a pair of verbs that function as synonymous parallels: *shama'* (to obey) and *'azan* (to listen). The root form of the first verb designates hearing, and this word came to have a significant role in instructional literature such as Deuteronomy and the Egyptian wisdom text Ptahhotep.[25] For these texts and others, hearing implies obedience. Those who conduct their lives in accord with their teacher's advice will judge accurately, with integrity, Ben Sira observes. The Greek text gives them a more exalted responsibility—that of judging nations. This ingenious reading takes the Hebrew word for truth to be a rare noun for nations and in this way brings Ben Sira's teaching in line with cosmopolitan concepts of philosopher kings going back to Plato. The same idea occurs in Wis 3:8 and in the Greek text of Prov 29:9.

Ben Sira promises more than accurate handling of judicial disputes, either in domestic settings or further afield. He promises listeners that they will be rewarded as lovers, dwelling in wisdom's inner chamber. Sleeping in her bedroom is a fantasy that rivals that of the strange or foreign woman in Proverbs, with one great difference. Whereas the devotees of that woman risk their lives for furtive sex, those who obey wisdom will dwell securely. In the second colon, the verb translated "dwells" (*yikhan*) is that for pitching a tent. Because the idea of judging nations is foreign to Ben Sira's thought elsewhere, some scholars read *yishkon* for *yishpot*, yielding "dwell."[26] This verb soon came to indicate a divine presence, the shekinah. Along with *shem* (name), *panim* (face), *dabar* (word), and *maqom* (place), this epithet enabled later Jews to avoid uttering the divine name. Other ways of achieving the same goal are seen in the New Testament, among which are passive forms and locatives such as "in heaven" or simply "heaven."

Verse 16 does not appear in the Hebrew text, but the Greek translator now introduces the idea of faithfulness that he removed from the previous verse to make room for wise rulers in civil government. The language of inheritance and progeny, dear to the authors of earlier narratives about the founding mothers and fathers, lies behind the thoughts expressed here. According to Exod 19:5–6, Israel is YHWH's private possession (cf. Isa 19:24–25); elsewhere she is promised the land as inheritance (Gen 13:14–17). Now, wisdom becomes the special property of those who obey her. Wisdom has replaced the land, and the possibility that descendants might not revere her does not even surface.

Thus far this brief poem has concentrated on the recipients of instruction, although wisdom initiates the discussion and appears throughout as the one who responds to them. With vv 17–19, the emphasis falls on wisdom herself.[27] She seems like a stranger, subjecting her students to arduous tests, then rewarding them on the basis of their conduct. The final verse shows that the stakes in this classroom are high. Life and death await in the wings.

The erotic hint in v 15 becomes more explicit here with the play on the well-known theme of a foreign woman. Verse 17 states that wisdom initially disguises herself as she and a learner walk together.[28] Like her rival who promises sensual pleasure, wisdom trades on the perception of strangeness to lure students into her camp. The attraction of the exotic enhances her seductive charm, a theme that plausibly flourished in the time of Ezra and Nehemiah, who strongly resisted marriages between Judeans and foreign women.[29]

Moreover, the image in this verse belongs to the Greek world of peripatetic instruction, which has its parallel in rabbinic and early Christian pedagogy, perhaps also in prophetic circles of an earlier time. Wisdom is depicted not as sitting in a classroom, but as a teacher wandering along hazardous byways, accompanied by eager students. To discern the extent of their knowledge, she does what teachers have done for as long as recorded history: she tests them. The noun *benisyonot* (trials) derives from the verb that describes YHWH's activity in Genesis 22, which produces harrowing results in the life of the patriarch Abraham and his family. The same verb occurs in the story about King Ahaz, who piously refuses to subject YHWH to a test, thinking himself secure from danger as a result of a treaty with the king of Assyria ("I should not petition nor test YHWH," Isa 7:12).

The mention of trials would arise naturally because of the difficulties faced by young students, from the necessary tedium associated with memorizing large blocks of text, oral or written, to the long hours committed to penmanship, obligatory recitation, and hard thinking. Worse by far, however, all this distraction kept boys from more enticing pursuits with members of the opposite sex and from exciting, risk-filled ventures like military service.[30]

As if to compensate for the limited excitement attached to scholarly pursuits, Ben Sira depicts wisdom as providing adequate risk. She brings a sense of unease: the ever-present fear of corporal punishment, which, according to scribal texts from Mesopotamia and Egypt, could be quite harsh. The third bicolon in v 17 alludes to the prolonged time of study necessary for mastery of the curriculum and for enculturation. The goal of knowledge, then, goes beyond the acquisition of skills inherent to functioning as a scribe. The primary aim is to cultivate the mind so that one's behavior accords with the truth that resides in the classic texts. When that occurs, Ben Sira remarks, wisdom can trust that the student's will has become her own.

Now that total accord has been achieved, wisdom freely bestows her secrets on the deserving student, bringing happiness to replace fear. The decisive words here echo the frequent expression for the blessed in the Psalms, along with a rare concept, the unveiling of hidden mysteries. This latter idea occurs in Job 11:6, "that God would tell you the secrets of wisdom" (cf. Dan 2:22, "He reveals the deep and the hidden; he knows what is in the darkness, and light dwells with him"). The association of deep secrets with both God and wisdom continues in the literature from Qumran. The search for wisdom in Job 28 lays the foundation for speculation about her secrets, inasmuch as she is thought to be deep beyond fathoming (cf. Eccl 7:24). Perhaps, too, Qoheleth thinks that God has placed mystery (the unknown) in the human mind but has withheld access to this treasure (Eccl 3:11, reading a nominal form of the verb 'lm, to conceal).[31]

The final verse of this poem concedes what is surely present in all instances of intellectual inquiry: there is no guarantee of success. The possibility of failure, always lingering nearby, can either energize the mind or bring atrophy through frozen fear. The image of a lazy person attempting to negotiate life by his own resources and ending up like the ruins of a deserted village or in the hands of robbers, those who plunder by night (Obad 5), brings this unit to an effective conclusion. The double use of the verb sur (to go aside) adds poignancy to the threat.

For some, the beauty of intellectual pursuit is its open-endedness, the fact that no one ever achieves the ultimate goal. The treasure at rainbow's end simply remains there, always beckoning but ever receding into the distance. The excitement comes from the search; those who sit and wait for wisdom to descend from above in some miraculous disclosure miss everything. Nevertheless, occasional reinforcement in the quest should not be scoffed at, as Ben Sira well understands. That is probably why he offers promises of happiness and success.

How does this poem function as theodicy? It belongs to the broader world of divine discipline, where YHWH subjects individuals to difficulty for the purpose of forming moral character. In this scheme of things, adversity serves a useful purpose, however painful it may be. Those who subscribe to this theory of divine pedagogy accept trials as a necessary means to a greater good. Rather than indicating an inattentive or cruel deity, these anomalies that try the faithful actually point to a caring figure in the transcendent realm, one who does not shrink from inflicting pain to effect growth in character.

Obviously, this understanding of divine discipline has a serious flaw when applied generally, for excessive evil often strikes fatally, without warning, or strikes deeply or relentlessly to the point of debilitation. In such instances no moral formation can occur. And what of the suffering of innocent children, whose circumstances preclude any possibility of growth? Moreover, for modern readers, a revulsion for corporal punishment renders this response to the problem of theodicy less than ideal. Perhaps the other texts I examine here will offer more promise.

Wisdom of Solomon 11:15–12:27

The Alexandrian source to which we now turn appears to have been composed a little later than Sirach, somewhere in the late second century BCE, possibly even as late as the early first century CE.[32] Written in learned Greek, it is part of a treatise heavily influenced by middle Platonic ideas.[33] These range from a theory that humans possess a spark of the divine to belief that knowledge is a hypostasis, an actual attribute of deity manifesting itself below. The wider text employs various rhetorical devices to defend God's fundamental justice in the face of troubling events that seem to undercut it, especially the early demise of good people[34] and the divine particularism that expressed itself in the slaughter of the Egyptian firstborn as told in the book of Exodus.

The brief unit under consideration has been aptly called a Mercy Dialogue,[35] for it labors to show how God always tempers judgment with compassion, applying two principles whenever punishing the guilty: (1) measure, number, and weight, and (2) little by little. The traditional belief that the punishment must match the crime governs this entire discussion, as does the philosophical ideal of wise rulers. Power exists, the author asserts, to make mercy possible. The dialogue is fueled by a series of questions related to justice, and the examples chosen for analysis clearly represent objections raised by the intellectual community about the biblical narrative of the exodus and the conquest of the land that eventually came to be called Canaan.

The initial section (11:15–20) lays out the principle of measure, number, and weight as applied to the plagues that afflicted the Egyptians. The text contends that wrong thinking led the Egyptians to worship repulsive animals rather than the creator, who, in turn, used irrational creatures to punish them. Recalling biblical narrative about bears and lions as agents of divine punishment (1 Kgs 13:1–32; 2 Kgs 17:25), it supposes that God could easily have continued that tradition, or even raised it a degree by forming terrifying dragons of mythic lore. Indeed, justice alone could have pursued the guilty, stopping them in their tracks. Instead of resorting to such dreadful means of slaying the Egyptians, a just deity carefully distributed punishment by measure, number, and weight.

Religious polemic against idolatry has a long and checkered history; its early expression in sixth-century prophecy and specific psalms set the tone of caustic ridicule:

> Their gods are silver and gold, the work of human hands.
> They have mouths but cannot speak, eyes but cannot see.
> They have ears but cannot hear, noses but cannot smell.
> They have hands but cannot feel, feet but cannot walk.
> No sound rises from their throats. (Ps 115:4–7; cf. Ps 135:15–17)

By the time of the Mercy Dialogue, that mockery has reached new heights. Idols are said to be unable to protect themselves from fire, theft, impure hands, and bird droppings.[36] At the same time, rational explanations for the practice of worshiping idols are put forward: an emperor's desire to be honored from afar, a father's grief over the loss of a son, artistic pride in the product of human craft.[37]

Israelite authors were able to appreciate the function of icons as sacred presence—for example, the ark, the brazen serpent, and the table of bread—but they strongly resisted all devotion to other human artifacts or creatures. The elaborate dressing, feeding, and exercising of idols among Israel's neighbors struck worshipers of YHWH as ludicrous. The idols' vulnerability, as mocked in the story of Bel and the Dragon, clinched the case for biblical opposition to the practice. Still, in subtle ways, the Torah scroll, followed by the menorah, gradually filled the role left vacant by this opposition. Perceptive religious leaders realized that divine presence is best symbolized by objects that can be seen and touched.[38]

The Dialogue's first question, stated rhetorically, occurs in v 21. In the face of divine power, "who can withstand the might of thy arm?" This reminder of the creator's sovereignty leads to two observations about the imbalance between the artisan and what he has made. In God's eyes the whole world is like a speck that tips scales, or a drop of dew—an admission that looks stunningly modern as scientists learn more about the vast universe. How much more remarkable, then, is divine solicitude for such insubstantial creatures (11:23). A merciful deity overlooks sin, giving the guilty ample time to repent. Here is the author's answer to delayed punishment for the wicked, one that puts a positive spin on the lack of immediate response.

This divine patience arises from love, according to the text. The existence of something is sufficient proof of God's love for it, for the creator would not have made what was loathsome. Then come two more questions: "How would anything have endured if you had not willed it? Or how would anything not called forth by you have been preserved?" (11:25 NRSV). Because God loves the living, he spares all things, correcting them little by little until they develop strong character. Now comes an astonishing claim—that God has deposited divine substance in humans, endowing them with qualities of the eternal (12:1). Here is a decisive step beyond the concept of the image of God found in Gen 1:26–27. That earlier notion implies that women and men are mortal, although in some sense a reflection of the creator. Scholars see various possibilities in that language about a divine image: dominion over earth, sexual distinction, speech, self-transcendence—but not immortality. That limitation does not appear in the Mercy Dialogue. The divine mind has a corollary in the human mind, a familiar Stoic concept that eventually permits speculation about the *logos* and its partial distribution among humans.

The next section of the Mercy Dialogue (12:3–11) addresses the problem that arises from YHWH's harsh treatment of the native inhabitants of the land seized by the Israelites as their own. The text turns these indigenous peoples into monsters, accusing them of human sacrifice and cannibalism, by this means endeavoring to justify their eradication. Such despicable people and their religious cult so defiled the land, it contends, that YHWH recolonized the area with deserving people. Even then YHWH sent advance warning to elicit repentance, all the while applying the principle of little by little as a controlling factor in the administration of punishment. That check against the full release of divine fury served little purpose, however, for God knew that the people belonged to an accursed race. This curious comment echoes the story of the curse that Noah placed on Ham, the father of Canaan, in Gen 9:25, and the additional remark about inborn evil seems to reflect the sentiment attributed to the deity in Gen 6:5, although that observation applied to all humanity.

The biblical story about a gradual conquest of the land provides both a problem and an opportunity, or so it seems to the author of the Mercy Dialogue. The problem: Why did it take so long to occupy the land that YHWH loved? The opportunity: God's compassion was operative throughout. Thus the text states that YHWH could easily have conquered the land by different means, whether by wild animals or a mere word. The latter would easily have sufficed, just as it did at creation. Elsewhere the author attributes final judgment to God's powerful word, a stern warrior that comes down from heaven to effect death (18:14–16).

A series of four questions introduces the next section (12:12–18), all of them asking in one way or another who can challenge the deity for destroying his own workmanship, especially when it is flawed. No one can call the deity to account; the same incapacity applies to earthly rulers, none of whom dare contest God's actions. The text then expounds on idealized kingship—the use of power for good ends—and views divine strength in this light. The appropriate wielder of power neither judges unjustly nor sits idly by while ruthless people take advantage of seeming weakness. Divine power, in this author's view, sustains righteousness, working to evoke virtue in those who are spared.

What about the chosen people who replaced the Canaanites? The next section (12:19–22) addresses this issue, contrasting the divine treatment of the two groups. The eradication of the wicked serves as an example to the righteous, teaching them virtue. Failing to profit from the instruction carries a heavy penalty, for the deity demands a higher moral standard from the recipients of divine promise. The children of God are chastened to make them worthy judges, an idea we encountered in the Greek text of Sir 4:15. The enemies of God's people, however, fall under harsher punishment by far. The picture of merciful human judges who anticipate being shown mercy by the heavenly judge brings to a close this treatment of contrasting discipline.

The final section of the Mercy Dialogue (12:23–27) returns to the opening topic, the worship of creatures rather than the true God, and judges practitioners of such idolatry to be deserving of punishment. YHWH is thus exonerated from their destruction. The mention of children in the previous unit has opened the way for describing idolaters as foolish infants. The moderate rebukes that came in the form of animals served as a warning to the Egyptians, making them culpable before God, whom they came to recognize as the true God. The author makes a dramatic claim here, hardly supported by the biblical narrative in Exodus, that nevertheless serves his theodicy well.[39] Even condemned Egyptians were forced to acknowledge the justice of their fate. By turning their own putative gods against them, a just and merciful deity led the Egyptians to see the error of their ways. Discipline in divine hands can have beneficent results, but everything depends on the human response. Divine mercy is dispensed in proportion to human acceptance of the moral law.

When we pause to compare the two texts discussed thus far in this chapter, Sir 4:11–19 and Wisd 11:15–12:27, one major difference stands out. Ben Sira writes to exalt wisdom, the agent of divine discipline, whereas the unknown author of Wisdom of Solomon engages in a deliberate theological meditation, a sort of internal dialogue with the deity about discipline. For Ben Sira, personified wisdom is distinct from God; for the author of Wisdom of Solomon, she is a divine attribute, similar to *logos* and spirit. The third example of divine pedagogy that we shall examine purports to be divine speech, albeit transmitted through prophetic mediation.

Amos 4:6–11 and Hosea 11:1–7

The prophets Amos and Hosea were active in the northern kingdom during the eighth century BCE, roughly 750 to 722. During those years, a prosperous Israel fell before an expansive Assyrian empire, and both Amos and Hosea saw the people's unbridled optimism fade as social turmoil led to regicide and abuse of the powerless. Each prophet in his own way tried to communicate a divine word of judgment while holding out a remote chance of reprieve if the people would amend their ways. By and large, Amos emphasized social injustice,[40] while Hosea focused on cultic abuses,[41] but this assessment of their messages is an oversimplification. Hosea's use of marital and parental imagery to depict YHWH's relationship with Israel lends itself more readily to the notion of discipline than does Amos's approach. Nevertheless, the prophet from Tekoa does not shrink from using the concept of discipline, nor does he sugarcoat it.

Amos 4:6–11

(6) As for me, I gave you
    clean teeth in all your towns
    and lack of bread everywhere.
  Yet you did not return to me.
  Oracle of YHWH.
(7) I also withheld rain from you
    three months prior to harvest.

I made it rain on one town
    but not on another.
One area would be rained on
    and another portion, on which it did not rain, dried up.

(8) Two or three towns wandered
    to one town to drink water
    but were not satisfied.
Yet you did not return to me.
Oracle of YHWH.

(9) I smote you with blight and mildew repeatedly.
Your gardens and vineyards,
    your fig trees and olive trees
    were devoured by locusts.
Yet you did not return to me.
Oracle of YHWH.

(10) I dispatched pestilence against you
    in the manner of Egypt.
I slew your young men with the sword,
    along with captured horses,
    and I made the stench of your encampments
    go up into your nostrils.
Yet you did not return to me.
Oracle of YHWH.

(11) I overthrew you
    just as Elohim overthrew Sodom and Gomorrah.
You became like a brand
    pulled from fire.
Yet you did not return to me.
Oracle of YHWH.

This textual unit is set off from its immediate context by a fivefold refrain—"Yet you did not return to me"—which builds to a climax, yielding a final threat in v 12:

(12) Therefore thus I will do to you, Israel;
    because I will do this to you,
    prepare to meet your God, Israel.

In the manner of oaths in the ancient world, the precise threat remains unexpressed to increase its horror. A hymnic fragment follows, appropriately placed to serve as a sort of doxology of judgment (4:13).[42] It declares that the creator who knows human thoughts also brings darkness and destruction in battle, and it identifies this powerful figure with the God of Israel, YHWH of hosts.

The divine disciplinary acts that Amos mentions seem patterned on the ancient practice of liturgical recitation, but in place of the customary saving deeds that brought a sense of special privilege to an elect people, Amos substitutes acts of punishment. The effect must have been devastating, like that of the events described. The punishments relate to nature and history, revealing the deity as active in both realms. In five consecutive blows, YHWH's punishment is said to have struck the people, who nevertheless remained unrepentant: first famine, then drought randomly dispensed, followed by failed crops, pestilence spread by war, and finally earthquake.

Amos minces no words. The famine was severe, as graphically portrayed in the image of clean teeth from lack of bread. The seemingly random pattern of storm clouds and their release of water is revealed as a function of design for maximal effect—namely, the timing of drought to coincide with the specific moment when the barley most needs rain. The erratic rainfall brought social unrest, forcing some residents to journey to nearby villages in search of water, but the meager supply failed to slake their thirst. As if loss of the grain crops were not enough, locusts arrived, along with various fungi in the vineyards, ruining the grapes, figs, and olives. Locusts alone, according to the poetic description in the book of Joel, possessed the power to denude all vegetation, leaving behind empty granaries and stomachs.

The next disciplinary punishment brought dreaded warriors who brandished swords. Accompanying them, pestilence wreaked havoc among the starving citizens as bodies rotted and their stench diffused over the blighted land. The first to suffer, young men, represent the future, now bleak. Even the prized war horse, a source of such pride to YHWH in the divine speeches to Job, shifted allegiance, going over to the invaders.

Finally, a devastating earthquake leveled houses, reviving the faint memory of a legendary destruction that sent Sodom and Gomorrah into the waters of the Sea of Salt. As there, so here only a few survived, resembling a partially burned stick removed from a fire. The severity of this cataclysmic event was still remembered by the later editor who composed the superscription to the book of Amos (1:1).

What is the point of all this? The prophet wishes to justify the divine decision to bring fire on this people—to use the language of his threats against foreign nations that introduce the book (1:3–2:3)—and to pave the way for a similar indictment of the two kingdoms, Israel and Judah (2:4–16). In his view, YHWH has sent repeated warnings that ought to have produced repentance.

Those warnings, coupled with prophetic admonitions laced with appeals to turn, have been ignored. The history of divine chastisement, presented as a liturgy of wasted opportunity,[43] justifies the horrific warning to prepare for the worst, still unspecified. Like a merciful sovereign, this deity has shown a willingness to forgive (7:3, 6), but the time has come for the execution of justice.

Hosea 11:1–7

Hosea's example of divine discipline is less direct but infinitely more intimate. He introduces us to the innermost thoughts of a disappointed deity who has acted as a parent to a rebellious child:

(1) When Israel was a child
    I loved him;
    from Egypt
    I called [him] my son.

(2) They called them,
    so they walked from me.[44]
    They sacrificed to Baalim
    and offered incense to idols.

(3) I led Ephraim,
    taking them in my[45] arms;
    but they did not know
    that I healed them.

(4) I drew them with human bonds,
    with loving cords;
    and I appeared to them
    like one who put a yoke on their jaws,
    though gently I offered them food.

The description of an affectionate parent teaching a child to walk and soothing hurts in loving arms effectively communicates YHWH's feelings toward Israel. The abrupt shift in imagery from children to livestock, disturbing to modern eyes, highlights the close affinity in Israel between humans and small cattle. Because the people's very existence often depended on the well-being of these animals, special care was directed toward them. Hence, Hosea moves on to describe YHWH's gentle treatment of oxen. The emphasis here falls on nurture, although set within a context of idolatry.

    With v 5 the prophet introduces a radical change in YHWH's treatment of the child whose origin was in Egyptian bondage. Israel's failure will result in a return to the land of its oppressors. Worse still, it will find itself divided, with some being subjected to Assyrian rule. The image of a yoke,[46] first mentioned in v 4 in terms of divine easing, returns in v 7 with no such relief.

Discipline, in Hosea's portrayal, is wielded by a loving parent whose deepest emotions are sharply conflicted, as we see in the sequel to this unit (11:8–9). An ambiguous text matches the turmoil it discloses, with modern interpreters divided over whether the contrast between God and man indicates forgiveness or punishment. YHWH appears to entertain the unthinkable, the total abandoning of Israel, and to wonder how he can possibly carry such a thing through. He admits that his thoughts stir warm feelings toward Israel, but do they eventuate in a stay of execution? The answer is not clear, but one thing shines through the text with blinding force: Israel must reckon with the demands of deity—"For I am God, not man, the Holy One among you."

The examples of divine discipline that we have studied in this chapter by no means exhaust the possibilities, but they illustrate the rich potential inherent in this approach to theodicy.[47] In the next chapter I consider the most common approach of all, the belief that whatever difficulties people experience are punishment for sin.

7

Punishment for Sin

Blaming the Victim

Were personal sins the cause of sickness, the entire world might not contain the necessary number of hospital beds.

—Stanley L. Jaki

Perhaps the oldest and most common explanation for evil in its different forms simply brings together sin and punishment in a one-to-one relationship. This view rests on the assumption that the universe operates by a rational system that somehow hands out reward and punishment relative to an individual's merit. In some religious systems, mostly Eastern, that principle extends over more than a single lifetime, with the total accumulation of karma determining both the scope and the nature of subsequent incarnations.

The conviction that one can expect justice from the deity or deities is grounded in a deep psychological need for order. Random instances of evil suggest that chaos has the upper hand, and no human society can survive in such an environment. Ancient myths dealt with this problem, each myth in its own way. Victory over chaos came at a high price, but in the end society found consolation in the knowledge that order had been assured.[1] The biblical covenant between God and Noah was accompanied by a visible sign, the rainbow, which served as a reminder of both the former chaos[2] and the divine promise that from that time forward the universe would be stable. Never again, it announced, would the deity lash out in a destructive manner that threatened survival itself.

Because of the importance of order within society, a recent theorist has argued that every community has developed a system of scapegoating as a means of overcoming violence and assuring society's well-being.[3] That is, faced with the threat of harm, a vulnerable group will sacrifice a convenient representative to appease the threatening power. The theory gets its name from a ritual in ancient Israel for removing evil by choosing a goat and symbolically laying on it the offenses of the people, then driving it into the wilderness, away from human habitation. I examine this phenomenon in the next chapter, but for now my concern is to emphasize the significance to humankind of predictability.

According to the principle of individual reward and retribution, there can be no victim, for all individuals receive their just deserts. A story about the learned rabbi Hillel illustrates the ease with which this simple response to disaster appears to remove any doubt about the rule of justice: "One day he was walking along the river and he saw a skull floating on the water and said to it, 'Because you drowned others, they drowned you, and in the end those who drowned you will be drowned'" (Abot 2:7). The reasoning is easily penetrated: the person who was drowned met an unwelcome death, which only befalls sinners. Virtuous people reach the grave peacefully, surrounded by loving descendants.

The anecdote highlights the insidious nature of this response to evil. On the assumption that the rule allows no exceptions, we easily arrive at the conclusion that whoever undergoes harm has brought it on himself. This kind of reasoning is illustrated in both testaments. Job is blamed by his friends for his troubles, and a man blind since birth prompts Jesus' disciples to ask, "Master, who sinned, this man, or his parents, that he was born blind?" (John 9:2). In the narrative world represented by the Gospel text, someone has brought blindness on the infant. To the ones seeking insight, the culprit can only be the unborn child or his parents. A third possibility—that there are random occurrences of evil—seems beyond their ken. Nor does Jesus seize this option, but he does reject the principle of exact retribution, arguing instead for an instrumental understanding of evil. In a word, evil exists, at least in this instance, to enable Jesus to demonstrate God's healing grace.

Both examples, Job and the man born blind, demonstrate the flaws in assuming that in every instance evil strikes in exact proportion to sin. Yet despite the rejection of this principle in both these and other instances, not a few religious people—and many nonreligious people—continue to adhere to it. The instinctive reaction of many to personal illness or tragic accident is the question, What have I done? That tendency to connect disaster with guilt is fueled by the overwhelming assumption throughout the Bible that God pun-

ishes misconduct and rewards goodness. Even the promised transference in
that final settling of accounts in a future existence has not entirely driven out
the old ways of thinking.

The pervasiveness of such attitudes in ancient Israel can be seen in the
way the psalmists view their own experiences, whether good or bad. The first
psalm presents an idyllic picture of a world governed by the principle that the
good always prosper and the wicked invariably fall into harm's way. The psalmist firmly believes that the righteous are protected by YHWH, while their opposites are destined to perish. The images that serve to illustrate their divergent
futures convey volumes. Virtuous people resemble well-irrigated trees, whereas
the wicked are like chaff in the wind.

This imaginary world brings comfort to those who believe, like the poet
responsible for Psalm 112, that the righteous will never be moved (112:6) and
the desire of the wicked will come to nothing (112:10). The close association of
charitable deeds and prosperity in this psalm shows what a powerful ethical
incentive the principle of reward and retribution can be. That stimulus to benevolent action partially justifies such thinking, for rare indeed is the person
who can measure up to the standard of Plato that the virtuous deed must
emanate from pure desire for good, not fear of punishment or hope of reward.
Loving God for the deity's sake rather than the blessings it brings is not unknown in the Bible, but its rarity matches the difficulty involved in making
such love manifest. The psalmist acknowledges the inevitable conflict between
the righteous and the wicked but asserts that good will ultimately triumph.
Indeed, the trouble the wicked might foment is barely considered, so secure
are the righteous in God's protective care.

The laments within the book of Psalms bear witness to the presence of
unexplained evil while also attesting to the belief that YHWH will act decisively
to rectify all wrongs.[4] With a single exception, Psalm 88, these complaints move
from petition to praise, implying that the deity has heard the plea and has
responded to remove the source of pain. The agony of Psalm 88 is contained
in its initial declaration: "YHWH, God of my salvation." Nothing that follows
lends credibility to the traditional epithet. In fact, this same deity is blamed for
the trouble that has overwhelmed the poet, who wonders aloud, somewhat
brazenly, whether the inhabitants of the grave can match his praise of YHWH,
now held in abeyance.

Ironically, the principle that individuals get what they deserve often does
apply, which goes a long way in explaining the tenacity of such a view. Many
good people conduct their lives in a manner that avoids unnecessary risk. Their
cautious lifestyle leaves them unexposed to the consequences that follow lawlessness, debauchery, and numerous other dangerous pursuits. Thus as a gen-

eral rule, those who live on the edge come to a bad end, while those who cultivate the mind and body as a divine temple find a degree of peace.

Nevertheless, the world has so much randomness that no individual can ever count on reaping the benefits of a noble life. The social interconnection of the human populace renders everyone vulnerable to the violence of a few. In the modern world, weapons of mass destruction threaten the extinction of humankind just as the ice age wiped out the majestic dinosaurs. In such a world, it becomes increasingly difficult to believe that a just judge actively dispenses reward and punishment, at least during the only life that we can be sure of experiencing.[5]

This modern shift in understanding removes us from the world of the Bible, except for the speculative books of Job and Ecclesiastes. Even there, the "modern" rejection of a causal link between act and consequence[6] appears alongside the opposite view. It has been plausibly argued that the sayings in the book of Proverbs represent popular sentiment that was absolutized into dogma in the same way that the principle of act and consequence, in response to popular questioning in the face of crisis, was solidified into dogma.[7] In all these instances, it is clear that simply asserting—or even formalizing—a cherished belief does not make it true.

Nor does historiography that interprets Israel's and Judah's past in the light of this principle do justice to what really happened, as modern scholars have long recognized. It matters little whether the deity under discussion is Chemosh from Moab,[8] Marduk from Babylon, or YHWH. The development of history involves numerous imponderables with deep interconnections, and any reading of the rise and fall of nations in terms of divine favor or wrath can only be categorized as theology—and bad theology at that.

The Four Friends of Job

To illustrate the inadequacy of this approach to theodicy, we shall begin by examining the arguments of the four friends of Job. Together, they reveal the weakness of trying to determine true character by things that are visible to the naked eye, especially in the instance of excessive evil.[9] I follow the arguments in the order that the friends appear as Job's partners in dialogue: Eliphaz, Bildad, Zophar, and Elihu.

Eliphaz: "Plowers of mischief and sowers of trouble reap the same"

Job's friend from neighboring Teman states the premise of his argument in agrarian imagery: "Precisely as I have observed, plowers of mischief ['awen] and sowers of trouble ['*amal*] reap the same" (Job 4:8). In typical sapiential fashion, Eliphaz gathers his information from observation,[10] relying on his own mental faculties to inform him about the way things operate in the world. To him, it is a well-known fact that farmers reap exactly what they sow; grains of wheat do not produce grapes or olives. By analogy, he concludes, anyone who wishes to harvest a crop of desirable circumstances must plant accordingly.

Eliphaz eases into this argument, briefly commending Job for his record of helping others stand tall during difficult times. But now that trouble has hit home, Job has become perturbed. The question that Eliphaz poses to his friend sums up his theology of suffering:[11] "Is not your piety your confidence, and the integrity of your conduct your hope?" (4:6). That is, don't you believe that your religious past assures you a pleasant future? With the word *tom* (integrity) Eliphaz picks up a concept that has been central to the prose narrative: the narrator, YHWH, and Job's wife have all affirmed Job's integrity. Personal wholeness brings reward in kind, Eliphaz assumes, and Job should trust in that hopeful scenario.

To support his positive spin on Job's circumstances and their immediate amelioration, Eliphaz appeals to tradition.[12] Have you ever seen a miscarriage of justice, he asks, then goes on to say that he certainly has not. Miscreants pay dearly for their evil deeds, he insists, for God acts in anger to negate their villainy. The illustration of might brought low returns to the natural realm: a lion and its young may roar in the night but starve for lack of available prey. Presumably, Eliphaz uses this image because of the close association of lions and royalty, as if to say that even powerful wielders of oppression perish when God's anger burns.

Not satisfied with arguments from personal observation, Eliphaz appeals to communication from the realm of the spirits. His graphic description of a numinous encounter enhances the force of its whispered message: "Can a human be more righteous than Eloah, or a person purer than the creator?" (4:17).[13] Profoundly aware of being in the presence of the holy, even if unable to clearly see his nocturnal visitor, Eliphaz reacted much like the prophet Isaiah in similar circumstances: he was terrified. The language of his account echoes that of theophanies to Abraham (*tardemah*, a deep sleep, Gen 15:12) and Elijah (*demamah daqqah*, a sound of silence, 1 Kgs 19:12).[14]

The extent of the word communicated by divine initiative is unclear, but what follows the question above may be Eliphaz's elaboration. It states by implication that the deity alone is pure, for even the heavenly messengers fail to measure up. How much less, Eliphaz remarks, do mortals have the right to claim purity, puny creatures who resemble moths in their extreme vulnerability. The images of mortality stand out here: houses of clay, ephemerality, tent cords, foundations of dust. If Eliphaz wishes to draw attention to human frailty, he has succeeded—but is that the issue? This anticipation of Job's theophany with its similar contrast between powerful creator and impotent human fails miserably as comfort, the stated purpose of the visit by the three friends.

At the conclusion of this low appraisal of human beings comes the harshest blow of all, at least from the perspective of the sages. Mortals die, it asserts, but not with wisdom (Job 4:21). The picture of breaking camp aptly describes human transience, as does the admission of failure in the ultimate quest for knowledge. Having come from dust, it says, mortals perish between morning and evening. The reversal of the usual reckoning, from evening to morning—the time of darkness and danger—merely exposes the irony of death in the hours when people feel most secure.

Not only are mortals guilty, they are born to trouble just as sparks fly up, for that is their nature. Furthermore, Eliphaz announces, fools may prosper momentarily, but their children are demolished in the gate. Once again, such an allusion can only bring increased pain to a friend who, according to the story, has lost his ten children in a single blow. In such a circumstance, Eliphaz urges Job to seek God. The subsequent hymnic praise expresses traditional piety: the one who sends rain and acts to save the poor from their enemies is a sure basis for hope. With this word, Eliphaz returns to his earlier question about Job's integrity as cause for expecting favor.

Having laid the ground for affirmation, Eliphaz waxes eloquent in describing divine discipline. Chastisement induces happiness, because the one who injures also heals. Job will laugh at danger—a theme that will reoccur when YHWH boasts about the valiant warhorse (39:22)—and will be at peace with nature itself.

The speech concludes with a splendid promise. Job will pitch his tent safely, defying the earlier image of the pulled-up tent cord. He will be surrounded by numerous children and domestic animals, at last coming to his grave like a shock of grain arriving at the threshing floor *in season*. How does Eliphaz know this? Not from a private theophany, as earlier, but from joint intellectual endeavor with Bildad and Zophar. Here Eliphaz wraps himself in the cloak of those from whom Job will soon hear additional words of wisdom. He also goes a step further, claiming veracity for his words and urging Job to listen and learn.

Age has taught Eliphaz, he avers in the second round of speeches, that mortals drink iniquity like water (15:16); however, there are degrees of evil, and the wicked fare less well than others. That conclusion seems to follow, given Eliphaz's insistence that evildoers ache continually, fearing darkness from which they cannot emerge. Once again Eliphaz paints a dismal portrait of the fate of the wicked: they are hungry, afraid, isolated, impoverished, unproductive, and barren. Their only stability, it seems, is emptiness—and this is their reward as well (15:31).

The invidious nature of Eliphaz's reasoning from misfortune to guilt reaches a pinnacle in his third speech, where the friend accuses Job of heinous crimes and simultaneously excludes human morality from the list of things precious to God. Integrity counts for nothing in the deity's eyes, and innocence brings no pleasure to the Almighty. Eliphaz's reflections on the puniness of mortals have produced this sharp separation of ethics from its transcendent source, yet he proceeds to justify God's conduct in sending calamity as punishment for Job's offenses.

The wicked, Eliphaz remarks, were snatched away before their time, a flood washing away their foundations (22:16). All their questioning of the deity's sight and might withered before YHWH's refutation of their arrogant reasoning, and the laughter of innocents filled the void. As his parting shot, Eliphaz urges Job to make peace with God, which will bring restoration. Esteem God more highly than gold, he says, and light will shine upon you, and through you, upon others. There could be no clearer articulation of the belief that piety brings generous reward.

Bildad: "Surely the light of the wicked will be extinguished"

The Shuhite wastes no time in asserting divine justice, asking testily: "Does El distort justice, or does Shaddai distort what is right?" (8:3). The intended answer to the rhetorical question is an emphatic "No." The twofold use of the verb 'awat (to distort) underlines the central idea in the sentence. In Bildad's mind, the deity cannot act unjustly; the matter has been settled once and for all. It follows that Job's children were egregious sinners, given their hasty demise. So, he advises, entreat the deity and amend your ways; if truly pure, you will receive blessing.

Like Eliphaz, Bildad appeals to collective experience and to lessons from nature. Our ephemerality requires that we supplement our own observations with accumulated lore, here summed up in an impossible question: "Can papyrus flourish in the absence of a marsh, or can reeds thrive where there is no water?" (8:11).[15] Devoid of moisture, these plants swiftly die; in like manner, those who forget El lose hope. With this word "hope" (tiqwah), Bildad echoes the language of Eliphaz. The images that follow combine two unrelated things—the fragile web of a spider and the spreading roots of a vine that are briefly impressive but short-lived because they are in rocky terrain. Job, however, still has hope, if he is truly without blame. The wicked, Bildad asserts, will not fare so well; their tent will cease to be. Once again, we hear an echo of Eliphaz.

Returning to the idea of a tent in his second speech, Bildad concentrates on the insecure environs of the wicked. The light of the wicked will be extinguished, he declares, and their lamp will burn out (18:5–6). Both images function metaphorically, suggesting death. To these Bildad adds images from hunting and warfare, a net and a hidden snare, as well as disease and terror.

Bildad's last speech (25:1–6), abbreviated by design or, much more probably, by accident, affirms God's greatness and emphasizes the lowliness of all else, including stars and moon. Like Eliphaz, Bildad celebrates God's purity to the detriment of those born of woman. What a vast difference between this understanding of mortals and the unrivaled expression of their grandeur in Psalm 8. It appears that divine justice can come only at the price of human worth.

Zophar: "Eloah exacts of you less than your guilt deserves"

Whereas Eliphaz introduced the frightening aspect of a theophany into the discussion, Zophar the Naamathite longs for divine disclosure to Job of the many-faceted secrets of wisdom (11:6). Does Zophar's remarkable insight about divine leniency belong to these hidden things? The text states that Eloah pardons some of Job's sins: "Know that Eloah exacts of you less than your guilt deserves" (11:6c).

Lacking knowledge of wisdom's secrets, Zophar muses, how can anyone expect to know the deep things of Eloah? This leads to further instancing of divine mystery and power in their transcending of heaven's height and Sheol's depth and ocean's breadth. Here Zophar refers to the three-tiered universe of ancient Near Eastern cosmology.[16] He then calls on the time-honored argument that power is somehow justified because no one can resist it.

Zophar, too, expresses the centrality of tents and hope. Counseling Job to entreat the deity in prayer, he assures his friend that he will experience light even during the night and that he will possess hope (11:18), resting securely. The wicked, however, will stumble blindly, lacking a way of escape. The final words of the speech highlight Zophar's conviction that the deity judges with precise scales: "Their hope is their last breath" (11:20b).

The second speech of Zophar focuses entirely on the sorry lot of the wicked, who may enjoy a brief moment of pleasure but will watch as everything is either consumed or taken from their tents and houses (20:1–29). In Zophar's view, divine justice is both alive and well. Evildoers will perish like dung; they will fly away like a dream, quickly forgotten. Sweet-tasting wickedness will turn poisonous inside, and God will feed them huge morsels of anger. Then at last their sins will be exposed in heaven, and the earth will rise up against them.

With this wrenching description of the fate of sinners, Zophar has come painfully close to describing Job's own physical and mental state. Job has known momentary happiness but has seen it snatched away in a scant second. His food has turned to venom within his aching body, and he has stood helplessly by as fire has consumed the contents of his tent, as it were. In truth, he has experienced the sorry fate that his friend links with the godless. While Job's integrity stubbornly refuses to give an inch, can we say the same for that of Job's three friends?

Elihu: "According to their deeds he will repay them"

Elihu suddenly enters the narrative just when readers expect a divine resolution of the problem, inasmuch as Job's three initial companions have been effectively silenced.[17] Worse, from a narrative standpoint, this fourth friend steals some of the divine thunder, anticipating what YHWH will say from the tempest. While Elihu has not been mentioned to this point, similarities in language with the other friends, as well as the transitional comments, imply that he has been an interested bystander all along. His self-referential introduction is suggestive of a buffoon, a bombastic windbag with an inflated sense of importance and a short fuse. Once he launches the actual debate, however, Elihu reveals flashes of an agile mind and deep piety.

The narrator's preliminary remarks about this young interloper make two important points concerning theodicy: first, that the three friends end the debate because Job considers himself innocent; second, that Elihu is furious over that very thing—specifically, that Job justifies himself rather than God. His anger is thus grounded in theodicy, an objection to innocence that is purchased at the deity's expense. Moreover, Elihu is peeved at the friends' inadequate defense of God's ways.

Responding to Job's insistence that he is innocent of any wrong and that God refuses to answer him, Elihu lays out various modes of divine disclosure, including nocturnal dreams and visions, disciplinary illness, and mediators. A lively scenario unfolds here. God visits a sinner at night, bringing distress to chasten the body and spirit until an angel, curiously called 'ekhad minni-'alep (one in a thousand), intervenes.[18] That intercessory act moves the deity to rescue the individual from Sheol. Once restored to his youthful strength, the person experiences something extraordinary: God repays him for his righteousness. More striking still, the former sinner sings about the triumph of mercy over justice in his relationship with God, who has pardoned his offense.

Not only does Job proclaim his innocence, Elihu remarks, but he also denies that serving God pays: "A person gains nothing for being in favor with God" (34:9). Elihu cannot even imagine that the deity could act unjustly, and he openly expresses his conviction that God compensates all people according to their conduct. This firm belief leads Elihu to assert that "God definitely cannot act wickedly, nor can Shaddai pervert justice" (34:12).

Elihu's confidence in the right governance of the universe arises from his understanding of divine rule. Because the creator is completely independent, obligated to no one, there are no subtle temptations to act deviously, whether from self-interest or fear. The ruler of the created world stands above all earthy kings, treating noble and peasant with similar impartiality. Moreover, Elihu claims, God keeps a vigilant eye on human rulers and punishes them for abuse of power.

This rousing tribute to a just deity who swiftly crushes cruel rulers contains one surprising reservation, stated guardedly: "When he [God] is silent, who can accuse; when he hides his face, who can gaze on him?" (34:29). A hidden, unresponsive deity is exactly what Job condemns much of the time, otherwise complaining of an abusive deity who refuses to leave him alone, even for a moment's respite.

Elihu's next point seems to rule out effective repentance, at least insofar as it brings reprieve from punishment. He asks Job if he thinks he can change his ways, even if instructed from above, and then expect a reduced sentence. The payback will be in full, doled out in precise measurement, Elihu believes, for divine justice is at work. Moreover, he charges, Job compounds his guilt, adding to his faulty knowledge rebellion. Mercilessly, Elihu desires that Job be tested to the limit of endurance. The reader is now face to face with a prime example of religious cruelty that originates in the identification of one's own belief with God's holy causes. Such equation of human and divine ideas has an insidious component: the certainty that one's adversaries are also enemies of God. Given that belief, the desire to see Job's trials increase makes narrative sense.

Actually, Elihu reminds Job, human conduct is a matter of indifference to the deity, like the bite of a mosquito to an elephant, in the popular saying from ancient Assyria.[19] Because God needs nothing, the complex realm of ethics relates to the human community alone. Like earlier arguments by the friends, Elihu's desire to place the deity above the fray comes perilously close to severing heaven and earth. "If you are righteous, what do you give to him, or what can he receive from your hand?" (35:7). At least one psalmist would answer, "Praise!"

Elihu offers another explanation for divine silence—namely, that the deity refuses to respond to those who are overcome by pride. Job, it follows, is a proud man, and God will not heed his cry until he conquers that vice. Those who listen and serve God, Elihu insists, will be restored. Job's trial is the result of guilt; of that, Elihu is sure (36:21). The unparalleled teacher has sent afflictions, and now it is Job's responsibility to learn from them.

Elihu's closing remarks venture beyond a justification of God's treatment of Job. Now the defender of religious tradition begins to extol the creator and to marvel at meteorological phenomena. In this context he makes a curious observation about divine motive: "Whether for instruction, or for his land, or for loving-kindness, he brings it about" (37:13). Both the created order and its human inhabitants enter this picture, but so also does the divine nature. The majesty on exhibit during a thunderstorm or snow shower serves as a constant reminder that God is profoundly attentive to his creation.

With that ascription of praise as background, Elihu urges Job to consider such wonders, insofar as possible. How can anyone penetrate the darkness that conceals the creator? he asks. Unable to see God, how can you prepare a case against him? Do you really want to be swallowed up for rash action? Look at the sun, if you dare, for it surrounds the deity. What is this invisible God like? "He cannot be found, but he is great in strength and justice, and abounding in righteousness. He does not afflict" (37:23). It is obvious that Job's misery has made little impression on Elihu, whose sole purpose is to depict God in the best possible light, even if that means accusing Job of serious misconduct.

Psalm 37

The problem with this type of theodicy is the way it ignores facts. Perhaps the most glaring example of this separation of fact from an imaginary religious realm is found in Psalm 37, where an aged poet makes an astonishing proclamation:

> I have been young and am now old,
>> but I have not observed a righteous person forsaken
>> nor his descendants hunting for bread. (Ps 37:25)

We might say that this psalmist has lived a remarkably sheltered existence— or that he is willfully blind. The entire psalm gives no evidence that the poet recognizes the weakness of his position. In his limited view, "all is right with the world." True, evil exists, but always under God's watchful eye and destined soon to vanish:

> Yet a short time and the wicked will be no more;
>> you will look at their place, but they will not exist. (v 10)

The two verses that follow suggest a distinction often made in the Bible: God's time differs from human measurement of days and years. For this reason, God laughs when evildoers plot harm against the righteous. The poet omits to mention, however, the confounding pain associated with the human experience of God's time.

The psalmist appears to want to have things both ways. The righteous may have little, but that is better than the evildoers' abundance, and during times of famine the virtuous will enjoy a surplus. In the end, the evildoers will vanish like smoke or wither like grass in the heat of the sun. For the poet, the matter is unequivocal:

> For YHWH loves justice;
>> he will not abandon his loyal ones.
> They will be guarded forever,
>> but the descendants of the wicked will be cut off. (v 28)

Thus the psalmist finds no compelling reason for concern in the face of oppression. He even claims to have observed an example of gross evil but at a later time to have looked in vain for the sinners. Their flourishing, in this author's view, was only momentary, whereas the pious will inherit the land.

The marvel is that this psalm stands alongside the many laments that present a much more realistic view of evil and its burdensome weight on worshipers. Perhaps Psalm 37 authentically depicted some people's experience, although its alphabetic form suggests calculated design rather than spontaneity of expression. Be that as it may, the simplistic response to evil's existence lends itself to untenable conclusions about guilt and innocence. The author of this psalm would likely have joined Job's friends in accusing him of grievous transgression.[20]

Israelite Historiography

What about Israelite historiography? Does the record of failure as told in the large historical complexes of the Bible and as presupposed by many of the prophets amount to an indictment of the victims? From the perspective of the Deuteronomistic historian, the collapse of the Davidic dynasty and the razing of the temple, coupled with loss of the land, were directly attributable to Israel's sin.

In addition to the Deuteronomistic History, various prophets charge the people with abandoning the Mosaic law and committing all types of crimes against humanity. Ezekiel 22:23–31 best sums up the prophetic indictment of the Israelites: princes resemble lions and wolves tearing their prey; priests betray their sacred trust, making no distinction between sacred and profane; prophets assist in covering up crimes and proclaim lies as divine oracles; and ordinary people commit robbery and oppress the powerless. In such a context, YHWH's search for someone to stand between the deity and the land comes up empty. Only then does divine wrath fall on a worthless people. From Ezekiel's perspective, the judgment is entirely appropriate.

The later author of Chronicles takes this idea of national guilt one step further, emphasizing individual responsibility so rigorously that it changes the way some rulers are portrayed, especially Josiah and Manasseh. According to the older account, these men are prime examples of the miscarriage of justice, divine retribution gone amok, for Josiah died too early and Manasseh too late. The Chronicler brings their lives into line with his idea that YHWH repays everyone on the basis of merit.[21] Manasseh's long reign becomes an instance of divine patience, delayed punishment giving the wicked king time to change his ways (2 Chr 33:1–20), and Josiah's early death becomes a consequence of his insistence on fighting Pharaoh Neco despite a warning "from the mouth of God" (2 Chr 35:20–24).

The sacred historiography and the prophetic indictments issued in an abiding sense of unworthiness, at least when Israel's leaders bowed in prayer. Acknowledgment of YHWH's justice and confession of the people's guilt run through the late liturgical prayers in an endless refrain.

Ezra's prayer in the book that bears his name opens with a confession of his sense of shame because of collective guilt that mounts upward like the famed tower of Babel. In his view, the calamities that have befallen the nation, including the subjection to foreigners, have come as well-deserved punishment. Despite this heavy burden of sin, YHWH has remained faithful, even now granting respite and restoring the holy temple. The punishments have been less than the people deserve (Ezra 9:13); indeed, Ezra declares, "YHWH, God of Israel, you are righteous, for we are an escaped remnant, as today" (v 15).

The book of Nehemiah preserves a prayer that is attributed to Ezra in the Septuagint (or to Levites, in the Hebrew text). In this prayer, too, YHWH's righteousness is proclaimed. Beginning with praise of the deity as creator, sustainer, and sole God, Ezra recalls the divine choice of Abram and the covenant with him that involved the land. He adds: "You kept your word, for you are righteous" (Neh 9:8b). He then recalls the bondage in Egypt, followed by deliverance dampened by disobedience, although YHWH was ready to forgive, gracious and merciful, patient and abounding in loyal love (v 17). Ezra contin- ues this rehearsal of Israel's wayward behavior and underscores the deity's persistent efforts through prophets to alter the people's conduct. Despite failure in this endeavor, YHWH remains gracious and merciful (v 31). Remembering Assyrian atrocities and Israel's suffering in exile, Ezra urges YHWH to rec- ognize the gravity of the punishment already imposed. He prays, nonetheless: "Yet you have been just in all that has come on us, for you have acted faithfully, and we have dealt treacherously" (v 33).[22]

A similar note sounds in the prayer of Daniel, who begins with confession of widespread sinfulness that constitutes rebellion against a righteous sover- eign (Dan 9:7–11).[23] Although YHWH declared the divine will through proph- ets and the law of Moses, the people did not obey these servants of a merciful and forgiving deity. In due time, Daniel says, YHWH brought punishment, "and yet the Lord our God is righteous in everything he has done" (v 14).

The prayer ends as it began, with a sharp contrast between human sin- fulness and divine justice: "For not on the basis of our righteousness do we offer our petitions to you but on your abundant mercy" (v 18). In this prayer, as in those credited to Ezra, a profound sense of human sinfulness associated with miserable circumstances is coupled with an equally deep conviction that YHWH has not forfeited the attributes once declared to Moses. Victims they certainly are, according to these prayers, but not innocent. YHWH alone is innocent—not guilty—and just.

If we inquire about the fundamental basis for the cause and effect rela- tionship at work in these texts, it must surely be the idea that YHWH has established a covenant with Israel to which stipulations of moral action are attached, along with promises of favor. The two sides of such a relationship can be seen, among other places, in Leviticus 26 and Deuteronomy 28–30. Here YHWH is represented as promising lavish blessing for obedience to the divine commandments, as well as severe punishment for failure to obey.[24] Lest anyone think that the oaths sworn by the originating ancestors of Israel have no binding force on subsequent generations, the author of Deut 29:13–14 has Moses anticipate such reasoning and pronounce it false: "It is not with you only that I make this covenant and this oath but with the one standing before YHWH our God this day as well as the one who is not with us." In short, Moses obligates all subsequent worshipers of the deity to abide by the covenant. They, too, stand under its blessings and curses.

We have by no means exhausted the possibilities for illustrating the direct link between sin and punishment that pervades the Bible. The idea is so prevalent that a thorough treatment would require an analysis of virtually all of the canon. In the next chapter I shift the emphasis away from the deity's character to the possibility of human atonement. I ask the question, Can someone suffer on my behalf?—and in so doing, move ever more in the direction of divine mystery.

PART III

Shifting to the Human Scene

8

Suffering as Atonement

Making the Most of a Bad Thing

Why has God created both wicked and good?
So that the one should atone for the other.

—Pesikta Rabbati 201a

If I am not for myself, who will be for me?
And if I am only for myself, what am I? And if not now, when?

—Hillel

The question posed by the famous first-century rabbi Hillel concerns a fundamental religious dilemma. Who reestablishes harmony between humans and their maker when things go awry? Does that monumental task fall to the sinful creature, or can someone else assume the role of redeemer? Traditional responses to this dilemma created two competing theological systems. In one, individuals depended on their own merit to earn acceptance in their creator's eyes; in the other, they looked to a substitute for redemption from their alienation under sin. Both systems hinged on divine justice. The theory of individual merit stressed personal responsibility and accountability; the theory of substitution opened the door for mercy, but only within a rigid framework of justice.

The idea that individual merit alone could overcome estrangement between God and sinners and the belief that an innocent individual could somehow make intercession with God and effect forgiveness for others offered powerful answers to sin's divisive nature.

Still, neither theory was entirely satisfactory. In their early expressions, neither provided a justification for innocent suffering. In this chapter I look at the development of these opposing systems of atonement and consider how each eventually came to incorporate a defense of perceived divine injustice.

Individual Merit

The Hebrew Bible juxtaposes the two systems of atonement but gives clear preeminence to individual merit. Personal responsibility for sin is the central theme of the prophets, priests, and sages; personal choice determines one's destiny. Ironically, even the substitutionary theory of atonement entails a personal decision to activate redemptive power in one's own life.

For ancient Judaism, human nature was not flawed to the core. To be sure, something very similar to original sin was associated with the story of Eve and that of Aaron and the worship of the golden bull. In both these traditions, however, the guilty stain that affected all humans subsequent to the sin was eventually removed. In the first case, it was obliterated by the flood. The idolatrous worship of the bull reintroduced the stain, but Israel's acceptance of the Law at Mount Sinai was said to have cleansed the people once again.

How, then, could Israel account for the human propensity to sin? Ben Sira takes up this issue in a remarkable section that highlights two quotations of opponents' views (Sir 15:11–16:23),[1] both introduced by a formula of debate, "Do not say." The first troublesome view places the blame for sin on God:

> Do not say, "My rebellion is from God";
>> for he does not do what he hates.
> Lest you say, "He led me astray";
>> for he has no need for violent men. (15:11–12; cf. Jas 1:13–15)

Ben Sira's refutation of such thinking takes the form of a syllogism:

> God hates evil.
> God does not do what he hates.
> God is not responsible for sin.

True, humans are endowed with an inclination, but it is neutral until acted upon through free choice. Ben Sira thus grounds his argument in creation. That is not all. He echoes Deut 30:15, 19, which stipulates that Israel has a choice between life and good, death and evil (v 15), life and death, blessing and curse (v 19). The combined arguments, universal and Sinaitic, serve to reinforce a teacher's private opinion. Human choice, untrammeled by divine sovereignty, determines one's destiny (15:14–20).

Like the prophets Ezekiel and Jeremiah, Ben Sira must deal with individual versus collective responsibility. He acknowledges the possibility that individuals may sin and bring destruction on the populace, a reality he says he has witnessed and Scripture attests. Still, Ben Sira insists, "He [God] judges a person on the basis of deeds . . . ; everyone will receive according to his actions" (16:12b, 14b).

At this point Ben Sira addresses the second troublesome view, a challenge to the notion of individual accountability:

> Do not say, "I shall be hidden from YHWH,
>   and who from above will remember me?
> Among so many people I shall not be known,
>   for what am I in a limitless creation?" (16:17)

Ben Sira emphasizes the deity's majesty and hiddenness, which render such thoughts as expressed by the opponent pure foolishness (16:23).

In a new section, Ben Sira returns to an idea briefly introduced in 15:19, the watchful divine eye, and argues that God sees every human action. He rejects the opponent's attempt to sever the relationship between God and the moral act and claims that no deed goes unnoticed by the creator of the universe (16:24–17:24).

Is divine surveillance cause for dismay? Not at all, Ben Sira contends, for God is compassionate toward humans, who combine extraordinary dignity with commensurate misery. While possessing the image of God, they are also finite. Still, in the face of certain death, they must not lose hope, for the Shepherd watches over those who turn to him. Employing seven imperatives in two verses (17:25–26), Ben Sira urges his students to turn from evil:

> Turn to YHWH and abandon your sins;
>   pray before him and lessen your offense.
> Return to Elyon, turn from iniquity,
>   and greatly despise the abominable thing.

Moreover, he urges them to praise God in the present moment, even if inadequately, for after death none can do so (17:25–18:14).

With these arguments, Ben Sira dismisses the charge that YHWH is responsible for human transgression and the claim that the vast distance that separates YHWH from mortals conceals their deeds. Still, he insists, the deity extends mercy to frail humans, who should use the short time allotted them to praise him. For Ben Sira, divine compassion stands alongside a strict principle of reward and retribution based on individual merit.

Such thinking continued to develop among the ancient rabbis, who understood the conflict within the inner self as a battle between two natures: *yetser hara'* and *yetser hattob*—an evil inclination and a good disposition. They based this notion on experience but grounded it in Scripture. The term *yetser* is derived from the story of the flood, which states that the people's inclination was overwhelmingly evil (Gen 6:5). Even the two different spellings in Hebrew for the nouns "heart" (*leb* and *lebab*) and "inclination" (*yētser* and *yêtser*) were used to support this theory of rival dispositions. The rabbis acknowledged the necessity for both natures in this life, noting that removal of the evil one would rid the world of procreation. Nevertheless, the evil inclination was to be strenuously resisted. Help in this endeavor might be entreated of the deity himself, hence the prayer attributed to Rabbi Tanchum:

> May it be Thy will, O Lord our God . . . that Thou break and remove the yoke of the Evil Inclination from our heart, since Thou hast created us to do Thy will, and we are duty-bound to do Thy will. Thou dost wish it and we wish it; who then prevents it? The leaven in the dough [i.e., the incitement of the Evil Inclination].[2]

Believing that a moral rule operated in the world, the rabbis held that punishment for sin was measured out exactly and appropriately.[3] Violence was met by violence, greed by loss of wealth, sexual offense by disease of the sexual organs, and so on. Nevertheless, life was never so neat nor punishment for transgression so exact. Therefore, the rabbis also held that suffering in the present age accorded credit against misery in the world to come. In this way unexplained suffering took on new, eschatological meaning.

How did an early death or the suffering of a child fit into this picture? The rabbis taught that divine prescience embraced the future—specifically, that those unfortunates who suffered or died early in life would otherwise have fallen into irredeemable sin.[4] God therefore showed them compassion, either taking them prematurely, from a human perspective, or allowing them to suffer as children to atone for subsequent sin.

Significantly, however, not all suffering was understood as atonement for one's own sin. In rare instances, human suffering was thought to serve a substitutionary function, redounding to the benefit of others.

Substitution

The substitutionary theory of atonement is grounded in a low view of human nature, assuming a near universal human propensity to transgress the divine will.[5] Salvation can be attained only by the righteous; it thus falls to some innocent "other" to remove the stain and penalty of sin. The complex development of this theory took root in antiquity, blossomed in the sixth century BCE, and bore abundant fruit in the third decade CE.

A gnawing sense of guilt accompanied misfortune in the ancient world, judging from the literature from Egypt and Mesopotamia that has survived. These widely separated people believed that sickness and other types of disaster were sent as punishment from the gods. The ones on whom such misery fell often had no idea how they had given offense, and they employed an intricate array of magic to gain some insight into the will of the higher powers.[6] Whether accidental or intentional, all transgression entailed punishment.[7] Very early in some societies the principle of substitution was entertained as a way of pacifying an angry deity or deities. Human sacrifice, often of a virgin, was one means of easing the collective guilt, but this dire measure eventually gave way to the substitution of a specially chosen animal. The Bible attests both types of sacrifices, although only vestiges of human sacrifice are evident, notably in the cult of Molech and its ritual of passing children through the fire (Lev 18: 21; 2 Kgs 23:10). Biblical prophets like Ezekiel denounced this practice with customary vehemence (Ezek 20:31; cf. Jer 32:35).

The principle of substitution lies embedded in biblical narrative. Three brief examples will highlight its troublesome features. First, the familiar story of David's adulterous act with Bathsheba, wife of Uriah the Hittite. Such sinful behavior, made even worse by David's role in arranging Uriah's death in battle, could not go unpunished, from the narrator's perspective. Accordingly, YHWH sent the prophet Nathan to reprimand the king. Strangely, however, YHWH allowed David to escape direct punishment, imposing the ultimate penalty on the child of the illicit union (2 Sam 12:14).

Second, the daughter of Jephthah. The story involves a rash vow, uttered during the heat of battle, that came home to haunt the warrior-judge. Here, too, someone other than the guilty individual bore the consequence, in this case, of thoughtless zeal. Modern interpreters may differ over the nature of the girl's suffering, either death or permanent celibacy,[8] but everyone agrees that the penalty, whatever its nature, fell on an innocent victim (Judg 11:39).

Third, Judah, brother of Joseph. The mere thought of Benjamin's prolonged stay in Egypt and its effect on an aged father prompted the older brother to plead that he be permitted to take Benjamin's place and remain with Joseph in the foreign land (Gen 44:33). At stake in all three stories is a substitution—of innocents in the first two incidents and of a manifestly changed person in the third. The beneficiaries of these acts of substitution represent humankind—villainous, foolish, and vulnerable.

The principle of substitution was crucial to Israelites in coping with sin and its consequences. In all probability Israel's sacrificial cult[9] was taken over from the indigenous peoples in the land of Canaan, for the similarities in names for sacrifices in the Bible and in texts from Ugarit are too close to be accidental. The old law that required the sacrifice of the firstborn was not deleted from the Covenant Code (Exod 22:28), but later codes such as that in Exodus 34 and the Priestly Code permitted the substitution of money for a human being (Exod 34:20; Num 3:44–48). This substitutionary principle was widespread in the ancient Near East, extending even to military service.

Perhaps the most striking instance of this principle in Israel concerns a goat that symbolized the people's sins. In an elaborate annual ritual,[10] the details of which are given in Leviticus 16, Aaron laid his hands on the head of a goat, determined by lot, and confessed over it the people's sins. Now symbolically bearing Israel's guilt, the scapegoat was driven into the wilderness, away from habitable land, and set free. Through this act the people hoped to escape the consequences of unatoned transgression.[11]

The whole sacrificial system in the broader culture was predicated on the assumption that reconciliation between humans and deity was possible through obligatory rituals and offerings. Because the gods were viewed anthropomorphically, it was thought that they needed to be fed, clothed, and exercised daily.[12] These basic understandings issued in an elaborate cultic apparatus throughout the ancient world. The Israelites were very much at home in this culture, as the laws about priests and their duties reveal in intricate detail. There were daily oblations, as well as various sacrifices at specified times, some burned entirely as an offering to God and others cooked and consumed by cultic personnel. Some offerings were poured out as a gift to YHWH; others were eaten by the family members making the gift. These offerings included meat, cereal, wine, and incense, and all were governed by strict rules that even made special concessions for those who could not afford the prescribed offering.

The goal of these gifts was to establish harmony between God and humans, thereby making peace. Some were understood as sin offerings aimed at effecting atonement, while others were viewed as communion meals. The implications of the communion meals were particularly rich, for in Israelite culture only friends sat down together to eat. By some incomprehensible mystery, symbolized by these meals, sinners were able to eat with God. Former enemies became friends, all wrongs forgiven.

What happened, however, when the cultic apparatus ceased to operate? A brief hiatus began in 587 BCE with the destruction of the temple in Jerusalem.

Then in 521 a beleaguered community heeded the advice of the prophets Haggai and Zechariah to rebuild the temple in hopes of restoring divine favor, and in 516 an unimpressive building was dedicated to YHWH. The brief period when there was no temple for the worship of the deity was but an earnest of a much longer duration inaugurated by the Romans in 70 CE, one that persists even today. In Babylonian exile religious leaders from Judah were forced to reimagine life without the normal means of handling sin and its consequences. Lacking the holy abode with its implicit assurance of divine presence, how could atonement occur? In short, was the principle of substitution now inoperative? Was the biblical God unable to defend Zion? If so, why not turn to a stronger god? Such questions were undoubtedly entertained by some of the exiled Judeans. This setting offered precisely the right conditions for an original thinker to press the principle of substitution one step further, to something radically new. In doing just that, an anonymous poet formulated a theological explanation for innocent suffering that eventually came to dominate Christian understanding of the death of Jesus. Briefly stated, undeserved suffering redounds to the benefit of others. Such suffering is therefore vicarious, bringing redemption to an unnamed larger group who somehow escape the punishment they are due.

The Suffering Servant in Isaiah 52:13–53:12

(52:13) My servant will succeed,
> be greatly exalted and lifted high.

(14)   Just as many were dismayed at him—
> so disfigured was his appearance, nonhuman;
> his form, unlike people—

(15)   So he will surprise many nations;
> because of him kings will be silent,
> for they will see what has not been told them,
> comprehend what they have not heard.

(53:1) Who has believed what we have heard?
> To whom has YHWH's arm been bared?

(2)   Before whom he grew like a young plant,
> like a root [taken] from dry ground.
> He lacked attractiveness, that we should gaze on him,
> had no beauty, that we should desire him.

(3)   Loathed and shunned by man,
> a man of grief, familiar with illness,

      he was despised like one from whom one hides,
         and we did not give him a thought.

(4)   Surely he has borne our sickness,
         endured our grief;
      we thought he was smitten,
         stricken by God and afflicted.

(5)   But he was wounded for our sins,
         crushed because of our iniquities.
      On him were our healing chastisements,
         and by his bruises we have been healed.

(6)   Like sheep, all of us have wandered;
      each has turned his own way;
      on him YHWH laid the iniquity of us all.

(7)   Mistreated and beaten,
         he did not speak;
         led like a lamb for the slaughter,
         like a ewe, silent before its shearers, he did not speak.

(8)   By a miscarriage of justice he was taken away;
         who could have imagined his future?
         For he was cut off from the land of the living,
         smitten for my people's offenses.

(9)   They made his grave with the wicked,
         with the rich at his death.
      He had done no violence,
         spoken no deceit.

(10) Yet YHWH chose to crush him with sickness;
         if he makes himself an offering,
      he will see its fruit, prolong his days,
      and through him YHWH's pleasure will thrive.

(11) He will see the result of his toil
         and be satisfied;
      by his knowledge the righteous one, my servant,
         will make many righteous
           and bear their iniquities.

(12) Surely I will give him a portion with the many,
         and with the mighty he will divide spoil,
         because he exposed himself to death;
           was counted among transgressors;
         it was he who bore the sin of many,
         and interceded for sinners.

The brief description of suffering and its aftermath in Isa 52:13–53:12 has generated an enormous volume of interpretation but little agreement.[13] The poem unfolds in this way: YHWH's servant will affect many nations in some manner despite his marred appearance. This servant's origin was unpromising, and all who knew him reacted with disdain instead of sharing his misery. Yet somehow his suffering was on "our" behalf, although "we" thought it was punishment for his own sins. Moreover, the entire transaction was YHWH's doing, an effecting of forgiveness for many by the suffering of one. This servant endured the pain without protest and was given a dishonorable burial. Nevertheless, YHWH afflicted the servant in order to make him an offering for sin, in the end granting him progeny. The poem ends with a divine promise to reward the servant for an ignominious death that bore the sins of many.[14]

Perhaps the first thing that strikes readers of this poem is bafflement over the identity of the servant. That is indeed the reaction of the Ethiopian eunuch in the story preserved in Acts 8:26–40, which has him ask Philip, "About whom, pray, does the prophet say this, about himself or about someone else?" (v 34 RSV). Candidates for this role of innocent sufferer are numerous, beginning with Moses, who suffered on Israel's behalf and interceded with YHWH, and extending as far into Israelite history as this poet, the unknown author of Isaiah 40–55, probably around 540 BCE. The problem of identifying the servant is exacerbated by the fact that elsewhere in this literary complex, in three other poems, the servant of YHWH is identified as Jacob or Israel—that is, a national entity (Isa 49:3). Moreover, the stated mission is to "the nations" (42:1, 49:6, 52:15), which has given rise to the suggestion that the servant is to be understood as a small righteous minority within Israel.

The other servant poems in this complex announce that the servant will bring justice through the power of the spirit to all the earth, discharging his mission with quiet strength (42:1–4). They use royal and prophetic language about a call from the womb and special divine protection. When the servant's efforts appear fruitless, they affirm his role as a light to the nations (49:1–6)—an idea that seems to reflect the promise to Abraham in Gen 12:3: "In you all the families of the earth will be blessed" (or "bless themselves"). The poems also describe the servant as one who is instructed by YHWH, like a capable scribe, and is mistreated by humans but does not resist. The servant endures calumny but expects vindication from YHWH; as for his adversaries, they will vanish like a moth, being burned by their own firebrands (Isa 50:4–11).

The existence of these other poems about YHWH's servant complicates the matter of identification even further, particularly because they seem to lead up to an account of extreme suffering. Linguistic links among the poems reinforce certain thematic affinities. The language of servanthood recalls depictions of Moses and Job; that of early selection for a gargantuan mission to the nations is highly reminiscent of descriptions of the prophet Jeremiah. Furthermore, links between these servant poems and the rest of Isaiah 40–55 indicate continuity, especially with respect to the role of Israel in bringing healing to all peoples.

Who, then, is the servant? In my view, two possibilities stand out from the rest, one prophetic and the other royal. The servant may be the poet himself, the great exilic prophet referred to as Deutero-Isaiah. The final poem could then be understood as the testimony of a small band of disciples who tried to come to terms with their leader's execution. The circumstances of the poet's death are unknown, as are the reasons for it, natural or otherwise, but we can easily imagine that his proclamation of imminent deliverance may have irked Babylonian or Persian authorities because of its hidden messianic implications, despite his careful avoidance of the actual Hebrew word *meshiakh* and use, instead, of *'ebed* (servant). Against this scenario, however, is the identification of the Persian king Cyrus as YHWH's shepherd and anointed one (Isa 44:28–45:1)—that is, the messiah (*meshiakh*)—chosen to set Israel free.[15]

The royal figure who best fits the description of a suffering servant is Josiah, whose tragic death at Megiddo must surely have provoked deep soul-searching in light of Deuteronomistic theology, including the divine promise that the throne of David would be established forever (2 Sam 7:11b–16). According to the king's biography, he had followed the Torah as specified in the earliest form of Deuteronomy, ridding the land of rival cults and centralizing worship in Jerusalem. Despite faithfully following divine instructions, so the record goes, Josiah met an untimely end at the hands of an Egyptian pharaoh in the battle-weary plain of Megiddo. Later reflection on the hidden meaning of this apparent contradiction of revered tradition may have yielded an explanation in terms of a death that benefited the nation. Scattered evidence within the Bible points to a ceremonial remembrance of Josiah's death that survived as late as the time of the Chronicler.

The second thing that strikes readers of this final servant poem is its hyperbolic language, even beyond the usual exaggeration found in ancient Near Eastern texts. It has been argued that here the genre of lament is turned on its head. This intensification of the funeral lament involves a reversal of the usual form for a eulogy. Instead of praising the servant's virtues, the poem speaks of his undesirable features; rather than calling him a pillar of the community, it identifies him as despised; instead of likening the dead one to a courageous, lionlike hero, it adopts the image of a lamb; and rather than mentioning an honorable burial, it relegates the servant to a grave among the wicked. Here is no ordinary death, so the poet claims, but one of extraordinary gravity and promise. The servant's afterlife echoes the nation's symbolic res- urrection in Ezekiel 37 but is now applied to an individual.[16]

Because the language is poetry and the thought unprecedented, the words must be allowed to bounce off previous traditions without suggesting a literal extension of old ideas. The language is passionate; the ideas, global and, hence, shocking as they interweave guilt and innocence, suffering and redemption, Israel and the nations, a remnant and all Israel. This confounding assessment of the servant and his discomfiture is enclosed within a frame, 52:13–15 and 53:10–12. In the opening half of the frame, the deity announces the astonishing news that his servant, who generated low expectations, will surprise the foreign rulers and make them understand what has until now been unclear. The clos- ing frame provides a brief theodicy by arguing that there was a hidden purpose at work, one that somehow justifies such suffering. By this act the servant will atone for the sins of others and, seeing this good, will be satisfied.

The unspecified speakers in 53:1–9 are either representatives of the nations, who deemed Israel of little value until discovering that the servant's suffering redounded to their benefit, or greater Israel, who deemed the afflic- tion of a minority of little consequence until discovering its redemptive power. Regardless of their identity, the speakers stress the vicarious nature of suffering and recognize its beneficial effects. The two occurrences of "many" in each frame highlight the difference between a lone sufferer and all those who prof- ited from his death.

Because of the text's hyperbolic language and highly unusual form, some interpreters deny that there was an actual death.[17] After all, many psalms of lament use such language about death metaphorically to emphasize extreme suffering. Just as the psalm in the second chapter of the book of Jonah pictures the reluctant prophet in waters that engulf but do not actually drown, so the suffering servant may not actually have expired. Against this reading of the text, however, is the reference in v 9 to a grave and burial with the wicked. It therefore seems best in this instance to understand the language about death literally.

A third observation about the poem arises from links with the ritual in- volving the scapegoat discussed above. The poet seems consciously to have associated the two victims, goat and human. Just as the scapegoat bore the iniquities of all the people (Lev 16:22), so the servant bore the sins of many (Isa 53:12). Moreover, just as the scapegoat was sent off to an uninhabited land, so the servant was cut off from the land of the living. The same root (*gzr*) occurs with reference to the land in both texts. In both stories, too, the noun *'erets* (earth) faintly recalls the Canaanite sense of this word as a deity.

A final observation concerns the poem's continued influence within a persecuted community that came to define its suffering as vicarious. In Dan 12: 3–4 the expression "those who justify many [*matsdiqe harabbim*]" and the reference to knowledge (*hammaskilim*) echo the words about the servant in Isa 53:11, "by his knowledge [*beda'to*] shall the righteous one, my servant, justify many [*yatsdiq tsaddiq 'abdi larabbim*]." Further, the successful effort of the righteous in Dan 12:3 recalls Isa 52:13, "Behold, my servant will succeed." It seems that the author of the twelfth chapter of the book of Daniel was forming a theodicy based on the Isaianic text.[18]

Fourth Maccabees, a philosophical treatise from first-century Judaism,[19] preserves a story about a devout figure of priestly lineage who was put to death by the Seleucid ruler Antiochus. Eleazar, the victim of a vicious policy to eradicate Judaism, did not go quietly but interpreted his martyrdom as an offering for others. According to the account, he offered this dying prayer: "Be merciful to your people and let our punishment be a satisfaction on their behalf. Make my blood their purification and take my life as a ransom for theirs" (4 Macc 6:28–29).

As noted above, early Christians interpreted Jesus' death on the cross in light of the suffering servant.[20] Some details of the Passion narrative were taken directly from the description in Isa 52:12–53:13, for instance, Jesus' submissive attitude to Roman authorities, recalling muteness when being slaughtered like a lamb, and the nature of his death and burial, with its links to the wicked and the rich. Theological reflection on the manner of Jesus' suffering and subsequent burial pales, however, in comparison with the proclamation of its redemptive power for the whole world burdened by sin. Christians believed that God in some mysterious way became flesh and blood in order to assume the role of suffering servant, thereby atoning for the sins of humankind. The precise mechanism of this atonement is unclear. Later theologians offered various theories to account for it, the most prominent of which was drawn from the realm of slavery. According to this theory, championed by Anselm, Jesus' death paid the ransom that purchased freedom for all. An obvious difficulty with this view is the implication that a price had to be paid to some powerful figure, which approaches a dualistic understanding of the world. Moreover, it isn't exactly clear how the death of Jesus could function as such a ransom, but the notion of vicarious suffering had already been introduced by Deutero-Isaiah. Another theory, formulated by Abelard, emphasized the exemplary character of Jesus' death, which possessed the inspirational power to motivate others to live faithfully.

Within the New Testament, the prevailing theory of atonement is that in Jesus God reconciled the world unto himself. This reading of the cross and its aftermath takes for granted its substitutionary, or vicarious, nature. According to Paul and the other disciples, a sinless Jesus died on behalf of sinners—that is, all humankind. Furthermore, he also rose from the grave, they affirm, and in so doing became the first fruits of believers' future resurrection. That conviction lies at the heart of the Christian faith. Belief in a reward in life beyond death is the ultimate theodicy. In the next chapter I trace the development of this belief among the followers of YHWH.

9

Justice Deferred

Banking on Life beyond the Grave

If there is no immortality, all is permitted.

—Fyodor Dostoyevsky

It can be argued that in scholarly pursuits ink is spilled on a given topic in inverse proportion to what can actually be known about it— hence, the large number of articles and books that deal with belief in life after death.[1] All such investigations stand under the honest assessment that for now we possess blurred vision, or, to quote the Apostle Paul, we see "in a mirror, dimly" (*di' esoptrou en ainigmati*, 1 Cor 13:12). Whether Paul was correct in his contrast of "now" with "then"—of present obscurity with future clarity in face-to-face encounter—must await the unfolding of history and the final tick of our personal clocks.

In all probability, Paul was echoing the traditional elevation accorded to the "prophet" Moses. In the eyes of the Mosaic narrator, the lesser prophets encountered the deity through riddles, visions, and dreams that required acts of demystification, whereas Moses experienced YHWH through the immediacy of one-on-one dialogue (Num 12:6–8).[2] Paul's contrast seems to apply the ancient distinction between modes of receiving an inspired word to the supreme mystery and the ultimate human question. Like God, the mystery belongs to the fragile province of faith, and the question—Is death final?—always retains a sense of utmost urgency.[3]

What did the peoples of the ancient Near East believe about the destiny of the dead? Two rival views have been traced back to the Paleolithic and Neolithic periods.[4] Wandering seminomads[5] seem to have thought that the dead rested in their graves as "living corpses." The principle articulated in Gen 3:19 that dust returns to dust had as its corollary a conviction that the animating breath was reclaimed at death by its bestower (Eccl 12:7).[6] In the rival conception, which seems to have characterized the city-dwellers in ancient Mesopotamia, the dead descended to a watery underworld, the equivalent of the biblical Sheol, and wandered there as restless "shades."[7] There was considerable ambiguity as to the exact conditions in either location, but on one point all were in agreement: no human being returned from the realm of the dead.

The Bible does record an instance of momentary return, the result of King Saul's desperate resort to the medium of Endor. The prophet Samuel's apparition, however, did not take kindly to someone's having disturbed his sleep (1 Sam 28:15). This understanding of the netherworld as a place of rest finds utterance in poetry that anticipates a sense of closure for every trial (Isa 57:1–2). The sufferer envisions an end to all inequities endured in the present lifetime—the antithesis of the rival notion of a world ruled by a king of terrors (Job 18:14).

No shuttle linked the present world with the domain of the dead, nor did the shadowy inhabitants of Sheol give any thought to those who remained behind. Downtrodden worshipers used this bit of lore to argue that YHWH should act promptly to maintain a steady stream of praise. Just as mortals on earth had no commerce with the underworld and its residents, so the sovereign of the living was thought by some to have nothing to do with Sheol.[8] The prophet Amos's hypothetical statement to the contrary (Amos 9:2–3) has more to do with power than establishing a relationship between YHWH and the dead.

Probably the most widespread picture of the underworld involved tempestuous waters. The idea that its boisterous waves threatened even citizens of the present world caused some slippage in the belief that an impenetrable wall separated the living from the dead. Such slippage played out in the notion that persons under the power of sickness, physical threat, and the like descended for a time into Sheol. Deliverance would come only at the hand of YHWH. Those caught in the dreaded waters lifted up their petitions to the heavens in the belief that the deity possessed the power to rescue them, even if for some unknown reason he had, until that moment, lacked the will to save.

A Daring Breakthrough

This unpromising picture yielded over time to a stunning reformulation of YHWH's conduct vis-à-vis the dead. Two seeds lay in fertile soil awaiting the moistening dew that would act as a catalyst to promote germination. The seeds: a profound sense of community with YHWH that could withstand any obstacle, and a firm conviction that there was no limit to the deity's power. The catalyst: grievous injustices, and ultimately martyrdom, which intensified the problem of theodicy. The peculiar nature of these seeds yielded unique plants, each with its own individual characteristics.

The former seed, passionate communion with the deity, gave rise to bold reflection about the possibility that mortals have some deep-seated faculty that unfailingly responds to divine wooing. The natural outcome of such speculation was belief in an immortal soul, or *nepesh* (like the Egyptian *ba*), an idea that sometimes carried with it a disparaging of the physical.[9]

The latter seed, trust in YHWH's unlimited might, eventuated in the affirmation that death will finally succumb to that force:

> He has swallowed death forever;
> Lord YHWH has wiped away every tear from their faces;
> the reproach of his people he has expunged from the earth,
> for YHWH has spoken. (Isa 25:8)

In retrospect, a victory over death might suggest immortality, but the underlying concept of death's finality also raises the question, What about all those who have already surrendered to its sting? That query was intensified by martyrdom. Justice seemed to require that individuals who had forfeited their lives through fidelity to YHWH be given a chance to live out a normal life span. Thus a daring thinker ventured the unthinkable, the mind-boggling notion of bodily resurrection, prompting a modern intellectual, Ernst Renan, to write: "The blood of the martyrs was the veritable creator of belief in a second life."[10]

Here and there tiny cracks became visible in the hardened crust of belief about two distinct realms, this world and the next. Scattered stories of revered prophets' reviving the dead functioned primarily to enhance the prophets' prestige, but they also affirmed the prevailing belief that YHWH held the keys to life and death:

> See now that I myself am he,
> There is no God beside me;
> I kill and I enliven;

> I wound and I heal;
> No one can snatch from my grasp. (Deut 32:39)

From this assertion about YHWH as the sole source of both weal and woe
flows a recognition that the instruments of human distress are subject to the
deity's command.

Across the Hebrew Bible, graphic imagery for the various agents of distress conveys poetically the idea that against their volition individuals are
caught up in a battle of mythic proportions. The dominant image, that of raging
waters, has roots in ancient Near Eastern mythology.[11] The prophet Jonah,
according to the psalm in Jonah 2, found himself at the mercy of the deep. In
the view of the author, neither those waters nor their awesome creatures could
hold the reluctant prophet. Small wonder that this narrative of Jonah's
rescue from the sea assumed such significance in later reflections about resurrection.

The stories of Enoch and Elijah illustrate slippage of yet another kind: a
willingness to conjecture that rare individuals managed to elude death's ten-
tacles altogether. Both stories contain the verb laqakh; its usual meaning, "to
take or receive," assumes new dimensions through the identity of the one
doing the receiving—God:

> Enoch walked with God,
> and he was not,
> for God took [laqakh] him. (Gen 5:24)

> Now the sons of the prophets at Bethel went out to Elisha and said
> to him: "Are you aware that today YHWH is going to take [loqeakh]
> your master from being your leader?" He responded: "I am in-
> formed. Keep it down." (2 Kgs 2:3; cf. 2:5, 9, 10)

The mystery associated with Enoch's vanishing is conveyed primarily through
understatement, while the opposite approach produces a similar effect in the
story of Elijah's departure. In the former account, a particle of nonexistence is
followed by an explanatory declaration: "For God took him." The latter narrative
uses repetition to create an air of eager expectation, and the explosive finale
with the fiery chariot does not disappoint. On seeing the extraordinary chariot
and its mode of locomotion, a whirlwind, an awestruck Elisha cannot follow
his own earlier advice and keep quiet:

> Elisha kept on watching, crying out: "My father! My father! The
> chariot of Israel and its horses." (2 Kgs 2:12)

The strange story concludes with a linguistic equivalent of a particle of non-existence: "He saw him no more."

The peculiar use of the verb *laqakh* with God as subject forges an impressive link with three additional contexts, two of them in the book of Psalms (49: 16 and 73:24) and the other in Isaiah (53:8). In combination, they take a tentative step toward challenging the dominant worldview with respect to human destiny. At the same time, the authors' reluctance to come right out and openly affirm such a radical notion can hardly be missed.

Psalm 49:16

The blend of subject matter, language, and style in Psalm 49 resembles wisdom literature.[12] The main topic, life's fleeting character, receives fuller treatment in Ecclesiastes, but without the exquisite metaphor of death as a personal shepherd (v 15). Structurally, the psalm consists of two units, each of which ends with a common refrain that compares humans' mortality to that of animals (vv 13, 21). Verses 2–5 constitute a rhetorical introduction that uses both prophetic and wisdom terminology. The universalizing summons to attention is balanced by an individualizing expression of personal introspection.

The extraordinary language of this introduction matches the singularity of the entire psalm's boldly innovative thought: the twofold reference to humankind as children of *'adam* and *'ish*; the contrasting yet unified (*yakhad*) rich and poor; the plural words for wisdom and understanding; the escalating complexity of the wisdom terms, *mashal* (proverb) and *khidati* (riddle). The references to the importance of the human body (mouth, ear, and heart) in communicating anomalies stand over against the final assessment of the psalm: "Humans in their splendor cannot understand; they resemble animals that perish" (v 21).

The first unit (vv 6–13) addresses the perennial problem of evil persons of financial means and thus power. The psalmist observes that their wealth cannot purchase release from death's sure clutches. Because no amount of money suffices to stave off that dreaded predator, the rich will surrender their estates for the grave, where they cannot lay claim to a single particle of dust. Why, then, should anyone fear them?

At the same time, the psalmist acknowledges that none can avoid the grave. Both foolish and wise will meet the same fate: endless residence in the Pit. The psalmist thus refuses to universalize the experiences of Enoch and Elijah.

The second unit (vv 14–21) treats the same theme but breaks away from this dismal picture momentarily. Suddenly, the psalmist contrasts the fate of

the foolish with his own destiny. They will rot in the grave, while he will be
ransomed by God—indeed, will be received (like Enoch and Elijah).

> Surely God ['elohim] will ransom me [napshi] from Sheol's grasp,
> for he will receive [yiqqakheni] me. (v 16)

The psalmist then draws a conclusion in behalf of others struggling to understand the prosperity of the wicked. These oppressors need not be feared, for
they are destined to spend their last days in Sheol, having left all their possessions behind. Like their ancestors, whom they will join, they will never again
look upon the light.

The ambiguity of this psalm bars any claim of certainty that it contemplates
life beyond the grave. On the one hand, it seems to include everyone in its
gloomy picture of mortals' fate. On the other hand, it suggests that God will
make an exception in the case of the psalmist. If 'akh in v 8 is an aural mistake
for 'ak, this contrast becomes even more explicit:[13]

> Surely ['ak] a person can never ransom him,
>   cannot give his price to God. . . . (v 8)
> Surely ['ak] God will ransom me from Sheol's grasp,
>   for he will receive me. (v 16)

The addition of "he will receive me" introduces the possibility that the psalmist
has advanced beyond the common understanding of divine deliverance from
the power of Sheol. At the same time, the contrast between the psalmist's being
received (luqqakh) by God and the fools' being unable to take (yiqqakh) anything
with them provides a nice play on the verb laqakh.

Psalm 73:24

The other psalm that uses language reminiscent of that associated with the
departure of Enoch and Elijah throws into relief the vexing problem addressed
in the book of Job. The inclusion of this psalm in wisdom literature is based
almost exclusively on thematic considerations. Psalm 73 ponders the issue of
theodicy, offering fresh insight into the true nature of love for God. That advance comes, however, after mind-stretching struggle.[14]

The psalm juxtaposes a ruthless throng and a worshiper who comes perilously close to joining them, if not actually, at least intellectually. The frame
narrative (vv 1–3, 27–28) articulates the creed that seems to be crumbling and
reformulates it to accord with experience. "Truly God ['el] is good to the upright,

God ['elohim] to those whose hearts are pure" (v 1) becomes "But for me, God's drawing near is good to me" (v 28). Having taken refuge in YHWH, the psalmist imagines the gradual dissipation of those he had earlier envied.

The word *lebab* (heart) functions thematically in the psalm. It occurs six times, all with a cognitive sense (vv 1, 7, 13, 21, 26 [2×]). The problem is an intellectual one: how to maintain integrity in the face of apparent disconfirmation of a religious dogma. The psalmist recognizes just in time the power of the temptation to join those who question the deity's knowledge of human activity. He thus enters the sanctuary, where lofty thoughts drive out the previous bestial ones (v 17).

A threefold repetition of the adverb *'ak* (truly) focuses a spotlight at decisive moments: (1) the opening creed, v 1; (2) its negation, v 13; and (3) a reaffirmation of the original creed, but now with the emphasis on the removal of the reason for the earlier doubt, v 18.

The relief of the psalmist's anxiety is only partially due to the discovery that sinners are no more substantial than figments of a divine dream. The true consolation comes from a sense of divine nearness, one so real that it seems as if God takes the psalmist by the hand, offers him counsel, and more. What is that "more," the third source of consolation?

> You lead me by your counsel,
>   and afterward you receive [*tiqqakheni*] me [in] honor. (v 24b)

God receives him—but after what? After taking him by the hand and giving him vital counsel? The notion of unmediated divine instruction that protects from all harm has enormous appeal; even if that is all the psalmist hopes for, it need not be viewed as lacking in religious profundity. But the word *'akhar* (after, afterward) invites comparison of this text with Job 19:26: "After ['akhar] my skin has been stripped off thus, from my flesh I shall see Eloah." There, too, the meaning is ambiguous. The textual problems in Job 19:23–27 did not prevent the early church from using this unit to argue for a physical resurrection, but modern scholars have been more cautious. Early in his debate with his friends, Job recognizes the importance of a permanent witness to injustice, one that endures long after his death (16:18–22). In 19:23–27 he takes up this issue again and imagines the improbable: a future day when his words will stand as a lasting testimony to his claim of innocence. The precise nature of this witness is unclear. It takes the form of a record preserved on three kinds of writing material—scroll, engraved tablet, and rock—or, more likely, a stela on which a message has been carved with iron stylus and lead inlay.[15]

Job considers this written record unlikely, as the introductory "Would that" implies, but he expresses certainty that a redeemer stands ready to avenge wrongdoing directed at him. The same confidence pervades the earlier discussion of a heavenly witness, in 16:18–19. Job's choice of the expression go'ali (my redeemer) carries heavy irony in light of the divine epithet "the champion of widows and orphans" (Prov 23:11; Jer 50:34).[16] A victim of injustice, Job stands in need of help from a kinsman and fantasizes that a heavenly redeemer will champion his cause against God, the wrongdoer.

When does Job think this forensic event will take place? The phrase "after my skin has been stripped off thus" (v 26a) demands that one think of Job's death. Does he actually believe that he will be raised from the grave or, like Samuel's ghost, brought back from Sheol for a special occasion on which Eloah will acknowledge his mistake?

For at least two reasons, this interpretation is unlikely. First, Job's rejection of life beyond the grave in 14:1–22 leaves no room for hope; second, such a resolution would make his cry throughout the book ring hollow. An answer to the difficulty presented by the text has been found by distinguishing between two opposing scenes. In 19:25–26a Job imagines a postmortem vindication, whereas in 19:26b–27 he expresses his preference to see things set right before death.[17] In short, over against Job's assurance that the redeemer will vindicate him after his skin has been peeled off, he says: "But I would [i.e., want to] see God from my flesh, whom I would see for myself; my eyes would see, and not a stranger" (26b–27).

The word 'akhar (afterward) in Job 19:26 does not require that one read Ps 73:24 as a reference to life beyond the grave, but neither does it rule out such a reading. A combination of features in the psalm points to this bold interpretation: the words kabod (glory), le'olam (forever), tsur (rock), and khelqi (portion). If by kabod the psalmist meant earthly honor, we would expect something like "he will give me honor." The adverb le'olam normally applies to this world but eventually comes to be associated with the next age. In conjunction with the predicate nominative tsur, it may have the more exalted sense, for both the rock and the Rock of Ages endure. Even the noun khelqi may have this deeper meaning, for in sacred narrative the land as Israel's portion survived the death of generation after generation.

Anyone for whom God is the sole "possession and desire" in heaven and on earth has reached the stage where asking about the permanence of such a relationship is as natural as breathing. The fervor of this intimate relationship seems to give rise to the unthinkable. Death cannot blot out this love. It follows that the psalmist dares to hope for survival beyond death.

Isaiah 53:8

If Ps 49:16 leaves some doubt about whether the psalmist thinks of being
received by God after death, as opposed to being rescued in this life from dire
threat, and Ps 73:24 only obliquely refers to dying prior to YHWH's receiving
the worshiper in glory, Isa 53:8 explicitly mentions the servant's demise:

> By a miscarriage of justice he was taken away [luqqakh],
>> who could have imagined his future?
>> For he was cut off from the land of the living,
>>> smitten for my people's offenses.

This point is pressed by specific references to his grave and death in vv 9 and
12.

The question remains whether the verb luqqakh means simply "was taken
away"—that is, euphemistically, "died"—or whether it carries the weightier
sense of being received by YHWH. Even if we incline toward the latter interpretation, the exceptional nature of this servant, whether the ideal Israel or an
individual, rules out any universalizing of his fate.[18] The emancipation of an
exiled Israel paints YHWH's deliverance of an individual from Sheol's raging
waters on a broader canvas. The slippery use of metaphorical language in
discussions of death further complicates matters.[19] Exile, however unpleasant,
differs from death; life goes on, and death awaits the dispossessed just as it
does those who have taken over their land. If this servant is an individual,
death has already come, and luqqakh may echo tiqqakheni in Pss 49:16 and 73:
24.

Isaiah 26:19

Such modes of discourse that combine covenantal relationship with the ardor
of intimacy find expression in Ezekiel's vision of national revivification (Ezekiel
37). Dry bones receive new life through the activity of YHWH's spirit, and an
exiled people lives again. The same idea takes up residence in the little apocalypse embedded within First Isaiah (24–27). The much-quoted proof text for
belief in resurrection within the Hebrew Bible, Isa 26:19, can be explained as
a poetic reference to national resuscitation.[20] But is it more than that?

> Your dead will live, their corpses will rise;
> Inhabitants of the dust, awake and exult!

> For your dew is radiant,
> and the earth will give birth to the shades. (Isa 26:19)

Several observations about this text will keep it in perspective. First, it appears in an apocalyptic unit that bears witness to the collapsing of myth into metahistory. Events now transpire on two historical planes: ordinary experiences give way to extraordinary circumstances, this age moves to a new age. YHWH prepares a feast on a holy mountain, swallows death forever, and wipes away all tears (25:6–8).[21] Second, the victory song in chapter 26 both denies and affirms the rising of the dead (vv 14 and 19), indicating either a conflicted author or a gloss on an earlier text. Third, the people are experiencing YHWH's wrath, which evokes fervent cries for justice,[22] especially on behalf of the slain. Fourth, the momentary threat to civilization, expressed poetically in terms of futile pregnancies, will soon ease, and the reviving dew will bring new life.[23] Fifth, the song ends with the assuring word that YHWH will punish murderers, because the blood of the slain has finally been exposed, like that of Abel. This promise, and not the proclaimed resurrection, appears to be the main point of the song. "Your dead will live, their corpses will rise"—that may be, but for now the author advises the people to hide until the divine wrath is past. Clearly, Isa 26:19 does not suit the context very well. If it glosses v 14, it does so in the spirit of 25:8, the anticipated swallowing of death by a victorious YHWH.[24]

Daniel 12:1–3

The ambiguity vanishes when we turn to Dan 12:1–3, another apocalyptic text, this one a response to the horrific circumstances of the Maccabean revolt against a Seleucid threat to religious freedom.

(1) Then the great prince, Michael,
who accompanies your people,
    will stand.
It will be a time of trouble,
unlike anything seen
    since the nation's inception.
At that time your people will be delivered,
all those found written in the book.
(2) Many who sleep in the land of dust will awake,
some to everlasting life and others to continual
    reproach and contempt.

(3) The wise will shine like the radiance
          of the firmament;
      and those who lead many to righteousness,
          like stars forever and ever.

Several things mark this memorable text as extraordinary within the Bible: it introduces a new figure, Michael, the angelic protector of God's people; it views the conflagration of the future time of deliverance as entirely unprecedented; it suggests that a heavenly book contains a written record of the faithful;[25] it limits the bodily resurrection of the dead to a select group, presumably the exceptionally good and evil (note the *min* partitive); it echoes the language of Isa 53:12 and 66:24; it expands the concept of a radiant dew in Isa 26:19 to that of the risen dead;[26] and it stresses the witnessing power of such an event.[27]

2 Maccabees 7:1–42

Daniel's daring solution to the problem of theodicy is matched by the martyrology in 2 Macc 7:1–42. Readers of this fictional account of the death of seven brothers and their mother at the instigation of the Seleucid ruler Antiochus may concur in the closing sentiment that enough has been said about such hideous persecution. Despite its repellent detail, the rhetoric functions to encourage Jews to remain faithful to the law even to the point of violent death.

The several speeches attributed to the martyrs reinforce their hope in the resurrection, together with their conviction that God will punish their persecutors. That twofold belief is grounded in a theology of YHWH's power and character. The mother speaks about the wonderful mystery of birth, concluding that life comes originally from an act of divine benevolence and that the giver of life can bestow it again on those from whom it has been taken. An affirmation of YHWH's mercy accompanies this first explicit biblical reference to *creatio ex nihilo*. The narrator cannot resist observing that the devout mother has reinforced her woman's reasoning with a man's courage. This surprising acknowledgment that women were appreciated for their intellectual astuteness (and men for courage) contrasts pleasantly with proverbial wisdom from the ancient Near East that disparages women's minds.[28]

The third son thrusts his hands forward, sticks out his tongue, and insists that they are divine gifts that he hopes to get back. The recurring theme of the final four brothers concerns the question of divine justice. In short, the sons admit that their death is the result of sin; at the same time, they insist that God will eventually punish the murderers, excluding them from the hope of the resurrection. The seventh brother affirms present victory over death's sting; in his view, the brothers and mother have already drunk ever-flowing life, under the covenant.[29]

Wisdom of Solomon

The Hellenistic author of Wisdom of Solomon drew on a different intellectual tradition to answer the challenge to divine justice.[30] Death, in his unprecedented view, does not derive from God (1:13) but results from the devil's envy (2:24), and humankind is created in the divine image, hence immortal (2:23). A perishable body weighs down the pure soul, resulting in ignorance of divine mystery (9:15), but Wisdom bestows immortality (8:13, 17)—as does faithfulness to the law (6:18–19). Alongside the Platonic disparaging of the body lies a tinge of docetism. The author insists that the righteous dead only seem to have died, for they have the hope of immortality; their souls will shine forth, running like sparks through stubble (3:7).

The wicked who provoke this portrait of the righteous express the old-fashioned view that no one returns from Sheol (2:1) and that the dead are extinguished, their separable parts becoming ashes and dissolving into thin air (2:3). Images from nature depict the gloomy fate of the dead—clouds dissipating and shadows vanishing. In short, the opponents of the wise believe that no one returns from the grave, for the dead are sealed in a tomb with no hope of escape (2:4–5). Consequently, they advocate and practice the concept often referred to as *carpe diem*.

According to Wisdom of Solomon, the test presented by these greedy opportunists becomes an occasion for the virtuous to demonstrate the reality that they have found shelter in the divine hand. Safe from torment (3:1–4), the righteous claim the promise of eternal life (5:15). Clearly, for this author, belief in an immortal soul does not imply future bliss for everyone. To the contrary, only the righteous reap its benefits.

The views expressed here are thoroughly Greek, but they lack consistency. On the one hand, the soul is immortal, but on the other hand, immortality is bestowed only on the deserving. Similar ambiguity surrounds the concept of death.[31] For the righteous, death is only apparent, as if spiritual; for the wicked, death is real. The fate of the wicked, however, is not specified—whether complete obliteration or eternal punishment. Finally, in 8:20 the author makes an astonishing assertion, correcting himself to include a notion of preexistence alongside the concept of an immortal soul.

Resistance to Belief in a Resurrection

Ancient tradition was not easily overturned, even by an apparent answer to the perplexing problem of theodicy. Those who valued the insights of ancestral heroes more than modern innovations registered an emphatic "no" to belief in life after death. The issue came to divide Jews along party lines—the Pharisees opting for the new ideas, and the Sadducees refusing to accept them. A purely sociological explanation for these differences oversimplifies the issue. For some, the evidence of nature itself implies that death is final.

Possibly the most extensive expression of this negative view occurs in Job 14:1–22. Here the question is posed in its simplest form: "If mortals die, will they live again?" (v 14). In ancient myth the gods died and rose again, and their fecundity was celebrated annually in the royal cult. Mortals, however, fell into a different category; access to the tree of life was withheld from them, except for Utnapishtim, the hero of the flood in the Gilgamesh Epic from Mesopotamian lore.[32] In a text from Ugarit, Aqhat makes this point emphatically when promised eternal life in exchange for his bow. He rejects the goddess Anath's offer with these words:

> Further life—how can mortal attain it?
> How can mortal attain life enduring?
> Glaze will be poured [on] my head,
> Plaster upon my pate;
> And I'll die as everyone dies,
> I too shall assuredly die.[33]

To reaffirm the limitation of resurrection to the gods, Job reflects on life's brevity and undesirable limitations (14:1–6), death's finality (vv 7–12), and the deity's destruction of human hope (vv 18–22). For a brief moment, Job is drawn into the language of prayer (vv 13–17), but he does not linger there.

Job establishes the fact of human brevity by noting the kinship with nature. The similes of a flower and a shadow point to ephemerality and insubstantiality. Mortals' limited life spans, known only to God, remind one and all that humans do not exercise exclusive control over their destiny. Complicating matters further, divine surveillance shortens the lives of hapless offenders and innocents alike.

It occurs to Job that the link with nature could suggest permanence. He thinks of a stately tree that has been cut down and recalls the way a stump, given sufficient moisture, produces new growth. Can mortals anticipate a similar resuscitation? Job replies with a categorical negative, then proceeds to point out that the revivifying agent, water, dries up even in large quantities, suggesting to him that mortals vanish for all eternity.

Job finds additional analogies from nature in vv 18–22, this time contemplating durable entities such as mountains and rocks, which over time succumb to the eroding power of cascading streams. God's excessive force works like water on rocks, wearing away human affection and human perceptions to sorrow and pain.

Facing this grim prospect, Job wishes that God would hide him in Sheol until his wrath has passed—and only then remember him. In this imaginary world God would not spy on him but would have compassion on his miserable subject. There would be mutual calling and answering. Job's mental turmoil and physical distress, however, refuse to take comfort in unrealistic fantasy.[34]

Job's soul mate, Qoheleth, takes up the issue of life beyond the grave and responds with cool detachment: "Who knows?" His linking of humans and animals suggests, however, that he thinks of death as final. Indeed, Qoheleth's question, "Who knows whether the human breath goes upward and the breath of animals goes down to the earth?" (Eccl 3:21) may constitute his rejection of belief in immortality.[35] If mortals awaited blissful existence beyond this veil of tears, Qoheleth's skepticism would lack credibility. Nothing in the book indicates that Qoheleth's teachings are hollow; instead, his words are said to carry sharp barbs that prick those who dare to think radically like him.

Ben Sira continues his predecessors' resistance to the notion that the dead return from the grave. One could hardly express the view more strongly than Ben Sira does in observing that at death a person inherits creeping things, wild beasts, and worms (Sir 10:11). As he understands things, death ushers humans into eternal rest (30:17, 38:23), a state preferable to chronic illness, the disabilities associated with aging, and poverty. "Do not forget, there is no coming back" is punctuated with a wry epitaph: "Mine yesterday; yours today" (38:21–23). Behind this grim humor stands divine decree, "You must die" (14:17), and curse, "Unto dust you must return" (41:9–10). Ben Sira subscribes to the earlier theory that in Sheol no one inquires about things that occupy the daily thoughts of earth's inhabitants. Nevertheless, he thinks that God's attitude toward humankind is compassionate precisely because of life's brevity and its miserable end (18:8–14).

Like Job, Ben Sira uses an analogy from nature to make his point. Life, he writes, resembles a tree in that it constantly sheds leaves and grows new ones in their place. Like a used garment, the old ones decay and pass away (14:17–19). Modern naturalists say that nature recycles the old, and new organisms emerge from the decaying matter. Ben Sira would probably agree, although emphasizing the adjective "new."

The conviction that death inaugurates an era of eternal rest does not lead Ben Sira to rule out exceptions. He recalls Elijah's raising of the dead (48:5) and his ascension in the whirlwind (48:9), and he assigns to this prophet the special role of calming the divine fury at the decisive eschatological moment (48:10). Ben Sira also mentions Enoch as one who escaped death, noting that Enoch provides an example of repentance (44:16).[36]

This analysis of Israelite belief in life beyond the grave argues that a powerful sense of communion with YHWH and belief in the deity's creative might provided the seeds for the notion of an immortal soul and a bodily resurrection. The catalyst that broke those seeds open and produced full-blown concepts of immortality and resurrection was bitter persecution of the righteous, along with the ensuing apocalyptic. The driving force and intellectual dynamic was the problem of theodicy. Greek influence, hardly generative here, did bring decisive innovations. Old views exercised surprising tenacity in the face of attractive concepts, as if striving to keep theological discourse honest.[37] Proponents of both views, old and new, were nevertheless subject to the limits of human knowledge, so that in the end neither could claim authentication. In the next chapter I explore yet another response to the problem of theodicy—namely, the acknowledgment that we simply don't have an answer. Mystery therefore surrounds ultimate questions.

IO

Mystery

Appealing to Human Ignorance

What is finite to the understanding is nothing to the heart.
                                        —Ludwig Feuerbach

The Bible speaks often about God. It does so as if God is an active player in the human drama.[1] The various writers appear to know God's innermost thoughts and deepest emotions, and they freely share them with readers. We are told exactly what the creator said before transforming chaos into habitable order, and we are even informed about this supreme being's likes and dislikes. In short, from the purported beginnings of the human race, the deity's nature and activity are assumed to be transparent to omniscient narrators.

Moreover, the assumption that the maker can be intimately known endures in spite of frequent warnings that God dwells in darkness impenetrable to human eyes. This paradox of a self-revelatory God who is at the same time hidden from human sight created a lively dynamic in Israelite understandings of YHWH.[2] Rarely, however, did the notion that God's ways and thoughts are inaccessible become dominant, even if religious thinkers now and again reacted against the idea that humans have a direct line to heaven.

Indeed, we can hardly imagine the story of human origins and the long history of Israel and Judah apart from the vivid description of YHWH's indispensable role in it. Whether that divine activity is portrayed as favorably leading the chosen people toward some unseen

destiny or disciplining them for stubborn resistance, the narrators of this remarkable story give the impression that they are describing reality, not constructing fiction. Yet had anyone pressed the issue, I suspect they would have
conceded that their knowledge of God was not susceptible to rational examination.

It is precisely this problem that surfaces momentarily in the quintessential
proclamation of the divine will in the Torah, in the book of Deuteronomy. Here
amid a vivid description of YHWH's statutes as proclaimed by Moses we find
an amazing reminder that Israel must not think she has been granted full
disclosure. To the contrary, the author has Moses say, "The secret things belong
to YHWH our God; but the things that have been revealed are ours and our
children's forever, so that we may do all the words of this law" (Deut 29:28).[3]

Such caveats against presuming too great a knowledge of the deity take
poetic form in the twenty-eighth chapter of the book of Job, placed there because the preceding debate has centered on proper speech about God.[4] Much
has been asserted about the deity, pro and con, by Job and his three friends,
but can any of it be trusted? That is the question posed by the exquisite poem,
which does not denigrate human achievements, intellectual or otherwise, but
does put them in perspective. True wisdom, the poem insists, cannot be found
in the land of the living, for it resides with God. In lapidary fashion the poet
pronounces the whole intellectual enterprise a failure by its very nature. In a
word, it cannot answer the big question, a mystery known to God alone.[5]

Ecclesiastes

The agnostic position fails to overcome conventional wisdom in the book of
Job, but it finds embodiment in Qoheleth, the unknown author of the book of
Ecclesiastes.[6] For him, God's inaccessibility renders the deity unfathomable.
Human beings simply cannot know what God is doing at any given moment,
for the deity is not subject to rational calculation.[7] There is, in Qoheleth's view,
too much absurdity in life. No one can know—or secure—the future, because
virtue is not always rewarded nor vice always punished. Both humans and
animals have a common fate, and no distinction is made in the end between
wise and fool. These troubling thoughts amount to an existential crisis for
Qoheleth,[8] who has abandoned the belief that intellectual inquiry guarantees
long life, wealth, and descendants.

For someone who believes that God is truly a *Deus absconditus*, a hidden
God,[9] Qoheleth talks at length about this deity who towers above rational cal-

culation. In fact, Qoheleth uses the deity as both the subject and the object of verbs.[10] As acting subject, God makes or does, gives, judges, keeps one occupied with, and chases after. Above all, God sees to the continued creation of the world. As creator and thus the one who determines everything that happens, God is considered generous to a fault. That generosity has no rhyme or reason, however, for it appears to select recipients at random. God's judicial function has nothing in common with traditional views of calling individuals to give an account of their deeds. Instead, Qoheleth redefines the verb *shapat* (to judge) to convey a sense of propriety and timing. Similarly, the verb *'anah* (to answer or afflict) assumes a new meaning for him, approximating "to busy oneself with a particular task." Most striking of all, Qoheleth applies a form of the verb *radap* (to chase after) to God's activity in repeating the cyclic pattern of nature. Finally, God brings events to pass and tests, or purifies, humans. They, on their part, should fear God—that is, keep a proper awe, maintaining a safe distance and refraining from antagonizing this deity.[11]

Perhaps the most perplexing statement in the book concerns an act of combined divine generosity and stinginess: "God makes everything appropriate for its time; also he has placed *ha'olam* in the human mind yet without letting anyone find the work that God has done from beginning to end" (Eccl 3:11). The untranslated word has been rendered in various ways, but two quite different meanings fit the context. Either God has put darkness, the ultimate mystery, in the intellect, or God has placed there duration, a sense of eternity. The context suggests something positive, but the verse goes on to preclude human access to this gift. Humans are aware of the unknown and unknowable. That is the first meaning above. Alternatively, they know that time resists their grasp, that eternity eludes them absolutely.[12] Regardless of which meaning is chosen, Qoheleth's point can hardly be missed. The beauty of the precious intellectual possession aside, it does humans no good in their efforts to discern traces of divine activity. Moreover, the search itself is deemed a sorry business—although imposed on them by God (3:10).

This surprising assessment of everyday reality is set within a larger context that deals with the rhythms of life. A list of fourteen pairs of opposing experiences begins with the twin events that comprehend individual existence and nonexistence, birth and death, and concludes with the states of global existence, war and peace. Between these two pairs, the familiar poem covers many aspects of human existence—planting, healing, building, laughing, dancing, cohabiting(?),[13] embracing, searching, saving, sewing, speaking, and loving—each, with its opposite, relegated to a specific time. Unfortunately, however, no amount of intelligence can discern the proper time for any of them.[14] Qoheleth underlines this point with a rhetorical question, a device that he uses some thirty times in the course of the book: "What gain does the one who does [these things] have in that he toils?" (3:9).

Practical experience has taught Qoheleth that the only good thing is to enjoy life, for God alone makes that possible. With the words that follow, Qoheleth places himself squarely in the camp of determinists, possibly influenced by Hellenistic philosophy: "I know that everything God does will be for a long time; unto it none can add, and from it none can take away. God has done [it] so that they will fear his presence. What preceded and what follows existed already, and God seeks after what has been pursued" (3:14–15). It is difficult to imagine a stronger denial of human potential to live to any effect. In short, God's deeds are permanent, inalterable, and iterative. All of this provides a sharp contrast with ephemeral humans, who, in the brief span between birth and death, are destined to knock at the door of wisdom, only to be barred from entering by divine decree. In depicting God as withholding access to a dubious gift, Qoheleth's account resembles the Genesis portrayal of a jealous deity who denied the original couple access to the mythical tree of life (Gen 3:22–24).

It seems to irk Qoheleth no end that the means for coping with life's difficulties formulated by earlier sages have been proven bankrupt by close observation. An empirical approach,[15] testing everything by personal examination, has demonstrated the glaring exceptions to a just world order. Qoheleth carries this analysis to its logical conclusion: humans fare no better than beasts. Just as the author of Psalm 37 proclaims the traditional credo and grounds it in personal experience, Qoheleth refutes that testimony on the basis of the totality of his experience: he has seen that all creatures have a common destiny. The much-touted moral order does not exist, he finds, and the principle of reward and retribution does not hold. Qoheleth affirms a verdict from the myth of the primordial pair in the garden of Eden: "Everyone came from dust, and everyone will return to dust" (Eccl 3:20b). Epistemological agnosticism leaves him no recourse but to ask, "Who knows whether the human breath ascends and that of beasts descends?" (3:21).

In another context Qoheleth brings up this disturbing failure in expected reward and retribution (8:11–13, 9:1–3); here, too, he quotes traditional belief and then exposes it in the harsh light of experience. In this case, however, he comes perilously close to blaming God for the spread of wickedness. In short, delayed punishment encourages evildoers to commit further misdeeds. Qoheleth considers the resulting situation totally absurd. Moreover, ordinary distinctions on the basis of morality and piety seem to play no part in human destiny. Qoheleth tests the theory of individual justice and declares it wanting; although he concedes that everyone is subject to divine control, none can know whether love prevails, or hate. All are treated the same: wise or foolish, saint or sinner, pious or impious, cautious or bold. In his experience, humankind is beset by trouble while death lurks in the shadows.[16] Like life itself, Qoheleth's sentence trails off into nothingness: "and afterwards, to the dead" (9:3c).

Fully aware that his minority views clash with established teachings, Qoheleth actually asserts that his own interpretation of things will stand the test of time. Anyone who claims to understand the divine workings, he states, is simply mistaken (8:17). The deity's activity is impenetrable, just as mysterious as human gestation (11:5). Even were one able to discover God's work, it could not be changed one iota: "The crooked cannot be straightened, and the missing cannot be listed" (1:15).

Living in a period of deep interest in predicting the future, Qoheleth reacts strongly against this popular trend in Greek and Jewish circles.[17] No one, he declares, knows what is yet to occur (8:7, 10:14, 11:6). A deep chasm separates this world from the heavenly realm where destinies are determined, and the two never meet. To Qoheleth, the consequences of this fact seem obvious: "Do not rush to speak or quicken your thought to bring a matter before God, for God is in heaven and you are on earth. Therefore, let your words be few" (5:1).

On the basis of such comments, we might conclude that Qoheleth offers no defense of divine justice. While that is true up to a point, it can still be argued that he provides an indirect theodicy.[18] If God stands entirely outside rational argument, and if human beings cannot know anything about the deity's conduct, there remains no basis for accusation. Because reason cannot fathom God, neither can it convict. The problem is no longer God; it has now become the limits of rational discourse about deity. Theodicy, then, is insoluble, a mystery that is embedded in the unfathomable mystery of God. Human knowledge is restricted to what takes place under the sun, and God is not a factor in this intellectual pursuit. The most anyone can do is explore the world of sensory pleasure and enjoy the few benefits of existence, knowing that time and chance share a random dance, as do good and evil.

Fourth Ezra

Toward the end of the first century CE, an anonymous Jewish author wrote a series of seven visions in which the problem of theodicy takes center stage.[19]

Readers are treated to an odyssey of the soul as the author journeys from perplexity over the apparent injustice of God to jubilant praise of this same deity. As the medium for his message, the author chose apocalyptic,[20] a genre that commanded a huge audience beginning in the second century BCE.

In this literature, bizarre dreams, which necessitate a divine interpreter, usually an angel, divide history into distinct periods that steadily progress toward an end time of war between the forces of good and evil. The present age is characterized as controlled by evil, but a messianic deliverance is anticipated, after which the devout will either enjoy earthly paradise for a specified period or have eternal bliss. Frequently in this literature, a hero from antiquity is taken on a heavenly journey and given secret knowledge concerning the history of the world. The actual authors of these tracts for perilous times are concealed by the names of ancient worthies; favorites are Enoch, Daniel, Baruch, Ezra, Abraham, and Adam.[21] The New Testament apocalypse, Revelation, is attributed to the disciple John.[22]

These apocalypses describe Rome—symbolized by Babylon, in accord with their fiction of great antiquity—as the embodiment of evil. The authors purport to predict the future, which for the most part had already occurred; modern scholars determine the actual date of an account by noting when accurate history ends. As time passed and the predictions of the end time were inevitably shown to be wrong, revised interpretations were put forth, beginning with Jeremiah's prediction of the years between exile and restoration, progressing through two revisions in the book of Daniel, and so on.

Fourth Ezra towers over these texts for sheer intellectual passion and integrity. The author speaks in the voice of Ezra, a venerated scribe whose orthodox credentials are second to none. He struggles to understand God's treatment of the elect, who by any fair assessment are no worse than the Romans who rule over them. Sin, to him, is universal, and the punishment for lawlessness is eternal damnation, which seems to contradict divine mercy. Moreover, God could easily have given the ability to abide by the law as an accompaniment to the commandments. Why did the deity withhold that necessary power? Worse still, why have humans been entrusted with an intellect but prevented from discovering the secrets that open up the universe? Again, what is the benefit of free will if that element of the mind is corrupt from the beginning? These are some of the questions that Ezra puts to the angelic mediator, who functions as the author's alter ego.

The first of the book's visions (3:1–5:20) launches the painful dialogue and hints that the problem that has brought such deep agony to Ezra has no solution but resides in divine mystery. A brief historical retrospect leads him to question God's judgment of nations rather than individuals. This tension between the many and the few—which, as we have seen, pervades the servant poems in Second Isaiah—runs throughout the visions. Under the principle of national righteousness, even Israel, God's elect, cannot stand. The angel's response echoes the agnosticism of Qoheleth: "Your understanding has utterly failed regarding this world, and do you think you can comprehend the way of the Most High?" (4 Ezra 4:2).[23]

The angel reinforces this point by posing three impossible problems: how to weigh fire, measure the wind, and conquer time.[24] Naturally, Ezra must admit an inability to solve a single one of them. Pressing the point, the angel adds some hypothetical questions about the oceans above and below, the exits of hell, and the entrances to paradise. These lie outside Ezra's experience, he concedes, but fire, wind, and time do not. Therefore, the angel concludes: "You cannot understand the things with which you have grown up; how then can your mind comprehend the way of the Most High?" (4:10–11a). As a reminder that Ezra needs to recognize his rightful place, the angel tells a parable about the attempts by sea and forest to extend their domains.[25] Undaunted, Ezra replies that his inquiry is firmly planted in earthly reality. He asks only to know why Rome rules over Judeans, why covenants have been broken, why life is ephemeral, why mercy is withheld, and why God has not acted to preserve the divine reputation.

The remainder of the first vision takes up the matter of the history that has elapsed and the time that remains, using homely examples like the nine months of pregnancy to illustrate the urgency and inevitability of the decisive moment. The whole discussion stands under the heavy burden of sin that is blamed on Adam, into whose heart an evil seed was sown. This taint will be taken up later in the book and given considerably more exposure.

The second vision (5:21–6:34) returns to the matter of individual responsibility for one's destiny. Ezra reminds the angel that God has a long history of selecting a single thing as a gift to the many: one vine, one land, one flower, one river, one city, one dove, one sheep, one people, one Torah. Why, then, Ezra asks, has the one been given over to the many? (5:23–30). The angel's feeble response that God's love for Israel surpasses that of Ezra does not satisfy, hence the return to impossible undertakings:

Count up for me those who have not yet come, and gather for me the scattered raindrops, and make the withered flowers bloom again for me; open for me the closed chambers, and bring forth for me the winds shut up in them, or show me the picture of a voice; and then I will explain to you the travail that you ask to understand. (5: 36–37)

In short, perform what only God can do if you want answers from me. Ezra's predictable response leads the angel to reiterate divine mystery: "So you cannot discover my judgment, or the goal of the love that I have promised my people" (5:40b). The discussion moves once more to the time that has already elapsed and the years yet to come. This entire treatment of past and present presupposes earth's increasing senescence, a view that elsewhere is expressed in the description of history as descending from a golden age to ages of silver, bronze, iron, and clay (Dan 2:36–45).

The third vision (6:35–9:25) opens with an account of creation. A brief anecdote about two mythic creatures who represent chaos, Leviathan and Behemoth, implies that the flaw in creation reaches beyond Adam's bad seed. Ezra inquires why Israel does not own the world, if God created it for her. The intense nationalism of the author surfaces here in an allusion to Second Isaiah's description of the nations as spit (Isa 40:15).[26] The angel reverts to the use of parable, speaking about broad and narrow entrances. Entrances in this world are exceedingly narrow, whereas those in the world to come are broad— the reverse of a similar analogy attributed to Jesus.

The preoccupation with the many and the few returns in this vision, along with the theme of an evil heart that has captured virtually everyone. Ezra resolutely declares that it would have been better if the earth had not produced Adam. The cautious way he avoids specifying God as creator here, substituting earth, speaks volumes, as Ezra goes on to reprimand Adam for incurring guilt on all who follow, a view also endorsed by later Christians. The angel reminds Ezra of yet another gift: free will. In this context of the primacy of choice comes an intriguing midrash on the covenant formulary in Exod 34:6–7, with emphasis falling on God as merciful, gracious, patient, bountiful, compassionate, benevolent, and judicial (7:62–70 [132–140]).[27] Finally, Ezra gets an answer to his dilemma over the many and the few—to wit, that God made this world for the many but the world to come for the few (8:1). This understanding later came to characterize Christian responses to the same problem.

The third vision introduces the idea of intercession for the dead but declares that a decisive juncture will be reached on the day of judgment. For the present, intercessory prayer has its place, but from that decisive day forward such prayer will serve no purpose. The reason: those who perish "also received freedom, but they despised the Most High, and were contemptuous of his law, and forsook his ways" (8:56). In this exchange with the angel, Ezra pleads for mercy for the unrighteous. He tries argument, lament, proof from Scripture, prayer, and request; he succeeds only in being reprimanded for low self-esteem and in being assured that he belongs to the few who are deemed righteous.

When the author progresses to the fourth vision (9:26–10:59), he describes more than a single transformation. Ezra has left his bed, the scene of the earlier visions, and now walks in a field, where he encounters a woman grieving over the loss of her only son. Ezra offers not comfort but reproof, telling her that her own loss is dwarfed by the national disaster, the destruction of the temple. Then he says an astonishing thing: "For if you acknowledge the decree of God to be just, you will receive your son back in due time, and will be praised among women" (10:16 NRSV). What has happened? Has Ezra undergone a conversion?[28] Whatever the case, he is now privileged to watch a remarkable transformation that mirrors his own change as the woman becomes a celestial city. Lest he misunderstand what he has seen, Ezra receives instruction from the angel: this woman is Zion.

The next two visions (11:1–12:51, 13:1–58) abound in strange animal imagery similar to that in the book of Daniel. In both cases the animals represent foreign kingdoms and the Messiah. The author's intent is to describe the history of the world in such a way as to leave the impression that readers are living in the last days. Ezra prays for insight, and God interprets the visions, commanding him to write everything down and commending him for forsaking his own ways and following God's. Ezra alone has been granted divine secrets, and he is to teach them to the wise (12:36–38). Such revelation has come as reward for wisdom, God assures him, "for you have devoted your life to wisdom, and called understanding your mother" (13:55).

Ezra's final vision (14:1–48) echoes God's appearance to Abraham under a tree and to Moses in a burning bush. Even the double address "Ezra, Ezra" resembles the biblical story of God's appearance to these worthies. Ezra becomes a second Moses, restoring the law that has been burned. Taking with him five able scribes, Ezra dictates for forty days, and the scribes write his words in characters with which they have no familiarity. In the end they produce ninety-four books, seventy of which are kept hidden for the wise, because they contain "the spring of understanding, the fountain of wisdom, and the river of knowledge" (14:47).[29]

It cannot be said that Fourth Ezra takes the argument about divine justice to new horizons. Actually, the author's responses to the problem are the usual ones: God's actions are mysterious; God will vindicate Israel in the end; God exults in the salvation of a few; God's mercy prevails in this world, justice in the next. None of these responses addresses Ezra's fundamental problem, the sentence of eternal damnation hanging over the masses. Least comforting of all is the angel's word that God does not grieve over these miserable creatures. The book teems with unresolved tensions, chief of which is its location in a genre that suggests full disclosure over against its constant disclaimer of what cannot be known—the unfathomable mystery of God's ways. This daring author may not have solved the dilemma he explored with such passion, but he did succeed in exposing it in such a way that it could no longer be swept under the carpet.[30]

Second Baruch

Another apocalypse from about the same time as Fourth Ezra belongs to an extensive tradition about Baruch, Jeremiah's scribe.[31] The similarities with Fourth Ezra are striking. Agonizing over many of the same issues that vexed Ezra, Baruch reaches the same conclusion about the unfathomable God. The failure of the few virtuous people to influence God sufficiently to forestall Zion's destruction compels Baruch to ask:

> O Lord, my Lord, who can understand your judgment?
> Or who can explore the depth of your way?
> Or who can discern the majesty of your path?
> Or who can discern your incomprehensible counsel?
> Or who of those who are born has ever discovered
>   the beginning and the end of your wisdom? (2 Bar 14:8–9)[32]

In response to a vision concerning the final days, Baruch wonders aloud:

> Who can equal your goodness, O Lord?
>   for it is incomprehensible.
> Or who can fathom your grace
>   which is without end?
> Or who can understand your intelligence?
> Or who can narrate the thoughts of your spirit?
> Or who of those born can hope to arrive at these things,
>   apart from those to whom you are merciful and gracious? (75:1–5)

Baruch, too, believes that the foreign nations are as nothing—like spit (82:5)—but that Israel has a special place in the divine heart.

Like Fourth Ezra, this author emphasizes Adam's sin but insists that everyone has become his own Adam. This shifting of the onus for sin from Adam to the individual sinner makes the case for free will more emphatically than the former's appeal to the injunction of Moses to choose either good or evil (4 Ezra 7:59 [129]). Neither author sees much comfort in divine promises that cannot be claimed until the next world. Furthermore, both complain that the assurance that the earth was created for humans is hollow when they depart and it remains.

Second Baruch defends God's reputation in the face of apparent defeat by Roman soldiers, who destroyed the divine abode. That did not happen, he insists, until angels came to Zion, removed the holy things and committed them to the earth, breached the wall to the city, and invited the enemy to enter, since its guard had departed (2 Baruch 6–8). In this way the author tries to silence those whose faith has begun to flag before Rome's might. Israel's prophets showed less ingenuity when placing responsibility for the calamity on the sins of the people. Still, Second Baruch does not entirely retreat from their explanation, for he later adds that God punished his sons before turning to judge the nations (13:9).

Both authors demonstrate the capacity to press intellectual doubt to the limit without forsaking praise of the deity, whom neither can understand. Ezra walks in a field while singing God's praises, and Baruch exclaims that were his members mouths and the hairs of his head voices, even so he would be unable to honor the deity properly (2 Bar 54:8)—this despite the conviction that God determines everyone's destiny, recording it in a heavenly book (23:4–24:2). Eventually God will rectify all wrongs, nourishing the righteous with Leviathan and Behemoth, now gourmet food instead of dreadful foes (29:4). Through all Baruch's dismay shines the belief that God's ways are inscrutable *and* right (44:6), for Israel has suffered less than her guilt requires (78:5). As this allusion to Second Isaiah reveals, Baruch's familiarity with the biblical tradition is close.[33]

Now if, as this chapter suggests, all knowledge of God and his ways is partial, might the characterization of YHWH in the Bible—which depends on that knowledge—be only partially accurate? In the final chapter I examine the role of human projection in theological discourse and suggest a way to conquer anthropocentricity.

II

Disinterested Righteousness

Questioning the Problem

Not *how* the world is, is the mystical, but *that* it is.
                                                —Ludwig Wittgenstein

How much do we really know about God? The preceding chapter examined the attitude among ancient followers of the deity that a cloud of mystery conceals the living God. The same reluctance to claim absolute knowledge of the divine characterized other peoples as well, bearing witness to genuine humility with respect to transcendence. To be sure, the ancients peered into the cloud in an effort to descry appropriate images—verbal or otherwise—by which to depict their gods,[1] but the remove between those icons and the mystery they represented was never forgotten.

The huge chasm that separates icon and reality has since been seriously compromised by the reification of a literary construct. If the biblical depiction of the deity is a product of human understanding, we may assume that it carries the same limitations as human knowledge about God, colored by the same tendency toward anthropocentricity. However, as this literary construct has become absolutized—a by-product of the canonical process—its representational character has become obscured. Human perceptions of the deity have been accorded absolute veracity, with monumental consequences for the problem of theodicy.

The implications of anthropocentricity are nowhere more evident than in the book of Job. The tenacious illusion that the deity must conform to human standards of justice and mercy, that God must punish evil and—especially—reward good, produces a shallow, self-serving piety that cannot be sustained. To the extent that mortals set limits and impose them on the deity, they have constructed an idol. The author of the book of Job excels as an iconoclast, removing human beings from center stage and rejecting all forms of idolatry. His God refuses to appear in the palace of justice, choosing instead the arena of creation. And, indeed, it is in this context that he hints at a corrective for the self-imposed poverty of anthropocentricity.

The Reification of God

Let me begin by stating the obvious: a cruel streak exists in the biblical depiction of God. The overwhelming evidence permits no other conclusion. A parade of witnesses to this fiendish behavior includes, among countless others, entire ethnic populations—Amalekites, Canaanites, Edomites—and single individuals, including Moses, the victim of attempted homicide, and an unnamed pharaoh whose free will was overridden.[2] The generation of the flood and the inhabitants of Sodom and Gomorrah would readily confirm the testimony of those who have experienced the deity's bestial nature. So would certain fringe groups within society—specifically, slaves, homosexuals, and those who would tap into the powers of witchcraft.[3] Perplexed individuals like Cain, Esau, and Saul could ask with dismay about arbitrary favoritism with dreadful consequences, and loyal devotees like Abraham and Jeremiah might well question a monstrous test and seductive rape.[4] The priests Nadab and Abihu present a prime example of a punishment in search of a crime,[5] as does Uzzah, whose effort to steady the ark was rewarded by instant death. David's innocent child who paid the ultimate price for his father's adultery and thousands of slain Israelites who fell because of David's census-taking at the divine command join prophets used as puppets in a cruel game aimed at eradicating King Ahab. These throngs readily attest to a harsh divine shepherd.[6]

Four recent examinations of the evidence suggest that the issue of divine cruelty can no longer be ignored.[7] Jack Miles uses the word "fiend," Norman Whybray opts for my language of oppressing the innocent, David Penchansky prefers Yeats's phrase "What rough beast?," and Otto Kaiser looks at theological categories that indicate divine concealment and disclosure. Miles examines a single example of devilish conduct on God's part, while Whybray, Penchansky, and Kaiser cut a wider swath.

For Miles, God's test of Job exposes an evil side, one that operates on the principle that might makes right. Over against an immoral deity stands an innocent Job whose defiance persists to the end, forcing God to acknowledge this fiendish streak. Job has spoken the truth: God does both good and evil. This insight, true to reality, coincides with divine silence; never again does God speak in Tanak. Job's God is truly inscrutable, being savage on Monday and lavish on Tuesday, idly slaughtering a family only to provide a suitable replacement.

Beginning with the prologue to the Decalogue, Whybray offers a sweeping analysis of biblical texts in which YHWH behaves in a manner that strikes mortals as ethically questionable. Whybray remarks about the rarity of scholars who face up to the question of a dark side of God and exposes the lengths to which some interpreters go to deconstruct the offensive materials. The God of Genesis feels threatened by the first mortals and resorts to mass destruction, wipes out specific towns, and poses a monstrous test to a loyal subject without giving any apparent thought to its influence on the three affected persons. The penchant for violence continues in Exodus and Numbers, with God trying to kill Moses and executing thousands of Israelites, in addition to Pharaoh's subjects. Similarly, the Deuteronomistic History abounds in stories of divine ire with no rational justification, and the Latter Prophets contain personal testimony about an untrustworthy deity, in Jeremiah's case, and a horrid one who demands human sacrifice, in the eyes of Ezekiel. Within the Writings, the psalms of complaint and the Joban combination of fable and dialogue attest to an experience of divine indifference and affront. Whybray designates this behavior atypical[8] but nevertheless calls for theological reflection to make sense of a troublesome feature of the Bible.

Penchansky restricts himself to six instances: (1) the insecure monster-God in Genesis 3, (2) the irrational God in 2 Samuel 6, (3) the vindictive God in 2 Samuel 24, (4) the dangerous God in Leviticus 10, (5) the malevolent God in Exod 4:24–26, and (6) the abusive God in 2 Kgs 2:23–25. Both Penchansky and Whybray draw inspiration from my *Prophetic Conflict*[9] and *A Whirlpool of Torment*, which treat a popular perception[10] of an all too scrutable deity and specific instances of divine testing (Abraham, Jeremiah, Job, Qoheleth, and the author of Psalm 73), respectively.

Otto Kaiser's exploration of two theological concepts, *Deus revelatus* and *Deus absconditus*, leads readers through an analysis of three dreadful texts (Gen 22:1–19; Gen 32:23–33; Exod 4:24–26) to an observation that divine self-disclosure is shrouded in mystery for the purpose of testing individuals by adversity and richly rewarding them for faithful obedience. This positive reading of difficult stories fails to deal with the many instances in which divine cruelty produces nothing but havoc in the lives of innocents.[11] One wishes that the sensitive voice of Ezra in the book of Fourth Ezra might echo through the writing of modern theologians, for if the masses are doomed, there can be no justification for God's having created the universe.

Contrary to widespread belief among those visited by Marcion's ghost, the problem of a dark side of God is not limited to the Hebrew Bible. The Apocalypse of John portrays a vindictive God bent on destroying civilization except for a few celibate men. Seven bowls of wrath have replaced water, but the result is the same as the ancient deluge. Furthermore, the scandal of the cross, however it is construed, exposes a shadow in the deity that only an Abelardian theory of redemption can render moderately palatable.[12]

In short, the Bible describes God as cruel; of that there can be no doubt. What shall we make of this fact? *First*, a concession. Such a description is one-sided. The Bible also depicts a compassionate deity whose long-suffering extends to personal involvement in overcoming evil. I take that familiar picture as one panel in a diptych; it stands as a permanent corrective, a reminder that the truth is always far from simple. Nevertheless, persistent unlovable features in the divine portrait force devotees to pick and choose which character traits to imitate, and this issue becomes particularly acute where children are concerned. Who wants them to become bellicose, to play a cat-and-mouse game with people's affections, to boast endlessly, to punish mercilessly, to show favoritism, and to adopt different standards of judgment depending on ethnicity, class, and gender?[13]

Second, a methodological observation. The views expressed in the Bible reflect an ancient construction of reality, one quite alien to modern thinking. One response to the biblical picture of God would take into account evolutionary history, relegating undesirable traits to past misconceptions easily correctable by modern standards. In this view, Israel's conception of God became increasingly more ethical but suffered from a heavy constraint, the necessity to explain both good and evil as the domain of a single deity. Unfortunately, the evidence for sustained progress in ethical sensitivity is hardly persuasive.

Third, a theological axiom. Mortals construct their theology from anthropology.[14] Precisely how this axiom works may not be as obvious as Ludwig Feuerbach believed.[15] We do fashion God in our own image and look on this figure whom we have projected into the heavens as the answer to human hunger for wholeness. This deity embodies everything that is noble but also possesses the power to meet every human need. We may challenge Feuerbach's claim that in Christianity mortals finally admit to worshiping themselves, for he failed to give adequate consideration to the few who expect no reward for selfless devotion. Still, he recognized the vital part that humans play in constructing deity.

Fourth, a literary fact. Authors create an imaginary world as a means of telling a particular story to entertain, to shape character, to advance a desired ideology, or perhaps simply to satisfy a personal artistic impulse. Biblical authors are not exempt from these rules of literary fiction, regardless of their muse—human or divine. The characters in their stories must accommodate themselves to observable reality or to fantasy, else the story quickly aborts.

Fifth, a personal thesis. The Judeo-Christian world has put itself in a straitjacket by reifying a literary construct. It has failed to distinguish between poetic imagination in the service of theology and reality itself. In so doing, it has forgotten a fundamental tenet of theism, that God cannot be known. The self-concealment of the divine arises from the nature of transcendence. Even Romanticism's three avenues to transcendence—poetry, music, and art—have not succeeded in bridging the gulf between the earthly and heavenly realms. Left with nothing but *via analogia* and *via negativa*, theologians in the Judeo-Christian tradition who turn to the Bible come up against similar restraint. The great tautology, YHWH's self-revelation to Moses as "I am that I am" (Exod 3:14), reveals precious little while concealing much.[16] Everyone who persists in the search for clues to the divine character must eventually join Deutero-Isaiah in a humble acknowledgment: "Truly, you are a God who hides" (Isa 45:15).[17]

That insight alone casts a heavy shadow on every depiction of God, biblical or otherwise. It follows that all knowledge of God is partial, which may mean that some of it is altogether wrong—including perceptions in the Bible, on which we have unfortunately placed a stamp of authenticity. The terrible ramifications of that contested move have left a permanent stain on Christendom, and yet many today press ever closer toward deification of human words. For these, Scripture seems to have replaced God as supreme object of worship. Slowly and unknowingly, they have created an unholy trinity that comprises an authoritarian deity made in their own image, an inerrant and infallible Scripture, and self-proclaimed all-knowing interpreters who alone understand this nonexistent text.

The ambiguity of our own psyche, our tension-ridden combination of good and evil, which ancient rabbis identified as competing inclinations *yetser hattob* and *yetser hara'*, corresponds to the way we experience reality as both blessing and curse. Because life meets us sometimes as beneficent and sometimes as oppressive, we describe the Lord of life as both good and evil, if only to assure ourselves that we are not alone during adversity. We cannot imagine a deity who does not comprehend the fullness of our own experience, perhaps because we so desperately seek justice. In our best moments we believe that justice will prevail, but the reality of justice deferred points to a cruel deity, one who permits injustice to reign.

Confronted by mounting evidence of evil within God, we quickly endeavor to mitigate its consequences and to soften the blows of "the slings and arrows of outrageous fortune."[18] We assure ourselves that YHWH balances justice and mercy as we do. Ancient rabbis understood the alternation in divine names within the Pentateuch as expressions of divine attitudes, YHWH when mercy was dominant and Elohim when justice ruled. But this balancing act, which finds classic expression in the thirteen attributes of Exod 34:6–7, suffers from a fatal flaw—the notion of transgenerational punishment. The suffering of an innocent child is a scandal to religious faith, as Ivan in Dostoyevsky's *The Brothers Karamazov* perceived with stunning clarity. Modern science has pressed the issue further, denying telos and highlighting genetic flaws. The universe is destined for burnout, and DNA is a shaping force in our present lives, along with economic and cultural factors. The classic arguments for theism—ontology, cosmology, and teleology—have lost their cogency: a bankrupt church and synagogue face the apocalyptic threat of superviruses and nuclear holocaust. Clearly, evil has the upper hand as AIDS and religious wars compete with Shoah as the modern sequel to the devastating bubonic plague. Where is God in all this human misery? Is the literary construct that describes a transcendent creator devoid of any external referent?

For some, the only viable answer to the cosmic joke being played on mortals is to face reality without any illusions. Freud and Nietzsche stand as courageous witnesses to the self-sufficiency of adulthood. For others, placing God at the center of evil and suffering seems a worthy alternative. In the process,[19] traditional notions of divine power and knowledge must be jettisoned in favor of vulnerability. The gain is real. God suffers along with mortals, in a sense redeeming the dark side. The loss is real. Why should anyone worship a vulnerable deity? Shades of Feuerbach!

The intellectual journey in this brief consideration matches the ambiguity of which it speaks. It underlines the reification of God, the absolutization of a literary fiction, at the same time that it grasps at straws in positing an element of truth in that construction of reality. While I cannot subscribe to the validity of the portrait of God in the Bible, I draw my own painting from it, together with my religious longing, and offer it as a viable alternative. Consistency would require me to abandon the enterprise altogether. That I am not yet willing to do so is testimony to the power of a literary construct and a religious community shaped by poetic imagination.

Some Reflections on the Book of Job

The courageous author who composed the book of Job must surely have become a pariah in the community of exiled Judeans—like a historical critic in Southern Baptist circles or a liberal in an evangelical divinity school. The radical attack on traditional views is analogous to postmodernist and feminist rejections of authority centered in Western males of European descent. Anyone who dons the mantle of an iconoclast risks open hostility, as the name Job suggests.[20] Indeed, the interest of the story's innocent sufferer is thrust aside by his friends and the two heavenly instigators of his pain. The divine speeches serve to push Job further to the periphery, while mythic beasts assume center stage. Honesty compels the poet to acknowledge harsh reality: neither the universe nor its ruler accords any weight to human morality as a claim for preferential treatment. Ironically, the story implies that Job's exceptional virtue has invited preferential treatment of a savage nature.

"Does Job fear God for nothing?" In this simple question the fundamental problem that the book of Job will explore is laid out for readers to ponder. Perhaps the strangest aspect of all is the one who is providing this clue to the book, none other than the Adversary. To be sure, the question conceals deep suspicion, quickly expressed, that an emphatic "no" will be the correct answer. Nevertheless, the poet shows extraordinary boldness by letting the antagonist set the agenda rather than the omniscient narrator who pronounces on the hero's rectitude, a sentiment echoed by the deity.

With this formulation of the problem, the Adversary strikes at the core of the religious life. Does anyone love God for nothing in return? A story from medieval times depicts the issue in dramatic fashion. In it, a prophetess walks through the streets of a city carrying a torch in one hand and a pail of water in the other, her voice crying out above the noise of daily life: "Would that I could burn heaven with this flame and quench the fires of hell with this water, that men would love God for himself alone."[21] In the *Phaedrus*, the Athenian philosopher Plato put the matter another way. Glaucon, the spokesman for the view in question, remarks that a truly virtuous person would endure the most extreme torture without complaint. In short, character is demonstrated only by virtue that does not count the cost.

The carrot-and-stick mentality that lies embedded deep within religious expression seriously compromises the truly righteous life, for it provides selfish motives—the anticipation of heaven or avoidance of hell. Neither of these ideas had crystallized in the time of this book's composition, but their antecedents—

health, wealth, and progeny, or their absence—adequately compensated for the missing postmortem incentive to worship God.

The author of the book of Job perceived this dilemma that resulted from the religious system itself and drew from it an astute inference about the utility of evil. In a word, evil fulfills a vital function in sorting out those individuals who fear God for nothing, gratuitously, in vain. Without the presence of adversity, there would be no way of knowing whether people worship the deity simply because it pays dividends. After all, religion could function quite well as a business, a mercantile transaction of quid pro quo, this for that, in which accurate calculation of costs and benefits governs everything.

As the Adversary saw things, that is exactly what characterized religion. The claim was global, for it was grounded in wide experience, his shuttling about hither and yon as an observer of human religiosity. Although the subject whose integrity was thereby impugned was a non-Israelite, the judgment applied universally. A brief inspection of sacred texts within Yahwism quickly reveals just how self-centered this religion had become. Who could even imagine religious devotion that did not promise a worthwhile reward?

The author of the book of Job saw through the hypocrisy of self-serving piety, recognizing that it was both a lie and a farce. A lie, because life is far too complex to follow the simple rules of reward and retribution. A farce, because no one really fools God into thinking that the service is for nothing. How, then, can anyone—including God—really know that religion is authentic? This brilliant and daring poet devised a plan by which pure religion could be authenticated beyond the slightest doubt. The test required that God offer no hint as to the reasons behind Job's misery, for any insight into the cause of his distress would place Job right back in the situation of serving God for profit.

That probing of the hidden motive for piety is, in my judgment, the purpose of the book. Two other themes, secondary to this one, contribute to its universal appeal, for everyone suffers and everyone wishes to know how rightly to speak about the Ultimate. With the force of this threefold relevance, the book acts as a magnet, drawing readers of different persuasions to look at themselves in its pages.

Four Theological Cautions

Johannes Hempel refers to "the struggle for the last truth about God" as revealed in the book of Job.[22] I am more comfortable with a slightly different formulation, for I do not believe that anyone can discover the last truth about anything, however heroic the struggle. The author of the book of Job may well have grasped an important understanding of human belief about deity, but that is all. Theological claims are by nature unverifiable. It follows that the phrase "the last truth about God" is problematic in every way—its ultimacy, its absoluteness, and its unknowable object. In my view, this lonely voice that insists on theological complexity stands as a caution against established belief wherever it exists. How so?

First, the book of Job reminds readers of limits to all knowledge. In introducing this book, interpreters customarily admit an inability to establish with any degree of certainty its aim, audience, authorship, or genre. Does the book speak to the issue of disinterested righteousness, asking whether anyone actually worships without thought of the benefits that derive therefrom? After all, the viability of religion depends in the last analysis on faithfulness under duress, which falls outside every system based on reward and retribution for moral conduct. Does it address the vexing problem of innocent suffering or suffering in general? Given the prominence of pain in society at large, a probing of proper responses to suffering would surely serve a useful purpose, similar to the Babylonian text I Will Praise the Lord of Wisdom. Does it treat the matter of correct speech to and about God? In questionable circumstances, is honest reproach preferable to high praise? If so, do the differences in the two depictions of Job within chapters 1 and 2 of the prose introduction obscure this understanding—to wit, the choice of the Tetragrammaton versus the general Elohim; speech *to* God versus talk *about* God; divine praise of Job that includes a blessing versus praise alone; the declarative mood versus the interrogative; the narrator's observation that Job did not sin versus the same assertion qualified by the phrase "with his lips"; the divine perspective versus the human perspective?[23] Is the hero infected with the same virus as his comforters? His argument carries no force apart from an operative system of reward and retribution.

To whom was the book addressed—the intelligentsia within Israelite society? elite scribes and their aspiring students? ordinary exiles facing difficult decisions but without their customary religious base, the temple and its priestly ministry? Does Job represent Israel and its present suffering, or—perish the thought—everyone? Why the mythicization of land and ethnic identity? Why the bow toward religious teaching within the context of radical epistemological skepticism in chapter 28?

Who wrote this remarkable work—a sage? a prophet? a proto-apocalyptist? What religious traditions does the unknown author use? In what literary context does a sage employ folktale, lament, theophany, oracular vision, and oath of innocence? Why the retrojection of the story into the patriarchal epoch? Why the peppering of irony throughout the work?

Who speaks for the author—the narrator who holds the puppet strings, even those that control the deity? Job himself? the friends? Elihu? the oracle? the theophany? the Adversary, a verbal expression of the deity's hidden side?

The preceding questions cannot be answered in multiple-choice fashion, with one correct response hidden among a couple of remotely possible ones and at least one that is far-fetched. A plausible case can be made for virtually all of the options presented, depending on one's operating assumptions. This situation merely calls attention to the poverty of human intellect when confronted with an ancient text like the book of Job.

Second, the book of Job offers incontrovertible proof that a text functions as a mirror, revealing the minds of interpreters in addition to its own contours. A quick glance at Jewish attitudes to the figure Job confirms this point. Over the centuries he has been viewed as a saint (Testament of Job); an imperfectly pious man (Rashi); a rebel (Ibn Ezra); a dualist (Sforno); a devout man in search of an answer (Saadia Gaon); a person who lacks true knowledge (Maimonides); an Aristotelian denier of providence (Gersonides); one who confuses God's work and Satan's (Simeon ben Semah Duran); a determinist (Albo); a man who fails to give Satan his due, a scapegoat, an isolationist, and a sign of divine love (the Zohar).[24]

Christian interpreters have fared no better, whether they lived prior to the blossoming of higher criticism or during its heyday.[25] The multiple understandings of Job among modern critics who subscribe to the same hermeneutical principles tellingly illustrate this fact: readers bring as much to a text as they discover in it. How else could they view the book as blemished perfection and flawed editing; a literary masterpiece and an unfinished or damaged work; naive religiosity and studied irony; heroic dissidence and failure of nerve; growth in spiritual perception and progress toward productive hypocrisy? The putative shift in paradigm from history to literature in recent scholarship only calls attention to the power of an intellectual climate over supposedly objective thinkers.

Third, questioning belongs to the essence of faith. The religion that settles for the declarative mode as formulated in creed and sacred narrative belongs in a museum, for it attests to the human struggle to exert power over the deity and worshipers. Even when reinforced by the imperative, such sacred fantasy threatens to become merely moralism, embodied law in desperate need of the interrogative. Only as reason tames fantasy and moralism can a viable form of worship evolve. The book of Job elevates the questioning spirit over sacred narrative and law. In the end, divine approbation conveyed through a narrator falls on the one who dares to utter the unutterable and to question even the most sacred dogma.[26]

Fourth, no one can bring together such vastly different perspectives as the heavenly and the earthly. We are hardly capable of understanding the view from below, as it were; how can we possibly perceive things from above? Creating dialogue for the deity runs the risk of hubris; having that fictional character laud a human as perfect in every way is hubris in the extreme. Neither Job nor his maker deserves such praise. Both are flawed beings. That insight may be the permanent legacy of the ancient poet.[27]

The Divine Speeches and Job's Response

Questions far outnumber answers in the book of Job; indeed, the divine speeches have been compared to teachers' examinations. Their most noteworthy aspect is what they do not say, or better still, the dimension of reality they leave wholly unmentioned. The voice from the whirlwind interrogates Job at length about meteorological phenomena and zoological creatures, real and imagined, but remains strangely silent about human beings. Their only appearance is as the object of derision and challenge. Although boasting about a power that subjects heavenly objects and the forces of nature to its direct control, sustains the animal kingdom, and subdues recalcitrant chaos, YHWH says absolutely nothing about providential care with respect to the human species. The effect is to relegate humans to the perimeter of divine concern—in direct contrast to their reigning assumption.

Furthermore, the world that unfolds before Job's eyes brings little comfort, for it is characterized by the violence of red tooth and claw, as well as lightning, hail, and treacherous ice. Lions go in search of prey, as do ravens and eagles. From the first reference to the king of the jungle to the final observation that the young of eagles suck up blood, a single theme, predation, dominates. Thus the conclusion to the first divine speech sums up its message: "Where the slain are, there is he [the eagle]" (Job 39:30b).

While the first divine speech concentrates on visible objects, the second one ventures into the realm of the imagination—the human psyche, where evil resides and is given external expression. YHWH issues a challenge to Job: conquer wickedness and pride among human beings if you hope to usurp my place in the heavens. The monstrosity of the task is dramatized in the form of Behemoth and Leviathan, twin mythical creatures, symbols of chaos, that embody evil itself. Elsewhere wisdom is identified as YHWH's first work (Prov 8: 22), but in the present context Behemoth has preempted that favored place: "He is the first of God's mighty works" (Job 40:19). In Genesis 1, waters of chaos are considered preexistent, the first divine act being the separation of this primordial matter into a habitable universe. The author of the divine speeches in the book of Job seems to attribute the creation of chaos, or evil, to

YHWH, unless "first" here means preeminence of rank rather than chronological priority. The other creature, Leviathan, serves as a foil to human aspirations to perform wonders. Who would dare to stir up this fierce creature's ire? How much more serious, then, is Job's wish to stand in God's presence.

The statement that follows this stinging rebuke of Job absolves the deity of all debt: "Who has given to me that I should repay him? Everything under the entire heaven belongs to me" (Job 41:3).[28] With this concise formulation of the matter, the poet has YHWH refute an understanding of religion as a comfortable business deal. And yes, Leviathan too belongs to YHWH. This king of pride, partially bound when YHWH set restrictions on the sea, is still a formidable foe, at least to humankind. Obviously, his ultimate taming will not be at Job's hand.

Power, not justice, occupies the divine mind here, but Job has conceded that issue long before this heavenly harangue. The two attributes, power and justice, are not entirely separable, however, for the latter cannot be achieved in a power vacuum. Insofar as justice comes into being when righteousness is served, power is essential to equity in society. The same applies in the divine realm. Without the means of establishing justice universally, God cannot be deemed just. The divine speeches address the issue of potentiality but ignore the matter of actuality. They claim that YHWH could be just if that were a priority. Nothing spoken, however, indicates that it ranks high on the divine chart of values.

For this reason, among others, Job's response in 42:1–6 continues to mystify interpreters. In the context of his own words he has been vindicated, for he was earlier convinced that a sinner could not stand in the divine presence (13:16). On this reading his response suggests new insight beyond what he has been taught: "I had heard of you by listening, but now I behold you" (42:5). Personal observation has trumped transmitted tradition in making Job a new man, one whose eyes have been opened. Sight and sound function symbolically in this context, for the deity was believed to be hidden from human eyes. Rare exceptions are reported in the Bible: Jacob, who became a different man after the disclosure of the divine face; Moses, who died in obscurity; Isaiah, who heard words that announced the nation's virtual eradication. It is possible, therefore, that the Joban poet intended to convey a literal sense by the curious expression "now my eye sees you," but the singular form of the noun *'eni* (eye) then becomes all the more peculiar. The hearing of the ear is also ambiguous. It can signify rumor, but the present context suggests an educational connotation of attentive listening more typical of its use in wisdom literature. In any event, the exact nature of Job's newfound knowledge is not stated, making his "therefore" in the verse that follows less than transparent.

What does Job really say as a result of this clarity of vision? The gram-
matical ambiguity of his final words makes it impossible to determine with
confidence. At least five possible meanings for this verse (42:6) have been
proposed:[29]

1. Therefore I despise myself and repent upon dust and ashes.
2. Therefore I retract my words and repent of dust and ashes.
3. Therefore I reject and forswear dust and ashes.
4. Therefore I retract my words and have changed my mind concerning dust and ashes.
5. Therefore I retract my words, and I am comforted concerning dust
   and ashes.

The difficulty is compounded by the absence of an object for the verb *ma'as*
(to despise, reject), unless the prepositional object "dust and ashes" serves a
dual function. The absence of the direct object leads some interpreters to read
"I melt," in the sense of submission; this reading assumes a different verb,
masas. The phrase *wenikhamti 'al* also has several meanings: "I repent on account of or on"; "I forswear"; "I have changed my mind concerning"; "I am
comforted about." Furthermore, "dust and ashes" may indicate either humiliation or finitude, the human condition.

The ambiguity of Job's response matches that of the divine speeches. The
nature of the test has prevented the deity from giving Job a reason for his
suffering, which would legitimate Job's faithfulness and place him right back
in the position of serving God for the benefit it brings to him. Likewise, the
human condition requires that one face life's uncertainties with no simple
answers to its inequities.

To summarize this examination of the divine speeches and Job's response, they
seem to imply that God plays by different rules from those projected on the
deity by human rationality. God does not always reward goodness and punish
wickedness. Life is hardly that predictable, for the condition of finitude implies
both suffering and limited knowledge. Human beings therefore delude themselves in thinking that they can manipulate the deity and thereby achieve happiness. The truly exceptional person, like Job, either fears God for nothing,
according to the older prose narrative, or challenges the deity for injustice,
according to the poetry. Above the fray, God performs an indispensable task
for both types of individual. In a word, God maintains order, thus containing
chaos, and sustains creation. That being the case, neither criticism of the deity
for failing to implement justice by human standards nor defense of divine
conduct receives endorsement.

Creation, it follows, was an act of pure grace,[30] and in the presence of infinite bounty any suggestion of stinginess has no place. Life in its most fragile form far surpasses whatever evil exists in the world. Being has replaced non-being, and all creatures are empowered to pursue their own nature in an environment that promotes self-expression. Here is a universalism that negates every elevation of human beings to the center of things, a position that only one Being can occupy. That singular being is the creator and sustainer of everything. As recipients of the supreme gift of life, humans would do well to relinquish the notion that the deity owes them anything more than has been freely bestowed, irrespective of desert.

Conclusion

The injustices that warped so many lives in ancient Israel were too ubiquitous to be denied and too random to be blamed on human misconduct. Their presence, and the misery they produced for devout people, forced religious leaders to ponder the cause of this evil, human or otherwise. Of human culpability there was little doubt, but what about divine guilt as well? Biblical notions of YHWH laid themselves open to charges of injustice on several fronts.

First, the concept of election implies special favor for some and thus exclusion for others. To be sure, the real purpose of divine choice can be construed as blessing the many through the few, as expressed in the initial story of election, the choosing of Abraham and setting him apart as a source of well-being for everyone. The same idea finds different expression in Deutero-Isaiah's formulation about Israel the servant, who is called to be a light to the nations. This salvific function of a covenanted people was easily forgotten, however, amid the turmoil of daily life and conflicts between nations. Election for service was easily transmuted into election to superiority and privilege. An elevated sense of entitlement seemed to justify the taking of land from its owners by warfare, and the claim of superiority gave rise to cruel measures to exclude outsiders from the blessings of the elect. When election becomes ideology, as in the royal theology associated with Zion, it assumes international dimensions, with concomitant hubris and—ironically—dire consequences for powerless subjects who belong to the chosen group.

Second, the idea of divine zeal, essential to belief in justice, supports the covenantal ideology's exclusivity and is easily perverted into uncontrolled wrath. The danger of such divine fury even when placed in the service of justice is dramatically illustrated in the rebuke attributed to God when the Egyptian army encountered this wrath and the angels prepared to sing the daily hymn of praise: "The works of my hands are drowning in the sea and you sing my praises?" (B. Talmud Sanhedrin 39b). This silencing of heavenly praise carries its own deafening roar, the accompaniment to divine fury, but a roar that nonetheless did not quell the divine wrath unleashed on the pharaoh's army.

The dilemma faced by the deity is real. There can be no justice without vengeance, the sure demonstration that evil will not stand. Although a loving God cannot be indifferent to injustice, love also demands patience, a sure sign of mercy. The paradox is that providence must abandon humankind so that grace may work itself out in individual lives, but the ones who are thus forsaken experience suffering. That is why it is said that God cannot have both a world and justice. However much we put a positive spin on divine anger by calling it suspended love, concealed mercy, or a necessary interlude when violence and misery dominate, it remains a source of consternation.

Third, prolonged divine hiding brings too much suffering, evil in excess. Ironically, history cannot exist apart from divine hiding, which permits individuals to make free choices. The danger comes when that freedom generates so much pride that its destructiveness threatens civilization itself. Unlimited mercy, expressing itself in the form of patience, yields overweening pride. To prevent the destruction of humankind, God must break through the dark clouds that eclipse the divine presence. For many, God's failure to do so during calamitous events such as the destruction of the temple has thoroughly negated this explanation for divine silence.

Fourth, this dark side of God will last as long as the world exists, because the reason for divine hiding is evil's pervasiveness. In the suffering of innocents the reality of the world confronts the integrity of God, who for better or worse is caught up in the human experiment. Pathos, it follows, best characterizes the biblical concept of YHWH, much to the chagrin of all who prefer the God of philosophers.

Fifth, pathos draws the biblical God into the cauldron of suffering, as illustrated above by the silencing of angelic praise during human agony. The decision to create a world, God's experiment in self-disclosure, inevitably brought pain, the consequence of human freedom. The reality of free choice meant that not everyone would choose God over self, as the story of Adam and Eve portrays with telling effect. The offer of divine love was not always reciprocated, and the resulting rejection pierced the deity's heart at the same time that it aroused divine wrath. In reflecting on Genesis 1, I expressed this idea in the following way.

The Tear

Had God known the course of those first words,
He would ne'er have spoken,
Ripping night from day, land from sea, you from me.
Instead, God shattered eternity's silence and then cried,
A tear falling from divine eyes into mine,
Exploding in a shriek of eternity.

The rip in time, the cleft that separates creature from creator, also generates weeping and compassion essential to the mending of the rift, the healing of the sickness that isolates one and all.

Sixth, the shift from polytheism to henotheism and ultimately to monotheism has not had an entirely salutary effect. The commendable belief that a single creator is sovereign over all peoples easily lends itself to enforced conversion and rigid dogma; deeply held convictions that those with different theological views are agents of Satan and enemies of the true God can only lead to divisions among humankind. The temptation to assist God in destroying evil in this form is ever present—witness the religious wars that have blighted the landscape of human history.

The consequences of these six notions about the biblical deity are legion, but a single rabbinic story about a certain Elisha ben Abuyah reveals the necessity of facing them squarely. In one version of the story, Elisha sees a boy die as a result of obeying his father; in another, he sees the tongue of a martyr being drug on the ground by a pig. In both accounts he becomes an atheist because of apparent divine injustice. The biblical theodicies discussed in this volume could not forestall all such departures from Judaism, but at the very least they kept religious discourse honest. That in itself was no small achievement, given the propensity of even devout people to delude themselves, especially in the service of what has become orthodoxy.

The biblical theodicies spawned by these concepts of YHWH as a cause of evil reveal the depth of religious diversity in the ancient world and the profundity of theological reflection. The problem of reconciling real injustices with belief in YHWH was too complex for any single answer and too urgent to be ignored. The search for a convincing explanation for innocent suffering bore witness to compassion for the weak at the same time that it attested undying loyalty to the one being subjected to critical scrutiny.

Each response to the problem of evil in a supposedly moral universe came at considerable expense. The atheistic answer was tantamount to forsaking the worldview in which the Israelites had been nurtured. Beyond that turning away from everything sacred, it represented an abandonment of the initial problem at the expense of the human community, overlooking natural and primordial evil, which cannot be laid at the feet of humankind. The polytheistic solution entailed a reversion to a stage in religious evolution that had been cast off for good reasons, not the least of which was a momentum toward universalism, with its accompanying higher ethics. The flirtation with a dualistic understanding of reality ran counter to the biblical insistence that the created universe is very good, even if this response was fueled by features within the Bible itself. The serious flaw in this approach to theodicy lay in its quasi nature, the recognition that in the final analysis the biblical deity has ultimate power over the lesser being.

The redefining of God suffered from similar weaknesses. By admitting vulnerability in the deity, one risks the possibility that the reason for religious allegiance has at the same time been jettisoned. After all, can a deity who lacks full knowledge and whose power is subject to a countervailing freedom of will really establish justice in society? The answer would seem to be an emphatic "no" if the deity must balance the qualities of justice and mercy, which on logical grounds cannot be done. The shifting emphasis within the Bible, the constant effort to keep the attributes in equilibrium, attests the importance placed on this balancing act. The seemingly natural resolution to theodicy's pressing urgency in terms of the building of character through adversity failed in one significant respect: its limited application. Far too many instances of debilitating suffering, evil in excess, can be adduced to allow such a simple solution as discipline. Nevertheless, its superiority over the response that blamed the victim is obvious. The difficulty with a thorough application of the theory of individual retribution and reward is its insidious nature, despite its legitimacy in many cases. The easy leap from suffering to guilt, and the corollary, from prosperity to virtue, condemns far too many innocents to punishment not of their own making and exalts far too many guilty beyond their just desert.

Even the move to allow humans to shoulder the blame for evil cannot be deemed entirely satisfactory—first, because it necessitated an anthropodicy and, second, because it could offer only partial explanations for moral evil. The focus on a superhero as a vicarious sacrifice whose innocence somehow redounds to others' benefit had enormous power, but it depends on a concept of transferred merit that is activated, at least partially, by intellectual assent— that is, the grace itself must be merited, but this is a contradiction in terms. This slippery slope came perilously close to introducing magic into the equation. The most satisfying solution by far implied escape from temporal existence into eschatology, a settling of accounts in another world after one's personal history reached its end. The difficulty of this answer is that such a final balancing of the books requires a leap of faith; otherwise, it can hardly bring comfort to a troubled soul. The reminder that the problem of theodicy cannot be resolved, given human finitude, can lead to premature abandonment of a vital intellectual and spiritual odyssey. Mystery certainly abounds, but it should not stifle intellectual curiosity, especially in the face of existential doubt. The challenge, then, is daunting. Can anyone love God for nothing in return? This question suggests that the best response to theodicy demands a studious examination of the motive that lies behind piety. If life is the supreme gift, we are indeed debtors, and nothing we do in the way of virtuous acts can ever repay God for such generosity. Still, even this formulation of the issue relates only to the motive for being religious. It does not touch upon the deeper question: Why does evil in excess exist? Instead, this answer addresses the human sense of wonder and gives it a worthy means of expression.

Regardless of the theodicy that we choose, one thing seems certain. Both God and humankind present problems. Theodicy therefore has a twin—anthropodicy. Any attempt to justify human conduct must confront evidence of evil every bit as horrendous as the evil we would see on the part of God. Evidence that men and women are fundamentally flawed is irrefutable—witness rampant sexism, racism, nationalism, ad infinitum. Nor is this awful stain of recent vintage, for the biblical world had more than its share of these horrors. Still, a purely negative assessment of the human community, like a straight verdict of guilt for the deity, must be judged myopic in light of the redeeming goodness of a few. That quality, like evil itself, defies explanation. If understood to be sparked by divine intentionality, such redeeming goodness becomes the finest theodicy of all, as it calls others to participate in the noblest effort under the sun: establishing justice for the victims of oppression, empowered by the mercy of the God of all grace.

Notes

INTRODUCTION

1. Even the different divine names within the first five books of the Bible (Elohim and YHWH), were understood by later rabbis to be indicative of God's two primary attributes, justice and mercy.

2. This text has been widely discussed, most helpfully by Michael Fishbane, *Biblical Interpretation in Ancient Israel* (Oxford: Clarendon, 1985), 335–50. For more recent analysis, see James L. Crenshaw, "Who Knows What YHWH Will Do? The Character of God in the Book of Joel," in *Fortunate the Eyes That See: Essays in Honor of David Noel Freedman*, ed. Astrid Beck et al. (Grand Rapids, Mich.: Eerdmans, 1995), 185–96, esp. 185 n 1 and 191 n 29. Ruth Scoralick, *Gottes Güte und Gottes Zorn: Die Gottesprädikationen in Exodus 34,6f. und ihre intertextuellen Beziehungen zum Zwölfprophetenbuch*, HBS 33 (Freiburg: Herder, 2002), focuses on the influence of Exod 34:6–7 in the Book of the Twelve.

3. Other exceptions include Psalms 33, 103, 145, and—most notably—Psalms 146–150, which erupt in a mighty crescendo of praise, concluding with the imperative "Praise YHWH. . . . Let everything that breathes praise YHWH. Praise YHWH."

4. For this hymn, see M. Lichtheim, ed., *Ancient Egyptian Literature*, 3 vols. (Berkeley: University of California Press, 197–80), 2:96–100.

5. The masculine pronoun here could easily be replaced by the feminine equivalent, for I suspect that some psalms were composed by women, just as instruction within the book of Proverbs often comes from mothers. Formal education, specifically in guilds, was restricted to boys, on which see James L. Crenshaw, *Education in Ancient Israel: Across the Deadening Silence* (New York: Doubleday, 1998).

6. Instead of *rokeb*, the usual participle for "the one who rides," the psalmist uses *hamhallek*, a Piel participle of the verb *halak* (to walk), perhaps an instance of covert polemic against Baal worship. Compare the usual formulation:

> Mounted [*rokeb*] on a swift cloud
>> YHWH comes to Egypt. (Isa 19:1)
>
> Sing to God, chant his name,
>> laud the rider of the clouds [*larokeb ba'arabot*]. . . .
> Kingdoms of the earth,
>> sing to God;
>> chant to Adonai, (*selah*)
>> to the one who rides [*larokeb*] the ancient heavens,
>>> who thunders mightily. (Ps 68:5, 33)

The Baal cycle, one of three mythic texts in ancient Ugarit, is translated in J. B. Pritchard, ed., *Ancient Near Eastern Texts Relating to the Old Testament*, 3rd ed. (Princeton, NJ: Princeton, University Press, 1969), 129–42. See also Mark S. Smith, *The Ugaritic Baal Cycle*, vol. 1 (Leiden: Brill, 1994).

7. Hans-Peter Stähli, *Solare Elemente im Jahweglauben des Alten Testaments* (Freiburg: Universitätsverlag; Göttingen: Vandenhoeck & Ruprecht, 1985); Karel van der Toorn, "Sun," in *Anchor Bible Dictionary*, ed. D. N. Freedman, 6 vols. (New York: Doubleday 1992), 6:237–39; Mark S. Smith, "The Near Eastern Background of Solar Language for Yahweh," *Journal of Biblical Literature* 109 (1990): 29–39; and J. Glen Taylor, *Yahweh and the Sun: Biblical and Archaeological Evidence for Sun Worship in Ancient Israel*, JSOTSup 111 (Sheffield: Sheffield Academic Press, 1993). Similar solar imagery is developed more fully in Ps 19:1–7, frequently thought to be an ancient Canaanite hymn to the sun deity that involves celestial proclamation devoid of sound and words, on the one hand, and the sun's journey in the heavens—vigorous, like a bridegroom emerging from his tent, and ubiquitous, none escaping its heat—on the other hand. An illuminating discussion of Psalm 19 can be found in William P. Brown, *Seeing the Psalms: A Theology of Metaphor* (Louisville: Westminster John Knox, 2002), 81–103.

8. Michael Fishbane, *Biblical Myth and Rabbinic Mythmaking* (Oxford: Oxford University Press, 2003), 34–36, distinguishes between a *"logos* model" and an *"agon* model" in the myths about creation. The former type emphasizes the verbal power that brings about created matter; the latter stresses physical combat. For earlier studies, see Jon D. Levenson, *Creation and the Persistence of Evil: The Jewish Drama of Divine Omnipotence* (San Francisco: Harper & Row, 1988); Bernard F. Batto, *Slaying the Dragon: Mythmaking in the Biblical Tradition* (Louisville: Westminster John Knox, 1992); and John Day, *God's Conflict with the Dragon and the Sea* (Cambridge: Cambridge University Press, 1985).

9. The psalm omits to mention the tasks of transformation generally performed by women: changing the raw into the cooked, straw into baskets, flax into clothing, and children into social beings. Perhaps another thing distinguishes men and women

from nocturnal creatures: their dependence on daylight for productive labor (vv 20–23).

10. Two similar texts from the early second century, Sir 29:21 and 39:26, list the essentials of life as four in number (water, bread, clothing, house) or a more generous ten (water, fire, iron, salt, flour, milk, honey, wine, oil, clothing).

11. Bernd Feininger, " 'Denk ich an Gott, muss ich seufzen' Ps 77, 4: Schwierigkeiten und Hoffnungen in unserem Umgang mit den dunklen Seiten des Alttestamentlichen Gottesbildes," *Bibel und Kirche* 46 (1991): 152–58. All translations in this volume are mine, except when otherwise noted.

12. The other three are vv 2–4, 11–16, and 17–21, conveniently demarcated by the Hebrew word *selah*, which is often taken as an indication of a momentary pause.

13. Manoah's response to the revelation of the visitor's identity—specifically, the offering of a *minkhah* sacrifice—carries a subtle hint that he understands that he is in the presence of transcendence. The name of the offering has the same consonants that appear in the name "Manoah" (*mnkh*). See James L. Crenshaw, *Samson: A Secret Betrayed, a Vow Ignored* (Atlanta: John Knox; London: SPCK, 1978), 76.

14. Emmanuel Levinas, "The Trace," in *Meaning and Sense: Collected Philosophical Papers*, quoted in Jacques Derrida, *Adieu to Emmanuel Levinas* (Stanford, Calif.: Stanford University Press, 1999), 62, writes that "He [God] shows himself only by his trace, as . . . in Exodus 33"; that the divine revelation, or visitation, is a sort of "disturbance imprinting itself . . . with an irrecusable gravity."

15. On narrative style, see Simon B. Parker, *Stories in Scripture and Inscriptions: Comparative Studies on Narratives in Northwest Semitic Inscriptions and the Hebrew Bible* (New York: Oxford University Press, 1997); Meir Sternberg, *The Poetics of Biblical Narrative: Ideological Literature and the Drama of Reading* (Bloomington: Indiana University Press, 1985); Adele Berlin, *Poetics and Interpretation of Biblical Narrative* (Sheffield: Almond, 1983); and David M. Gunn and Danna Nolan Fewell, *Narrative in the Hebrew Bible* (Oxford: Oxford University Press, 1993).

16. Walter Brueggemann, *The Psalms and the Life of Faith* (Philadelphia: Fortress, 1995), 258–67, describes the psalmist's move from first person to second, from "the pool of Narcissus" in the first stanza to complete focus on God in the last two verses.

17. John G. Gammie, *Holiness in Israel* (Minneapolis: Fortress, 1989). For the nature of Israelite religious thought, see Patrick D. Miller, *The Religion of Ancient Israel* (London: SPCK; Louisville: Westminster John Knox, 2000), and Rainer Albertz, *A History of Israelite Religion in the Old Testament Period*, 2 vols. (Louisville: Westminster John Knox, 1994).

18. The long history of biblical scholarship regarding glosses is a complex one, reflecting the larger intellectual environment, especially classical studies. Unfortunately, we do not have access to sufficient manuscript evidence of glosses (compare, for example, some Mesopotamian texts such as the Gilgamesh Epic), but additions in the Greek translation of the Hebrew Bible document the practice in biblical texts. Modern scholars assume that ancient editors inserted their own interests, probably in the margins, and these were later integrated into the text itself. The result was a liv-

ing tradition. Detecting such additions is a complicated matter, given the differences in literary style between ancient and contemporary works.

19. Similarly, the last verse of the third stanza narrows the focus from the general to the specific—namely, the redemption of Jacob and Joseph's descendants.

20. Much of the conflict over the Bible is a result of ignoring its poetic character—of reading its metaphoric language prosaically and understanding it literally. The great contribution of increased knowledge about literature from the world of the Bible is an appreciation of the extent to which poetry was employed by ancient writers to convey deep religious convictions and the place of fiction and hyperbole in ancient narrative.

21. Still, deep introspection could produce lyrical poetry, no small gain. See Giorgio Buccellati, "Wisdom and Not: The Case of Mesopotamia," *Journal of the American Oriental Society* 101 (1981): 35–47.

22. Samuel E. Balentine, *The Hidden God: The Hiding of the Face of God in the Old Testament* (Oxford: Oxford University Press, 1983), and Samuel Terrien, *The Elusive Presence: Toward a New Biblical Theology* (New York: Harper & Row, 1978).

23. S. T. Katz, "Holocaust, Judaic Theology, and Theodicy," in *The Encyclopaedia of Judaism*, ed. Jacob Neusner, A. J. Avery-Peck, and W. Scott Green (Leiden: Brill, 2000), 1: 406–20. Eliezer Berkovits, *Faith after the Holocaust* (New York: Ktav, 1973), reveals the horrific impact of the Holocaust on Jewish religious thought and the hollow optimism generated by the war of 1967 in Israel.

24. See the spring 1975 issue of *Daedalus*, entitled *Wisdom, Revelation, and Doubt: Perspectives on the First Millennium*, especially Eric Weil, "What Is a Breakthrough in History?" *Daedalus* (Spring 1975): 21–36.

25. This threatening aspect of the biblical deity has been discussed at length by W. Dietrich and C. Link, *Die dunklen Seiten Gottes* (Neukirchen-Vluyn: Neukirchener, 2000). See also Denys Turner, *The Darkness of God* (Cambridge: Cambridge University Press, 1995), and Walter Gross and Karl-Josef Kuschel, *"Ich schaffe Finsternis und Unheil!" Ist Gott verantwortlich für das Übel?* (Mainz: M. Grünewald, 1992).

26. The prophetic book of Hosea treats the same problem, unreciprocated ardor, from the divine perspective. Israel, understood as the deity's wife, has turned to other lovers, that is, other deities, abandoning YHWH in the process.

27. The literature is vast, but the issues are discussed in Terry Eagleton, *Literary Theory: An Introduction*, 2d ed. (Oxford: Blackwell, 1996), and Regina Schwartz, ed., *The Book and the Text: The Bible and Literary Theory* (Oxford: Blackwell, 1990).

28. Michael Fishbane, *Text and Texture: Close Readings of Selected Biblical Texts* (New York: Schocken, 1979), and Fishbane, *The Garments of Torah: Essays in Biblical Hermeneutics* (Bloomington: Indiana University Press, 1989), demonstrates the richness of this approach. Basic to this reading is the assumption that a literary artifact requires an interpreter in a reciprocal relationship, one who acts as midwife to the text. Furthermore, texts are fragments of a broader culture, necessitating an awareness of intertextuality for full understanding. Carol A. Newsom, *The Book of Job: A Contest of Moral Imaginations* (Oxford: Oxford University Press, 2003), beautifully illustrates the necessity for and utility of attention to intertextuality.

29. See the monumental work by Antti Laato and Johannes C. de Moor, eds., *Theodicy in the World of the Bible* (Leiden: Brill, 2003).

30. "God, he [Epicurus] says, either wishes to take away evils, and is unable; or He is able, and is unwilling; or He is neither willing nor able, or He is both willing and able. If He is willing and is unable, He is feeble, which is not in accordance with the character of God; if He is able and unwilling, He is envious, which is equally at variance with God; if He is neither willing nor able, He is both envious and feeble, and therefore not God; if He is both willing and able, which alone is suitable to God, from what source then are evils? or why does He not remove them?" Lactantius, *De Ira Dei* 13.

31. Ernest Becker, *The Denial of Death* (New York: Free Press, 1973).

32. Paul Ricoeur, *The Symbolism of Evil*, trans. Emerson Buchanan (Boston: Beacon, 1967).

33. James L. Crenshaw, "Suffering," *The Oxford Companion to the Bible*, ed. Bruce M. Metzger and Michael D. Coogan (Oxford: Oxford University Press, 1993), 718–19; David Kraemer, *Responses to Suffering in Classical Rabbinic Literature* (New York: Oxford University Press, 1995); and Oliver Leaman, *Evil and Suffering in Jewish Philosophy* (Cambridge: Cambridge University Press, 1995).

34. Abraham Joshua Heschel, *The Prophets* (New York: Harper & Row, 1962), uses this concept as the key to understanding the biblical deity. The departure from the God of philosophy is fully intentional but presents major problems. For defense of divine suffering, see Paul Fiddes, *The Creative Suffering of God* (Oxford: Clarendon, 1988), and Terence E. Fretheim, *The Suffering of God* (Philadelphia: Fortress, 1984).

35. These responses to suffering approximate ancient theodicies as delineated by R. M. Green, "Theodicy," in *The Encyclopedia of Religion*, ed. M. Eliade (New York: Macmillan, 1987), 14:430–41: (1) the free-will theodicy, (2) educative theodicies, (3) eschatological (or recompense) theodicies, (4) theodicy deferred: the mystery of suffering, and (5) communion theodicies. David Nelson Duke, "Theodicy at the Turn of Another Century: An Introduction," *Perspectives in Religious Studies* 26 (1999): 241–48, prefers the following categories: (1) theodicies of fatalism, (2) theodicies of accountability and calculation, (3) theodicies of instrumental purpose, (4) theodicies of expressivity, and (5) theodicies of denial.

36. Another way of expressing the difficulty of traditional theology is as follows:

> God is omniscient and omnipotent.
> God is all-benevolent.
> Gratuitous evil exists.

Any two of these statements exclude the third one. In trying to reconcile the rival claims, apologists have sacrificed aspects of divine power, emphasized human ignorance, or denied the human claim to virtue.

37. As used here, "theodicy" refers to the attempt to pronounce God innocent of the evil that befalls human beings. This understanding of the term differs from post-Enlightenment efforts to demonstrate the intellectual credibility of an infinite being or power and to show that belief in deity can coincide with belief in a mechanistic

universe. Theodicy is an articulate response to the anomie of existence, one that goes beyond silence, submission, and rebellion to thoughtful justification of the deity in the face of apparently contradictory evidence. The concept antedates by millennia the origin of the word "theodicy," a neologism coined by G. W. Leibniz in 1710 (*Theodicy: Essays on the Goodness of God, the Freedom of Man, and the Origin of Evil*, trans. E. M. Huggard [New Haven: Yale University Press, 1952]).

38. The phrase is used freely by Gustavo Gutiérrez, *A Theology of Liberation: History, Politics, and Salvation* (Maryknoll, N.Y.: Orbis, 1973), with reference to YHWH's championing the cause of widows, orphans, the poor, and strangers.

39. David Birnbaum, *God and Evil* (Hoboken, N.J.: Ktav, 1989), 4. See also the contributions to Terence E. Fretheim and Curtis L. Thompson, eds., *God, Evil, and Suffering: Essays in Honor of Paul R. Sponheim* (St. Paul, Minn.: Luther Seminary, 2000). According to Terrence W. Tilley, *The Evils of Theodicy* (Eugene, Ore.: Wipf & Stock, 2000), every theodicy not only fails but also damages the intellectual endeavor among both theists and victims of injustice. The contributors to *Perspectives in Religious Studies* 26 (1999), a volume on theodicy edited by D. N. Duke and S. E. Balentine, do not share this negative view of theodicy.

40. The term "theodicy" is anachronistic when applied to the ancient world, but the phenomenon is real. To heed Karl Barth's warning that such thinking is illegitimate would be to suppress significant theological discourse concerning evil and its effect on the psyche. Biblical authors, like their counterparts in Egypt, Canaan, and Mesopotamia, did not hesitate to ask hard questions. Their manner of dealing with evil in its multiple forms offers insight into the civilization that to a large extent shaped the West.

41. Antonio Loprieno, "Theodicy in Ancient Egyptian Texts," in *Theodicy in the World of the Bible*, ed. Antti Laato and Johannes C. de Moor (Leiden: Brill, 2003), 56.

42. Antti Laato and Johannes C. de Moor, *Theodicy in the World of the Bible* (Leiden: Brill, 2003).

43. Midrash Genesis Rabbah 49:9.

CHAPTER 1

1. Harold M. Schulweis, *Evil and the Morality of God* (Cincinnati: Hebrew Union College Press, 1984), 1. Schulweis's illuminating assessment of various responses to the problem of evil is compelling. See also David Tracy and Hermann Häring, eds., *The Fascination of Evil, Concilium* 1998/1 (London: SCM; Maryknoll, N.Y.: Orbis, 1998), and David Birnbaum, *God and Evil* (Hoboken, N.J.: Ktav, 1989).

2. In contrast to theodicies in the ancient Near East, modern theodicies are intended to prove the existence of a deity in a society that has become increasingly secular. Philosophical theodicies, not saddled with this goal, have concentrated on the existential crisis caused by excessive evil. Both attempts are beset by insurmountable difficulties, and the shift to justifying humans has fared no better, given the horrifying blight on the human landscape that seems to worsen by the day. See James L.

Crenshaw, "Introduction: The Shift from Theodicy to Anthropodicy," in *Theodicy in the Old Testament,* ed. James L. Crenshaw, IRT 4 (Philadelphia: Fortress; London: SPCK, 1983), 1–16 (= Crenshaw, *Urgent Advice and Probing Questions,* 141–54).

3. Contrariwise, many contemporary readers would view the issue in intellectual categories, considering believers to be fools bereft of reason.

4. The precise meaning of the expression is "to think," for in biblical literature the heart is understood to be the locus of the intellect.

5. J. Clinton McCann Jr., "Psalms," *New Interpreter's Bible* 4:716–17, and Samuel Terrien, *The Psalms: Strophic Structure and Theological Commentary* (Grand Rapids, Mich.: Eerdmans, 2003), 138.

6. Either the alphabetic arrangement in alternating verses has been disturbed, or the poet failed to execute it fully. Four letters of the alphabet do not begin a line: the Hebrew equivalents of English *d, m, n,* and *s.* The letter *h* and a nonvocal consonant can both be made to introduce a line, but that is not their natural position. Interpreters frequently consider the use of alphabetic arrangement to be an aid to memory, but corruptions like those in Psalms 9–10 make this hypothesis less than persuasive. Terrien, *The Psalms,* 140 writes: "Most probably, the written stage was altered, in spite of the acrostic alphabetism, by faulty memory during the oral transmission."

7. McCann, "Psalms," 717.

8. Like the Torah (Genesis, Exodus, Leviticus, Numbers, and Deuteronomy), the book of Psalms consists of five major units (Psalms 1–41, 42–72, 73–89, 90–106, 107–150), each with a concluding doxology.

9. McCann, "Psalms," 719.

10. These indications of linguistic unity are offset by opposing features in Psalm 9 alone: the presence of the liturgical term *selah,* thought to indicate a pause; the use of the word *tebel* (world) instead of *'erets* (earth); a different word for the poor; the name Elyon for the deity; the epithet "righteous judge"; the nouns *misgab* (stronghold) and *le'ummim* (peoples); the verb *tabe'u* (sank); the idiom for avenging spilled blood; the reference to the outcry of the poor; the gates of Sheol and of daughter Zion; and the emphasis on a throne and judicial proceedings.

11. Jacob Neusner, "Theodicy in Judaism," in *Theodicy in the World of the Bible,* ed. Antti Laato and Johannes C. de Moor (Leiden: Brill, 2003), 685–727, emphasizes things other than divine hiding. Basically, Neusner discusses the covenantal foundation for belief in an orderly universe—namely, the election of Israel and the promises associated with that choice. He goes on to show the subtle ways in which the rabbis defended the moral order, despite overwhelming evidence to the contrary. His remark that all they had to do was walk outside the school and look around at the miscarriage of justice reminds one of Oscar Wilde's observation in *De Profundis* that any narrow street in London contains enough misery to refute the notion of a loving God. Neusner recognizes the importance of the resurrection to rabbinic theodicy, but whereas he stresses the rational element, Bruce Chilton, "Theodicy in the Targumim," in *Theodicy in the World of the Bible,* ed. Laato and de Moor, 728–52, brings the pastoral dimension into play, particularly as interpreters of the Scriptures translated the Hebrew

text into Aramaic, the everyday language of worshipers. Above all, these Targumists sought to explain the destruction of the temple as punishment for sin, while registering a strong promise of its restoration.

12. Psalm 10:3 uses the usual verb for praising the deity, the root of which occurs in the word "hallelujah" (praise YHWH), for the evildoer's self-referential boasting. The verb *barak* (to bless) is used in a rare opposite sense, meaning "to curse." On the six other instances of this use of *barak* in the Hebrew Bible, see C. A. Keller and G. Wehmeier, "*brk* pi. to bless," in *Theological Lexicon of the Old Testament*, ed. E. Jenni with assistance from C. Westermann, trans. M. E. Biddle, 3 vols. (Peabody, Mass.: Hendrickson, 1997), 1:266–82, and Meir Weiss, *The Story of Job's Beginning* (Jerusalem: Magnes, 1983). We might note in particular two of these instances, which also involve violence against innocent persons. In 1 Kgs 21:10 and 13, Queen Jezebel, about whom nothing good is said in the narrative, seals Naboth's fate by suborning witnesses to testify that he cursed God in his heart. The other instance involves Job's children, who he thinks may have cursed God in their hearts (Job 1:5), and Job himself. In the latter case, both the heavenly Adversary (usually called the satan in modern popular discourse) and Job's wife endeavor to make him curse God (Job 2:5, 9). Neither succeeds: in Job's view, one should bless God whether receiving good or evil— exactly what he does not do in the poetic section of the book.

13. This royal ideology has been discussed by Leonidas Kalugila, *The Wise King* (Lund: Gleerup, 1980). Not only did ancient civilizations expect rulers to embody intelligent action; they also entrusted the weak (widows, orphans, and the poor) to the care of the royal administration. Failing in this responsibility, a king could be asked to relinquish the throne. This point is made in the Canaanite myth of Keret, whose son accuses him of failing to judge the cause of the widow, the wretched, and the poor and of failing to feed orphans and widows. See J. B. Pritchard, ed., *Ancient Near Eastern Texts Relating to the Old Testament*, 3rd ed. (Princeton, N.J.: Princeton University Press, 1969), 149.

14. The author of Deuteronomy identifies the powerless quite specifically: widows, orphans, strangers, and the needy. Psalm 10 does not belong to the discourse that characterizes Deuteronomy, for two of the four elements are missing: the needy (*'ebyonim*) and strangers (*gerim*). The word for the needy does occur, however, in Psalm 9:

> For the needy (*'ebyon*) will not always be forgotten;
> the hope of the humble will never perish. (v 19)

Here the desires of lowly subjects are couched in terms of hope (*tiqwat*). In 10:17 a different noun is used for this concept, one that emphasizes longing (*ta'awat*).

15. Frank Crüsemann, "The Unchangeable World: The 'Crisis of Wisdom' in Koheleth," in *The God of the Lowly: Socio-historical Interpretations of the Bible*, ed. Willy Schottroff and Wolfgang Stegemann, trans. Matthew J. O'Connell (Maryknoll, N.Y.: Orbis, 1984), 57–77, places Qoheleth in the company of the wealthy who lack compassion for the poor. The changing status of the family under the monarchy created wide divisions in society, on which see Leo G. Perdue, Joseph Blenkinsopp, John J. Collins,

and Carol Meyers, eds., *Families in Ancient Israel* (Louisville: Westminster John Knox, 1997).

16. Magne Saebø, "*nābāl* fool," in *Theological Lexicon of the Old Testament*, ed. Jenni and Westermann, 2:710–14.

17. James L. Crenshaw, *Old Testament Wisdom: An Introduction*, revised and enlarged (Louisville: Westminster John Knox, 1998), 67–68. Stephen A. Mandry, *There Is No God! A Study of the Fool in the Old Testament, Particularly in Proverbs and Qoheleth* (Rome: Officium Libri Catholici; Catholic Book Agency, 1972), 55–56, summarizes the nuances of the eight words for fool. Of *nabal* he writes: "practical atheist; denies explicitly immanent divine presence in his life in the form of unrestrained violence against neighbor; sexual perversion notable in him; very proud, very rebellious; enormous powers of destruction; always meets a violent death" (56).

18. The later author of the Testament of Job endeavors to salvage the reputation of Job's much-maligned wife: in this document, she is both loyal and devout.

19. An interesting twist on this familiar story has been provided by Pamela Reis, *Reading the Lines: A Fresh Look at the Hebrew Bible* (Peabody, Mass.: Hendrickson, 2002). Reis finds sufficient hints in the narrative to argue that Tamar was not wholly innocent in this union of brother and sister.

20. Compare the prophet Jeremiah, who excludes himself from a Jerusalemite population that he considers devoid of a single virtuous person. A similar rhetorical stance is taken in the Greek story about Diogenes walking through the city of Athens with lantern in hand, searching for a single good person. Roman Garrison, *Why Are You Silent, Lord?* (Sheffield: Sheffield Academic Press, 2000), discusses the extent to which ancient Greeks and Romans reflected on theodicy, from Theognis to Epictetus and Seneca. Garrison traces the theme of innocent suffering in the Iliad, especially that of Hector and Sarpedon; the Heracles tradition in the writings of Euripides and Sophocles; the life of Socrates from the differing perspectives of Xenophon and Plato; and Stoic writings by Musonius Rufus, Epictetus, and Seneca. From his survey, it is clear that polytheism did not entirely escape the problem that plagues monotheism.

21. Myths of the destruction of humankind—often, to control a burgeoning population—are well known in the ancient Near East. The Babylonian flood story depicts the creation of humans as an attempt to free the gods from menial service in the temple. When the ever-increasing population disturbs their sleep, the deities decide to destroy the entire human race. This approach is soon shown to be too severe, so other means of reducing the population are devised, such as restricting marriage and procreation for certain groups and limiting humans by making them mortal. For this myth, see Benjamin R. Foster, *From Distant Days: Myths, Tales, and Poetry of Ancient Mesopotamia* (Bethesda, Md.: CDL, 1995), 52–77. The intended destruction of humanity is also the subject of Egyptian and Sumerian myths (see Pritchard, *Ancient Near Eastern Texts*, 10–11, 42–44) in which the endangered species is rescued by a god—Re in Egypt, Enki in Mesopotamia—each through secretive action.

22. The problem, therefore, in the biblical account of the flood and its immediate aftermath is something other than overpopulation. The Yahwist emphasizes an ethical breach that has become virtually universal as the sole cause of the flood. Still,

remnants of the Mesopotamian source are easily detected in the biblical version, the most glaring from a religious standpoint being the anthropomorphic picture of YHWH smelling the aroma of Noah's sacrifice. The exquisitely structured story of the building of a tower to heaven bears witness to ancient fascination with linguistic differences. The biblical deity is described as responsible for these varying language systems but also capable of transcending their differences (see Joel 3:1–2 and its use in Acts 2:1–21).

23. According to Sigmund Mowinckel, *The Psalms in Israel's Worship*, vol. 2 (Nashville: Abingdon, 1962), 209, the term *maskil* indicates something of the supranormal in a cultic poem. The verb itself refers to skill in achieving success at an endeavor; it also has a distinct intellectual bent. Terrien, *The Psalms*, 29, interprets the *maskil* as "an individual meditation, hummed or murmured as a private introspection." The contrasting opinions of these modern scholars indicate our inadequate grasp of many superscriptions in the Psalter. See M. Saebø, "*śkl* hi. to have insight," in *Theological Lexicon of the Old Testament*, ed. Jenni and Westermann, 3:1269–72, esp. 1271.

24. On the echoes of Amos's biography in the legend about the man of God from Judah and the old prophet from Bethel, see James L. Crenshaw, *Prophetic Conflict: Its Effect upon Israelite Religion* (Berlin: de Gruyter, 1971), 39–46.

25. Hans J. Stoebe, "*tôb* good," in *Theological Lexicon of the Old Testament*, ed. Jenni and Westermann, 2:486–95. Naturally, this word has a broad range of meanings, depending on the context. Applied to people, it originally referred to warriors' skill, later coming to have ethical connotations and forming a natural contrast to *ra'* (bad). Later texts, especially psalms, apply the word *tob* to YHWH.

26. If the initial interrogative carries over to the second colon, the sense is less forceful: "Do they not call on YHWH?"

27. Johan Renkema, "Theodicy in Lamentations," in *Theodicy in the World of the Bible*, ed. Laato and de Moor, 410–28, detects no absolute defense of YHWH in this book, even in Lam 1:18 and 3:37–39 or 3:42, where interpreters usually find an acknowledgment that the deity is the source of evil. Renkema emphasizes the structural centrality of famine, along with the people's gentle admission of some guilt, both unintentional and from ignorance about which prophets spoke the truth, those offering comfort or those threatening Jerusalem's downfall. He underlines the existential crisis brought on by the alien work of the deity but thinks that the miserable victims of the siege appeal to God beyond God. Even the formula "Righteous is he, YHWH" in 1:18 does not strike Renkema as a theodicy; similarly, his interpretation of 3:37–39 as having nothing to do with creating absolute evil removes the text from rational defense of God. For Renkema, the people described in Lamentations truly believe in YHWH's goodness even in the face of such horrible suffering.

28. Biblical interpreters have made considerable strides toward understanding the importance of irony to ancient authors, but less progress has been made in the area of exaggeration for effect. Certain types of literature invite excess, particularly petitionary laments directed at securing a favorable hearing from the deity or from roy-

alty. Here overstatement is the norm, and interpreters should be wary of pressing this language too far in the direction of its literal sense.

29. The psalmist's use of the expansive *bedor tsaddiq* (generation of the righteous) instead of the simple *tsaddiq* (righteous) recalls Prov 30:11–14, where distinct types of people are indicated by the word *dor* (generation). Some show disrespect for parents, others think of themselves as pure although definitely unclean, still others are arrogant, and some are vicious devourers of the poor. The reference to eating the defenseless links this text with the sentiment expressed in Psalm 14. On this unit as the logical conclusion to Agur's skepticism, see James L. Crenshaw, *Urgent Advice and Probing Questions: Collected Writings on Old Testament Wisdom* (Macon, Ga.: Mercer University Press, 1995), 371–82. This limited sense of the noun *dor* to refer to a specific group within the larger community is rare (see also Pss 24:6 and 112:2); see G. Gerleman, "*dôr* generation," in *Theological Lexicon of the Old Testament*, ed. Jenni and Westermann, 1:333–35. Its usual meaning is temporal, implying duration.

30. This construction, in which a noun is formed from the same consonants as the verb, generally indicates intensification or emphasis. See B. K. Waltke and M. O'Connor, *An Introduction to Biblical Hebrew Syntax* (Winona Lake, Ind.: Eisenbrauns, 1990), 167 (161–86 for accusatives in general); E. Kautzsh, ed., *Gesenius' Hebrew Grammar*, trans. A. E. Cowley, 2nd ed. (Oxford: Clarendon, 1910), §117 p–v.

31. A human aversion to mentioning an object of dread may be rooted in the belief that hostile forces lurk in the shadows waiting to be summoned by specific vocabulary. Sheol and the entry to that realm, death, belong to such potential harbingers of ill. The use of euphemisms for Sheol does not appear to relate to any belief in punishment during the afterlife, which did not develop in Israelite literature until the Persian period. The poet may have had in mind the common belief, grounded in the story of human origins, that the earth is both the source and the destiny of all mortals.

32. J. J. Scullion, "Righteousness," in *Anchor Bible Dictionary*, ed. D. N. Freedman, 6 vols. (New York: Doubleday, 1992), 5:724–36, and especially Henning Graf Reventlow and Yair Hoffman, eds., *Justice and Righteousness: Biblical Themes and Their Influence* (Sheffield: Sheffield Academic Press, 1992).

33. The notion of the deity as an asylum for endangered Israelites has been seen as an important structural device in the Psalter by Jerome F. D. Creach, *Yahweh as Refuge and the Editing of the Hebrew Psalter* (Sheffield: Sheffield Academic Press, 1996). See also P. Hugger, *Jahwe meine Zuflucht: Gestalt und Theologie des 91. Psalms* (Würzburg: Vier-Türme, 1971).

34. James L. Crenshaw, *Joel* (New York: Doubleday, 1995), 173–74.

35. A proper receptacle for the bones of the dead functioned symbolically to indicate respect and, in later times, to assure complete participation in the anticipated resurrection. Scattered bones were therefore a sign of disrespect and entailed restlessness in Sheol. Israel's experience with ruthless warriors who left the dead to scavengers' appetites gave birth to the hope that at some future date YHWH would gather up the scattered bones and renew life. Ben Sira links this hope with the twelve

Minor Prophets: "May the bones of the twelve prophets revive from where they lie, for they comforted the people of Jacob and delivered them with confident hope" (Sir 49:10), whereas Ezekiel 37 associates the idea with national resurgence.

36. The metaphor of the shepherd was widely applied to deities in the ancient world and, by extension, to earthly rulers. This concept fit nicely into a rural society where evidence of tending sheep and goats was everywhere. Experience taught the closely observant that not every shepherd was worthy of the label, and that disturbing fact applied frequently to royalty. Biblical acknowledgment of this tainted image occurs in Ezek 34:1–31 (with reference to faithless prophets in contrast to YHWH and the ideal prince, David) and in Zech 10:3 and 11:4–17.

37. Richard B. Hays, *Echoes of Scripture in the Letters of Paul* (New Haven, Conn.: Yale University Press, 1989), has developed criteria for recognizing direct allusion to earlier Scripture. This task is enormously complex, given the vitality of oral tradition in the ancient world. Antecedents to Christian "echoes" of Scripture have been detected by Michael Fishbane, *Biblical Interpretation in Ancient Israel* (Oxford: Clarendon, 1985), and Siegfried Bergler, *Joel als Schriftinterpret* (Frankfurt am Main: Peter Lang, 1988).

38. The sages' openness to the world stands in sharp contrast to the covenantal ideology in its normal expression, although nationalism was always subjected to criticism by individuals who understood election as responsibility rather than privilege. The authors of wisdom literature recognized truth regardless of its source, although the pressure to incorporate sacred tradition into these universal insights eventually prevailed. Ben Sira took the lead, even going so far as to introduce a synopsis of biblical history as depicted in the lives of leading figures, and the author of Wisdom of Solomon concentrated largely on the story of the exodus from Egypt.

39. On these collections, see Crenshaw, *Old Testament Wisdom*, 55–88, and the bibliography there. The solitary collection attributed to a female, Prov 31:1–9, is treated in Crenshaw, *Urgent Advice and Probing Questions*, 383–95.

40. Crenshaw, *Urgent Advice and Probing Questions*, 371–82.

41. The place of prayer in wisdom literature has yet to be studied to the degree that it has been examined in historical texts, but see Crenshaw, "The Restraint of Reason, the Humility of Prayer," in *The Echoes of Many Texts: Reflections on Jewish and Christian Traditions. Essays in Honor of Lou H. Silberman*, ed. William G. Dever and J. Edward Wright (Atlanta: Scholars Press, 1997), 81–97 (= Crenshaw, *Urgent Advice and Probing Questions*, 206–21). Samuel E. Balentine, "Prayers for Justice in the Old Testament: Theodicy and Theology," *Catholic Biblical Quarterly* 51 (2001): 597–616, and Balentine, "Prayer in the Wilderness Traditions: In Pursuit of Divine Justice," *Hebrew Annual Review* 9 (1985): 53–74, has begun to relate biblical prayer and theodicy, supplementing his perceptive study of prayer in general in Balentine, *Prayer in the Hebrew Bible* (Minneapolis: Fortress, 1993).

42. Speculation about an individual's ascension to the heavens has a long history in the ancient Near East. This myth of a mortal who was summoned to appear in heaven before the gods was used as an explanation for finitude. On Ea's advice, Adapa refuses the hospitality of the gods and forfeits his immortality because of his

faithfulness to the counsel of the normally kind patron deity (Foster, *From Distant Days*, 97–101). Later apocalyptic literature reenergizes such speculation, kept alive by texts like Prov 30:4, on which see Raymond C. Van Leeuwen, "The Background to Proverbs 30:4aα," in *Wisdom, You Are My Sister: Studies in Honor of Roland E. Murphy, O. Carm., on the Occasion of His Eightieth Birthday*, ed. Michael L. Barré (Washington, D.C.: Catholic Biblical Association, 1997), 102–21.

43. James C. Vanderkam, *Enoch: A Man for All Generations* (Columbia: University of South Carolina Press, 1995), explores the various traditions about this ancient figure and traces them back to Mesopotamian lore about seven sages.

44. Paul Franklyn, "The Sayings of Agur in Proverbs 30: Piety or Skepticism?" *Zeitschrift für die alttestamentliche Wissenschaft* 95 (1983): 238–52.

45. James L. Crenshaw, *Ecclesiastes* (Philadelphia: Westminster, 1987), 189–92. Michael V. Fox, *A Time to Tear Down and a Time to Build Up: A Re-reading of Ecclesiastes* (Grand Rapids, Mich.: Eerdmans, 1999), offers an alternative view based on different voices in the author's narrative strategy.

CHAPTER 2

1. Ancient peoples believed that gods could die, perhaps because of the association of some deities with the seasons but also because the gods were often portrayed in anthropological categories. Their exclusive claim to heaven, and heaven's eventual democratization, has been lucidly described by J. Edward Wright, *The Early History of Heaven* (Oxford: Oxford University Press, 2000). Concerning 1 Enoch, he writes: "Thus, as it was earlier formulated among the Persians and Greeks, heaven became a very exclusive club where only the truly deserving would go after death to join the divine" (137), and "Heaven was becoming [in 3 Baruch, 2 Enoch, and Apocalypse of Shedrach] a place with rigorously exclusive admission standards" (184). Wright notes the dark side of this thinking at Qumran, where such visions "also create[d] a dangerous sense of superiority over outsiders by dehumanizing or demonizing them" (202).

2. A sobering reminder that the psalmist's feet are firmly planted in reality concludes the remarkable psalm. Even the one remaining deity must be admonished to establish justice. In short, that much-sought-after goal continues to elude society; monotheism has not removed inequity among human beings.

3. For discussion of this sublime expression of self-examination, see James L. Crenshaw, *The Psalms: An Introduction* (Grand Rapids, Mich.: Eerdmans, 2001), 109–27, and the bibliography listed there.

4. The ancient notion of a divine kingdom on earth, seemingly confirming the philosophical concept of teleology, has persisted into modern liberalism, only to erode with each new conflict that has revealed the nature of humans as corrupt.

5. Nietzsche's well-known remark about the death of God and its aftermath appear to have left no permanent scars on the masses who still believe that the deity is alive and well. Even Dietrich Bonhoeffer's Christianity without God (despite his deeply christological and theocentric faith) has dimmed, although post-Holocaust Judaism has come close to jettisoning belief in a deity.

6. Christian reaction to such confident assertions has been especially intense among fundamentalists, who see their worldview under attack. They have countered with increased emphasis on the literal inerrancy of Scripture and its historical factic- ity. The tenacity with which they cling to cherished beliefs, however, makes them vul- nerable ultimately to self-delusion. From the perspective of many, Julian Huxley is right that anyone who believes in God is like a blind person in a dark room searching for a cat that isn't there *and finding it*; see Julian Huxley, "The Creed of a Scientific Humanist," in *The Meaning of Life*, ed. E. D. Klemke, 2d ed. (New York: Oxford Uni- versity Press, 2000), 79. The names of Nietzsche, Feuerbach, Freud, Sartre, and oth- ers linger in the background and demand honesty rather than reflexive denial. Many modern theists seem ignorant of the rich tradition of protest within the Bible itself. Honest wrestling with the uncertainties of the ancients links believers over millennia at the existential level. Perhaps one result of such struggle today would be a reduction of triumphalism, Christianity's greatest shame.

7. I refer to the title of a profoundly moving book by Neil Gillman, *The Death of Death: Resurrection and Immortality in Jewish Thought* (Woodstock, Vt.: Jewish Lights, 1997).

8. See Michael D. Goulder, *The Psalms of Asaph and the Pentateuch* (Sheffield: Sheffield Academic Press, 1996), and Samuel Terrien, *The Psalms: Strophic Structure and Theological Commentary* (Grand Rapids, Mich.: Eerdmans, 2003), 394–95 (for ex- tensive bibliography).

9. For an imaginative reconstruction of an ancient festival at Bethel during the 720s in which the psalms of Asaph were used, see Goulder, *Psalms of Asaph and the Pentateuch*. Every effort at reconstructing festivals in ancient Israel must rely on mea- ger data in the Bible and considerable imagination informed by analogy from cultic practices in Egypt and Mesopotamia. Even the pioneering work of Sigmund Mow- inckel, *The Psalms in Israel's Worship* (Nashville: Abingdon, 1962), did not successfully overcome that obstacle when postulating an annual New Year's ceremony of en- thronement.

10. David A. Carr, *The Erotic Word: Sexuality, Spirituality, and the Bible* (Oxford: Oxford University Press, 2003), 59–65, relates this text to others in the Bible that de- scribe YHWH as a jealous husband who resorts to violence against an unfaithful wife (Israel).

11. Attempts to reproduce the pun in English have not been successful. In He- brew the words are *mishpat/mispakh* (justice/bloodletting) and *tsedaqah/tse'aqah* (righteousness/outcry).

12. Within the Asaph collection, these questions explode with tremendous force in four psalms: 74, 79, 80, and 82.

13. The great tautology of Exod 3:13–14 has been interpreted by some to mean "I shall be present" in a compassionate sense.

14. Psalms 42–83 prefer the name Elohim over YHWH, although the differing versions complicate matters and encourage some scholars to reject the hypothesis of an Elohistic collection. Absent that explanation, however, it is difficult to account for

the use of Elohim in place of YHWH in a psalm that is duplicated—Psalm 14 [53]—even if the practice is inconsistent.

15. Philological interest controls the analysis of this psalm by James Ackerman, "An Exegetical Study of Psalm 82" (Ph.D. diss., Harvard University, 1966); theology and tradition occupy the attention of Hans-Winfried Jüngling in *Der Tod der Götter: Eine Untersuchung zu Psalm 82* (Stuttgart: Kathölisches Bibelwerk, 1969).

16. Conceivably, v 5 also derives from this same speaker, although its reference to earth's tottering foundations would be an appropriate conclusion to the divine sentence.

17. The absence of any reference to widows has yet to be explained, but the choice of *rash* (the oppressed) may have been dictated by a desire to create a pun on *resha'im* (the wicked), for the two words in Hebrew have the same consonants (with the exception of the *'ayin*, which is nonvocal).

18. Julien Morgenstern, "The Mythological Background of Psalm 82," *Hebrew Union College Annual* 14 (1939): 29–126.

19. Oswald Loretz, "Aspekte der kanaanäischen Gottes-So(‖ö)hn(e)-Tradition im Alten Testament," *Ugarit-Forschungen* 7 (1975): 587–88.

20. Peter Höffken, "Werden und Vergehen der Götter," *Theologische Zeitschrift* 39 (1983): 129–37, and Jüngling, *Tod der Götter*.

21. The debate continues into the modern era, as reflected in the following articles: Roger T. O'Callaghan, SJ, "A Note on the Canaanite Background of Psalm 82," *Catholic Biblical Quarterly* 15 (1953): 311–14; Matitiahu Tsevat, "God and the Gods in Assembly," *Hebrew Union College Annual* 40 (1969): 123–37; Gerald Cooke, "The Sons of (the) God(s)," *Zeitschrift für die alttestamentliche Wissenschaft* 76 (1974): 22–47; Höffken, "Werden und Vergehen der Götter"; Jerome H. Neyrey, SJ, " 'I Said: You Are Gods': Psalm 82:6 and John 10," *Journal of Biblical Literature* 108 (1989): 647–63; Morgenstern, "Mythological Background of Psalm 82"; Herbert Niehr, "Götter oder Menschen—eine falsche Alternative: Bemerkungen zu Psalm 82," *Zeitschrift für die alttestamentliche Wissenschaft* 99 (1987): 94–98; Simon Parker, "The Beginning of the Reign of God: Psalm 82 as Myth and Liturgy," *Revue biblique* 102 (1995): 532–59; W. W. Prinsloo, "Psalm 82: Once Again, Gods or Men?" *Biblica* 76 (1995): 219–28; and E. T. Mullen Jr., *The Assembly of the Gods: The Divine Council in Canaanite and Early Hebrew Literature* (Chico, Calif.: Scholars Press, 1980). Additional bibliography can be found in Erhard S. Gerstenberger, *Psalms, Part 2, and Lamentations* (Grand Rapids, Mich.: Eerdmans, 2001), 115–17.

22. Convenient discussions can be found in Patrick D. Miller, *The Religion of Ancient Israel* (London: Society for the Propagation of Christian Knowledge; Louisville: Westminster John Knox, 2000); Wright, *Early History of Heaven*; and Mark S. Smith, *The Early History of God: Yahweh and the Other Deities in Ancient Israel*, 2nd ed. (San Francisco: Harper & Row, 2002).

23. Victor P. Hamilton, "Satan," in *Anchor Bible Dictionary*, ed. D. N. Freedman, 6 vols. (New York: Doubleday, 1992), 5:985–89; Rivkah Schärf Kluger, *Satan in the Old Testament*, trans. Hildegard Nagel (Evanston, Ill.: Northwestern University Press,

1967); Peggy L. Day, *An Adversary in Heaven: Satan in the Hebrew Bible* (Atlanta: Scholars Press, 1988); Elaine Pagels, *The Origin of Satan* (New York: Oxford University Press, 1995); and Ruth Nanda Anshen, *The Reality of the Devil: Evil in Man* (New York: Harper & Row, 1972). Anshen's experience is hardly unique. She writes: "That evil is an inherent element in the universe I soon saw all around me: in the pitiless affliction of suffering on the innocent, the helpless, the just; in the relentless eruptions and devastations of nature against human life. Above all, I saw the unbearable indifference of the universe to human aspirations and human suffering. As Euripides said: This is a universe where justice is accidental and innocence no protection" (xii).

24. Gary A. Anderson, *The Genesis of Perfection: Adam and Eve in Jewish and Christian Imagination* (Louisville: Westminster John Knox, 2001), combines philology, artistic representation, and classical theological reflection to grasp the complex meaning of the biblical story of beginnings.

25. There seems to be little doubt that the early Israelites accepted the worldview of polytheism. The exact origin of belief in the deity YHWH cannot be determined, whether as a mountain warrior-god or as a spin-off of El worship. Those interpreters who emphasize YHWH's fierce nationalism favor the first option, while those who give more weight to the deity's universalistic features grounded in myths of creation prefer the second. Perhaps both understandings were held from the beginning, for ancient Near Eastern peoples were not constrained by later Greek rational thinking. Inconsistencies merely expressed different aspects of the same reality.

26. The midrash on Ps 82:6–7 interprets the statement in terms of Israel: exalted to immortality at Sinai, but stripped of this godlike status with the episode of the golden calf.

27. Höffken, "Werden und Vergehen der Götter," rightly underscores the significance of this difference.

28. See Tsevat, "God and the Gods in Assembly," 127.

29. According to Otto Eissfeldt, "El and Yahweh," in *Kleine Schriften*, ed. R. Sellheim and F. Maas, vol. 3 (Tübingen: Mohr, 1966), 386–97 (originally published in *Journal of Semitic Studies* 1 [1956]: 25–37).

30. Alternatively, might the words *ke'adam* (man) and *uke'akhad hassarim* (prince) constitute a merismus, meaning "commoner and prince, thus everyone"? I have opted for the mythic interpretation in both instances, reading "like Adam" and "like one of the Princes." The ancient orthography, a strengthening *n* attached to the verb *temutu*, supports an early tradition unless this reading is an instance of archaizing. So, too, does the parallel in Deut 32:8–9 in the Qumran fragment, which has *bene 'elim* (divine beings) rather than "Israelites" ("When Elyon allocated the nations, when he divided humankind, he fixed the people's boundaries according to the number of divine beings [*bene 'elim*], but YHWH's own portion was his people, Jacob his inheritance").

31. For discussion of Amos's oracles against the nations, see John Barton, *Understanding Old Testament Ethics: Approaches and Explorations* (Louisville: Westminster John Knox, 2003), 77–129.

CHAPTER 3

1. Cornelis Houtman, "Theodicy in the Pentateuch," in *Theodicy in the World of the Bible*, ed. Antti Laato and Johannes C. de Moor (Leiden: Brill, 2003), 151–82, writes that "the entire primeval history (Gen. 1–11) may be interpreted as a justification of God. Human sin and rebellion are the cause of all evils that beset men—death, pain, murder, violence, etc." (152 n 4). Houtman lays aside all criticism based on modern sensibilities—for example, YHWH's slaughter of Egyptian children—and discusses only what troubled ancient authors. As early as Wisdom of Solomon, however, this particular problem required a rationale, and it may antedate this first-century text. Houtman's approach raises an important question: Is objective analysis, assuming its possibility (which I do not), the proper approach to the study of a topic such as theodicy? The introduction to *Theodicy in the World of the Bible* favors descriptive analysis (xviii–xix) over ideological critique or existential analysis, but I believe that interpreters should be guided by the particular text they are examining, with descriptive analysis as the first step in every instance, but not necessarily the final step. Ancient authors were not insensitive to moral issues like the slaughtering of innocents, nor should we be—even out of respect for Scripture. Silence has allowed sacred texts free rein to wreak havoc on human lives. Perhaps that recognition surfaces in Houtman's concluding observations about the state of flux in images of YHWH.

2. Karel van der Toorn, Bob Becking, and Pieter W. van der Horst, eds., *Dictionary of Deities and Demons in the Bible*, 2d ed. (Leiden: Brill, 1999). The older standard work on the dark side of the biblical deity is Paul Volz, *Das Dämonische in Jahwe* (Tübingen: Mohr, 1924). This language has been challenged by Fredrick Lindström, *God and the Origin of Evil: A Contextual Analysis of Alleged Monistic Evidence in the Old Testament* (Lund: Gleerup, 1983). Nevertheless, the Bible preserves remnants of belief that can best be described as demonic, hence its retention in the title of this chapter.

3. A medieval poem expresses this triumph by indicating that the warrior's bow, the rainbow, has the arrow turned toward God so that mortals can let it fly should the deity forget the promise not to send destruction again.

4. On divine literacy, see Shalom M. Paul, "Heavenly Tablets and the Book of Life," *Journal of the Ancient Near Eastern Society of Columbia University* 5 (1973): 345–53.

5. This observation concerns literary strategy only, without making any judgment about the ultimate origin of these texts.

6. Jon L. Berquist, *Judaism in Persia's Shadow: A Social and Historical Approach* (Minneapolis: Fortress, 1995), and Charles E. Carter, *The Emergence of Yehud in the Persian Period: A Social and Demographic Study* (Sheffield: Sheffield Academic Press, 1999).

7. See, above all, David Penchansky and Paul L. Redditt, eds., *Shall Not the Judge of All the Earth Do What Is Right? Studies on the Nature of God in Tribute to James L. Crenshaw* (Winona Lake, Ind.: Eisenbrauns, 2000); David Penchansky, *What Rough*

Beast? Images of God in the Hebrew Bible (Louisville: Westminster John Knox, 1999); and Jack Miles, *God: A Biography* (New York: Knopf, 1995), 308–28.

8. Karl-Johan Illman, "Theodicy in Job," in *Theodicy in the World of the Bible*, ed. Laato and de Moor, 304–33, rightly insists that the prologue and epilogue of Job be studied contrastively with the rest of the book. He works with Green's types of theodicy, despite their inexact application to the book of Job.

9. From the massive literature on Genesis 22, I highlight the following studies, of different types: Shalom Spiegel, *The Last Trial* (New York: Schocken, 1967); Gerhard von Rad, *Das Opfer des Abraham* (Munich: Kaiser, 1971); Georg Steins, *Die "Bindung Isaaks im Kanon" (Gen 22): Grundlagen und Programm einer kanonisch-intertextuellen Lektüre* (Freiburg: Herder, 1999); Jürgen Ebach, *Gott im Wort: Drei Studien zur biblischen Exegese und Hermeneutik* (Neukirchen-Vluyn: Neukirchener, 1997), 1–25; Ellen F. Davis, "Self-Consciousness and Conversation: Reading Genesis 22," *Bulletin for Biblical Research* 1 (1991): 27–40; Mishael Maswari Caspi and Sascha Benjamin Cohen, *The Binding [Aqedah] and Its Transformations in Judaism and Islam* (Lewiston, N.Y.: Mellen Biblical Press, 1995); Andreas Michel, "Ijob und Abraham: Zur Rezeption von Gen 22 in Ijob 1–2 und 42,7–17," in *Gott, Mensch, Sprache: Schülerfestschrift für Walter Gross zum 60. Geburtstag*, ed. Andreas Michel and Hermann-Josef Stipp (St. Ottilien: EOS, 2001), 73–97; David Volgger, "Es geht um das Ganze: Gott prüft Abraham (Gen 22,1–19)," *Biblische Zeitschrift* 45 (2001): 1–19; Robin M. Jensen, "The Offering of Isaac in Jewish and Christian Tradition: Image and Text," *Biblical Illustrator* 2 (1994): 86–220; Peter Höffken, "Genesis 22 als religions pädagogisches Problem," in *Frömmigkeit und Freiheit: theologische, ethische, und seelsorgerliche Anfragen*, ed. Friedrich Wintzer, Henning Schröer, and Johannes Heide (Rheinbach-Merzbach: CMZ, 1995), 221–37; Géza Vermès, *Scripture and Tradition in Judaism: Haggadic Studies* (Leiden: Brill, 1961), 193–227; Bruce N. Fisk, "Offering Isaac Again and Again: Pseudo-Philo's Use of the Aqedah as Intertext," *Catholic Biblical Quarterly* 62 (2000): 481–507; Jon D. Levenson, *The Death and Resurrection of the Beloved Son: The Transformation of Child Sacrifice in Judaism and Christianity* (New Haven, Conn.: Yale University Press, 1993); and Andreas Michel, *Gott und Gewalt gegen Kinder in Alten Testament* (Tübingen: Mohr Siebeck, 2003).

10. See Höffken, "Genesis 22 als religions pädagogisches Problem."

11. Critics of this latter view point out that nowhere does the story actually oppose human sacrifice. Narratives operate more subtly than that, however, and this story certainly stops short of reporting an actual immolation of the son Isaac, even if it may presuppose it.

12. Steins, *"Bindung Isaaks im Kanon,"* emphasizes the associations between this story and the Pentateuch, especially the exodus narrative.

13. The necessity of reading Genesis 22 through a Christian lens has been emphasized by R. W. L. Moberly, "Christ as the Key to Scripture: Genesis 22 Reconsidered," in *He Swore an Oath: Biblical Themes from Genesis 12–50*, ed. R. S. Hess (Grand Rapids, Mich.: Eerdmans, 1994), 143–73, and Moberly *The Bible, Theology, and Faith: A Study of Abraham and Jesus* (Cambridge: Cambridge University Press, 2000).

14. Erich Auerbach, *Mimesis* (Princeton, N.J.: Princeton University Press, 1953).

Auerbach compared this story with the Homeric account of Odysseus' scar, describing the latter style as foregrounding.

15. Ephraim A. Speiser, *Genesis* (Garden City, N.Y: Doubleday, 1964), 165: "The short and simple sentence, 'And the two of them walked on together' (8), covers what is perhaps the most poignant and eloquent silence in all literature."

16. Sanhedrin 86b credits this insight to Rashi.

17. Spiegel, *Last Trial*, elegantly traces this development. Within the larger narrative, the story's effect shows up in subtle ways. Sarah does not speak from this point on, although she has been an active and vocal presence until now.

18. Vermès, *Scripture and Tradition in Judaism*.

19. The rabbis calculated Isaac's age as 37 from the haggadah that Sarah, who was 90 when Isaac was born and 127 at the time of her death, died upon hearing that Isaac had been killed.

20. Søren Kierkegaard, *Fear and Trembling* (Garden City, N.Y.: Doubleday, 1941).

21. James L. Crenshaw, *A Whirlpool of Torment: Israelite Traditions of God as an Oppressive Presence* (Philadelphia: Fortress, 1984), 9–29.

22. Ludwig Schmidt, *"De Deo": Studien zur Literaturkritik und Theologie des Buches Jona, des Gesprächs zwischen Abraham und Jahwe in Gen. 18,22ff. und von Hi 1* (Berlin: de Gruyter, 1976).

23. Steins, *"Bindung Isaaks im Kanon,"* 163–86.

24. James L. Mays, " 'Now I Know': An Exposition of Genesis 22:1–19 and Matthew 26:36–46," *Theology Today* 58 (2002): 519–25.

25. See Ellen F. Davis, "Vulnerability, the Condition of Covenant," in *The Art of Reading Scripture* ed. E. F. Davis and Richard Hays (Grand Rapids, Mich.: Eerdmans, 2003), 277–93. I pursue the notion of God's vulnerability in chapter 4.

26. Shelby Brown, *Late Carthaginian Child Sacrifice and Sacrificial Monuments in Their Mediterranean Context* (Sheffield: JSOT Press, 1991).

27. Spiegel, *Last Trial*.

28. "Abraham should have replied to this putative divine voice: 'That I may not kill my good son is absolutely certain. But that you who appear to me are God is not certain and cannot become certain, even though the voice were to sound from the very heavens.' [For] that a voice which one seems to hear cannot be divine one can be certain of . . . in case what is commanded is contrary to moral law. However majestic or supernatural it may appear to be, one must regard it as a deception." Kant, *Streit der Fakultagten*, cited in Emil Fackenheim, *Encounters between Judaism and Modern Philosophy: A Preface to Future Jewish Thought* (New York: Schocken, 1973), 34.

29. Davis, "Self-Consciousness and Conversation 2," 31–32.

30. Hermann Gunkel, *Genesis*, 8th ed. (Göttingen: Vandenhoeck & Ruprecht, 1969), 237.

31. Early Christian interpreters understood Isaac's burden as a prefigurement of the cross that Jesus was forced to carry on the road to Golgotha. R. W. L. Moberly, "The Earliest Commentary on the Akedah," *Vetus Testamentum* 38 (1988): 302–23.

32. Kierkegaard, *Fear and Trembling*, 27–28.

33. Ellen F. Davis, *Getting Involved with God: Rediscovering the Old Testament*

(Cambridge, Mass.: Cowley, 2001), 58. Rad, *Opfer des Abraham*, reproduces this gripping scene.

34. Spiegel, *Last Trial*, 15. The full text reads as follows: "Go and tell Father Abraham: Let not your heart swell with pride! You built one altar, but I have built seven altars and on them have offered up my seven sons. What is more: Yours was a trial; mine was an accomplished fact!" (Yalkut Deut 26, 938).

35. The literature on this book is staggering. For discussion of the main issues, see James L. Crenshaw, "Job, Book of," in *Anchor Bible Dictionary*, ed. D. N. Freedman, 6 vols. (New York: Doubleday, 1992), 3:858–68 (= Crenshaw, *Urgent Advice and Probing Questions*, 426–48), and W. A. M. Beuken, ed., *The Book of Job* (Leuven: Leuven University Press, 1994).

36. Modern readers may be puzzled by the abrupt transition in the conversation from a report of the adversary's roaming the earth to the possibility that Job has been overlooked. This is an instance of encoded script, recognizable to ancient readers but hidden from modern ones. Most people in the postexilic environment would have been familiar with the Zoroastrian concept of divine eyes that survey the earth. The adversary is like a secret spy for the government responsible for detecting genuine fealty (cf. Zech 4:10, "These seven are the eyes of YHWH roaming throughout the earth").

37. Moriah plays on the verbs *yare'* (to fear) and *ra'ah* (to see), while Uz resembles *'etsah* (counsel) and *yo'ets* (counselor).

38. Michel, "Ijob und Abraham."

39. Tryggve N. D. Mettinger, *In Search of God: The Meaning and Message of the Everlasting Names* (Philadelphia: Fortress, 1988), 175–200. Mettinger characterizes the God of Job's friends as "the merciless engineer of the mechanisms of divine retaliation" (178).

40. Johannes Hempel, "Das theologische Problem des Hiob," *Zeitschrift für systematische Theologie* 6 (1929); reprinted in Johannes Hempel, *Apoxysmata* (Berlin: de Gruyter, 1961).

41. No one has been able to satisfactorily relate the book's framing narrative to its central poetic dialogues. Perhaps the least troublesome hypothesis takes the story of a pious Job to be the context selected by the author of the dialogues as the proper medium for exposing alternative views about innocent suffering, appropriate speech about God, and disinterested righteousness. From a modern perspective, however, once the assumption of individual reward and retribution has been refuted, it seems strange to return in the epilogue to this dubious belief. Among the commentaries, Edwin M. Good, *In Turns of Tempest: A Reading of Job with a Translation* (Stanford: Stanford University Press, 1990), best controverts the magical assumption of religion.

42. The standard commentaries treat this issue to varying degrees. See Norman C. Habel, *The Book of Job* (Philadelphia: Fortress, 1984); Marvin H. Pope, *Job* (Garden City, N.Y.: Doubleday, 1973); David J. A. Clines, *Job 1–20* (Dallas: Word, 1989); Hans Strauss, *Hiob, Kapitel 19,1–42,17* (Neukirchen-Vluyn: Neukirchener, 1963); and Carol A. Newsom, "The Book of Job," *New Interpreter's Bible* 4:317–637.

43. Job 1:1–5, 1:6–12, 1:13–22, 2:1–6, 2:7–10, 2:11–13, 42:7–10, 42:11–17.

44. Yair Hoffman, *A Blemished Perfection: The Book of Job in Context* (Sheffield: Sheffield Academic Press, 1996), firmly establishes the importance of irony to the author of the biblical book. Newsom, "Book of Job," applies this insight to the work of writing a commentary.

45. This Hebrew word, *khinnam*, has the sense of gratuitous action and thus wonderfully sums up both the nature of Job's religious conduct and the deity's harsh treatment of him. Neither was for cause; hence, the arbitrariness of Job's misery.

46. Johannes Pedersen, *Israel, Its Life and Culture*, 4 vols. (London: Oxford University Press; Copenhagen: Branner, 1926–1940), contrasted blessing and curse in a pioneering sociological study of ancient Israel. C. A. Keller and G. Wehmeier, "*brk* pi to bless," in *Theological Lexicon of the Old Testament*, ed. E. Jenni with assistance from C. Westermann, trans. M. E. Biddle, 3 vols. (Peabody, Mass.: Hendrickson, 1997), I: 266–82, list subsequent investigations into the background of blessing.

47. Klaus Koch, "*tmm* to be complete," in *Theological Lexicon of the Old Testament*, ed. E. Jenni with assistance from C. Westermann, trans. M. E. Biddle, 3 vols. (Peabody, Mass.: Hendrickson, 1997), 3:1427, writes that "only in Job and Psa 37:37 does *tām* approach *tāmîm* and become synonymous with *yāšār* (→*yšr*; Job 1:1, 8; 2:3) and antonymous to '*qš* 'to pervert.' " Elsewhere the adjective *tam* has less weight and indicates a "fine" man.

48. *Tiplah* occurs elsewhere only in Jer 23:13 and Job 24:12 (and possibly Ps 109: 4). Once thought to have come from Arabic and to mean "spit" or "prayer as protest" (cf. *tepildah*), the word is now considered to be related to *tapel* (to be tasteless; Job 6:6 and Lam 2:14).

49. One thinks of Mephistopheles' sarcastic observation about the deity's gossiping with the devil (Goethe, *Faust*, concluding lines of the Prologue; "I like, at times, to hear The Ancient's word / and have a care to be most civil: It's really kind of such a noble Lord / So humanly to gossip with the Devil!").

50. Gustavo Gutiérrez, *On Job* (Maryknoll, N.Y.: Orbis, 1987), bases this conclusion on God's commendation of Job for speaking rightly about him, in direct contrast to his three friends (Job 42:7).

51. Meir Weiss, *The Story of Job's Beginning* (Jerusalem: Magnes, 1983), and Carl G. Jung, *Answer to Job* (Cleveland: World, 1970).

CHAPTER 4

1. The classic statement regarding human puppets in YHWH's hands comes from Gerhard von Rad, "The Joseph Narrative and Ancient Wisdom," in *The Problem of the Hexateuch and Other Essays* (Edinburgh and London: Oliver & Boyd, 1966), 297. He writes: "God has all the threads firmly in his hands even when men are least aware of it. But this is a bare statement of fact, and the way in which God's will is related to human purposes remains a mystery. Thus the statements of what 'you meant' and what 'God meant' are in the last analysis irreconcilable."

2. Biblical literature is not entirely consistent on this issue, as is attested by the various stories about YHWH hardening or turning the hearts of particular individu-

als. Similar ambiguity has been detected in wisdom literature, which describes the consequences of actions as both automatic and activated by the deity. At some points the sages suggest that deeds carry within themselves the seeds of reward or punishment, while at other points they imply that direct divine action precipitates the ensuing events. It is likely, then, that ancient peoples, like modern ones, realized that actions are governed by numerous types of constraint. Actors possess freedom—of that the ancient writers were sure—but freedom is far from absolute.

3. Other writers are unwilling to abandon the notion of divine omniscience: "All is foreseen but freedom of choice is given; and the world is judged by goodness, yet all is according to the magnitude of the deed" (Pirke Aboth 3:16). In either conception, however, the outcome is the same: YHWH's power and knowledge will not displace human freedom.

4. The pervasive influence of a theological historiography shaped by the ideas of Deuteronomy has led modern critics to what has recently been dubbed pan-Deuteronomism, on which see L. S. Schearing and S. L. McKenzie, eds., *Those Elusive Deuteronomists: The Phenomenon of Pan-Deuteronomism* (Sheffield: Sheffield Academic Press, 1999).

5. The slightest hint of weakness on YHWH's part continued to trouble Jewish writers during the period of Roman dominance. A fine example of sensitivity concerning this issue occurs in the Apocalypse of Baruch (early second century CE). Baruch has a vision in which angels come to a besieged Zion and take away for safekeeping the holy items, entrust them to the earth's care until the future restoration of the temple, demolish the wall that protects the city, and then tell the Babylonian soldiers that they can enter since the guard (YHWH) has left the house. The text goes on to proclaim that the conquerors have no reason to boast about their victory over Jerusalem (2 Baruch 6–7).

6. The lamentation over the destruction of Sumer and Ur gives voice to the pathos evoked by deities' abandonment of their temple and its environs to destruction; see J. B. Pritchard, ed., *Ancient Near Eastern Texts Relating to the Old Testament*, 3rd ed. (Princeton, N.J.: Princeton University Press, 1969), 455–63. The book of Lamentations expresses similar dismay over YHWH's seeming lack of interest in Zion's fate.

7. This negative account of Israelite history was demanded by the events of 587, for few historiographers were willing to surrender belief in YHWH's trustworthiness. The only alternative was to place responsibility for Jerusalem's fall on willful humans. By this means YHWH's reputation was salvaged, but at what cost? The extent to which the Israelites' low self-esteem fed upon itself is difficult to assess. For modern minimalists, this entire depiction of Israelite history is literary fiction, a retrojection into the past of the major concerns during the exile. Maximalists are more sanguine about the actual continuity between preexilic and exilic understandings of reality.

8. Leo G. Perdue, *The Collapse of History: Deconstructing Old Testament Theology* (Minneapolis: Fortress, 1994), and Robert Gnuse, *Heilsgeschichte as a Model for Biblical Theology* (Lanham, Md.: University Press of America, 1989).

9. Stanley Brice Frost, "The Death of Josiah: A Conspiracy of Silence," *Journal of Biblical Literature* 87 (1968): 369–82, expresses surprise over the biblical authors' fail-

ure to address this shocking affront to the dominant understanding of divine solicitude. The difficulty posed by Josiah's death was magnified by the prophecy of a certain Huldah, who had announced that the king would go to his grave in peace (2 Kgs 22:18–20).

10. On this prophet, see Adele Berlin, *Zephaniah* (New York: Doubleday, 1994).

11. Debate continues to rage over the proper way to describe Israelite society, given the disparate phases in its emergence: (1) peasant revolt against authoritarian rule by Canaanite city-states; (2) peaceful acculturation with these same peoples; or (3) hostile takeover of the Judean hills at the end of an exodus from Egypt. Early village life under the leadership of a "family" head, with a tiny plot of land as a basic means of subsistence, differed appreciably from later kingdom life under the monarchs, who centralized power in Jerusalem and imposed heavy taxes. Contrast both forms of living with urban residence as a subject population in exile, and then imagine eking out a living in an impoverished postexilic Yehud under Persian control. The early family-based solidarity encountered frequent strain, both from central authority and from youth who were eager to take possession of their inheritance from aging patriarchs. In such circumstances, the original family structure gradually eroded, threatening the well-being of the weak.

12. Jeremiah 31:29. Robert P. Carroll, *Jeremiah* (Philadelphia: Westminster, 1986), 607–9, treats the proverb as integral to the discussion of a future transformation of Israel. Lamentations 5:7 has virtually the same substance but lacks the aphoristic form: "Our parents sinned and no longer exist; we must bear their guilt."

13. A rabbinic anecdote illustrates the integral nature of society and the destructive effect of one individual's conduct on the well-being of society at large. The story uses the figure of a boat and its passengers to symbolize the human community, a figure that early Christians also used to signify the church. On the boat a certain man busies himself with drilling a hole in the floor beneath him and, when confronted about his dangerous actions, maintains that he is only making a hole under himself. We may deceive ourselves into thinking that our deeds affect only ourselves, the story suggests, but ultimately our foolish behavior may place everyone around us at risk. In a sense, a society's penal code rests on the principle that hazardous conduct must be punished in order to protect the innocent.

14. The origin of ancient proverbs is the subject of much speculation. Many of them probably arose in the everyday circumstances of ordinary people, a point that Claus Westermann, *Roots of Wisdom: The Oldest Proverbs of Israel and Other Peoples* (Louisville: Westminster John Knox, 1995), has persuasively argued. More debatable are literary proverbs, sayings with an obvious artistic influence. Hans-Jürgen Hermisson, *Studien zur israelitischen Spruchweisheit* (Neukirchen-Vluyn: Neukirchener, 1968), contends that polished literary proverbs were composed by professional students. The existence of collections of proverbs in Egypt and Mesopotamia further complicates the matter, for we can be certain that schools existed in these two cultures. In assessing biblical sayings, however, it should be remembered that elegant language is not unknown among ordinary people. On ancient proverbs in unexpected places, see James L. Crenshaw, "A Proverb in the Mouth of a Fool," forthcoming.

15. Accordingly, its performance differs with the setting, a point often made by Carole Rader Fontaine, *Traditional Sayings in the Old Testament: A Contextual Study* (Sheffield: Almond, 1982).

16. Ezekiel's discussion of this legal matter of guilt or innocence presupposes two courts, one on earth and one in heaven. The decision from above, however, is mediated by humans, which in a sense places the center of power below. The discussion's context often leaves matters obscure, and readers must guess who issues the verdict, from the perspective of the text.

17. Jon Levenson's impassioned defense of all Torah as equally binding grows out of a Judaism steeped in profound ritual; see Jon D. Levenson, "The Sources of Torah: Psalm 119 and the Modes of Revelation in Second Temple Judaism," in *Ancient Israelite Religion*, ed. Patrick D. Miller, Paul D. Hanson, and S. Dean McBride (Philadelphia: Fortress, 1987), 559–74. Scholars whose presuppositions are informed by Protestant suspicion of the cult are less inclined to view some prescriptions as eternal. Perhaps the growing appreciation for ritual among Protestants, coupled with the blossoming of Catholic biblical scholarship, will bring greater appreciation for those elements of Torah that have been downplayed in the last century of biblical criticism. One can hope that this new development will lessen the divide between Jewish and Christian interpreters.

18. To communicate these insights, Ezekiel employs three literary devices: dogmatic affirmation, rhetorical question, and a double imperative. No one has stressed more strongly the importance to this prophet of writing than Ellen F. Davis, *Swallowing the Scroll: Textuality and the Dynamics of Discourse in Ezekiel's Prophecy* (Sheffield: Almond, 1989). Davis's analysis has been challenged by Katheryn Pfisterer Darr, "Write or True: A Response to Ellen Francis Davis," in *Signs and Wonders: Biblical Texts in Literary Focus*, ed. J. Cheryl Exum (Atlanta: Scholars Press, 1989), 239–47.

19. The Murashû documents from Nippur (fifth century) that have been thought to indicate a thriving Jewish presence in high finance within the exilic community can scarcely carry such weight. The majority of Judeans probably had to forge a meager existence through menial chores. Two factors may suggest that some transplanted Judeans prospered economically: first, the analogy with Egypt; second, the hesitation of some to return to Yehud when Cyrus made that possible. Still, the analogy with Alexandrian Jewry is inexact, for the migration to Egypt took place under far different circumstances, even if not wholly voluntary. See Matthew W. Stolper, "Murashû, Archive of," in *Anchor Bible Dictionary*, ed. D. N. Freedman, 6 vols. (New York: Doubleday, 1992), 4:927–28.

20. In an agrarian economy a single bad year could imperil a family, and the potential causes of crop failure were many—drought, plague, infestation, fire, warfare. Children could be sold into slavery to erase debt, and the poor entered into whatever transactions were necessary for survival. As the economy became less and less rural, mercantile interests flourished and Yehud became a money-driven economy. The divide between the haves and have-nots widened, as the book of Ecclesiastes attests: "Again I observed all the oppressions that are done under the sun: the tears of

the oppressed with none to comfort them, and from the power of the oppressors, none to comfort them" (Eccl 4:1).

21. Estimates vary as to the extent of gouging, perhaps as high as 40 percent, but the system itself encouraged abuse, with the various levels in the hierarchy of tax collectors setting an example for greed.

22. This prophet's affinities with the earlier Hosea have often been noted. Hosea, too, focuses on the commandments relative to human relationships when citing from the Decalogue: "Because there is no integrity, kindness, and knowledge of God in the land, swearing, lying, murder, theft, and adultery break out, and bloodshed touches bloodshed" (Hos 4:1b–2). The antiquity of the Ten Commandments is hotly disputed, but they probably existed in some form as early as the late eighth century.

23. Compare Ezekiel's visionary description of proscribed religious practices in the temple at Jerusalem shortly before its destruction (Ezek 8:1–18). The reliability of this portrayal of syncretism in the cult at Jerusalem is contested, not least because Ezekiel's prophetic ministry took place in Babylonian exile. Modern interpreters largely discredit the psychic powers that would have been necessary to give authenticity to Ezekiel's account, even while emphasizing the scope of such syncretism. Fresh light on this prophet's theology comes from John F. Kutsko, *Between Heaven and Earth: Divine Presence and Absence in the Book of Ezekiel* (Winona Lake, Ind.: Eisenbrauns, 2000).

24. The most striking example of a reactive audience is in the book of Malachi, where questions are posed by YHWH or his messenger and an audience responds to the charges. Such literature has rightly been called "discussion" or, better still, "contentious discussion." On this development in Israelite literature, see Julia M. O'Brien, *Priest and Levite in Malachi* (Atlanta: Scholars Press, 1990) and Eileen M. Schuller, "The Book of Malachi," *New Interpreters Bible* 7:841–77. Andrew E. Hill, *Malachi* (New York: Doubleday, 1998), 34–37, favors a didactic interpretation of the discussions, dubiously relating them to sapiential circles.

25. See the painting in Raymond O. Faulkner, *The Ancient Egyptian Book of the Dead* (New York: Macmillan, 1972), 30–31.

26. Both the location and the timing of the judicial decree, whether for life or for death, are complicating factors in Ezekiel's argument. Neither the place nor the occasion has anything to do with existence beyond the grave. Lacking any enforcement of the priestly judgment "He shall die," the words ring hollow. Ezekiel implies that YHWH will enforce the decisions granting life or imposing death, but things are not that simple. His further observations assume the deity's ownership of human beings, like that of a master with respect to his slaves, which conflicts with the stress on freedom of choice in the text.

27. Michael E. Stone, *Fourth Ezra: A Commentary on the Book of Fourth Ezra* (Minneapolis: Fortress, 1990), writes: "The answers given by the angel, however, are rather conventional. God's workings are a mystery and beyond human comprehension; God loves Israel and will vindicate Israel in the end; God rejoices over the few saved and is not concerned over the many damned; God's mercy works in this world, while his justice is fully active only in the world to come" (36).

CHAPTER 5

1. The attitude expressed by the people of Sodom is common even today in response to the boldness of "sojourners": an African American professor who assails the culture that has welcomed her, a freshman congressman who resists doing things the traditional way, a new law clerk who dares to raise objections to company policy, a novice minister who challenges ecclesiastical procedure.

2. That is, the initial identification of himself with them as brothers and the subsequent offer of two virginal daughters for their pleasure. The expressions for brotherhood (*'akhay*) and evil behavior (*tare'u* . . . *kattob be'enekem*) link this text with Judg 19:23–24, where the citizens of Gibeah demand a visitor for homosexual purposes and are offered a virgin daughter and a concubine instead.

3. The term "sodomy" derives from this biblical story and should not be projected onto the narrative, hence the quotation marks.

4. Hermann Gunkel, *Genesis* (Göttingen: Vandenhoeck & Ruprecht, 1922), 203, follows Julius Wellhausen in understanding Abraham's intercession for Sodom as a late interpolation into the Yahwistic narrative, primarily because of the way it deals with the problem of divine justice in the abstract. Classical prophets, he points out, saw no difficulty with the total punishment of a given community. Gerhard von Rad, *Genesis* (London: SCM, 1961), accepts Gunkel's general understanding of the two episodes in terms of the history of religions but goes on to emphasize the narrative's theological dimensions. Terence Fretheim's *Genesis* (Nashville: Abingdon, 1994) stands out among the several commentaries consulted in its sensitivity to the religious dimensions of the text.

5. In ancient Egypt the notion of divine judgment at death led to the picture of scales on which were placed the human heart and a feather, symbolizing justice. This powerful ethical motivation was familiar throughout the ancient Near East, as demonstrated by the frequent epithets for "divine judge."

6. John Bunyan's classic, *Pilgrim's Progress*, gives expression to the idea that human beings merely pitch their tents on earth, that their earthly existence merely offers opportunity to form character for the life to come. Given the brevity of human life, whatever understanding accrues is limited from the standpoints of time and space. This insight lies behind Immanuel Kant's observation, "It is arrogant to attempt to defend God's justice; it is still more arrogant to assail the deity" ("Uber das Misslingen aller philosophischen Versuche in der Theodizee," in *Werke*, ed. W. Weischedel [Darmstadt: Wissenschaftliche Buchgesellschaft, 1964] 6:103–24).

7. Considerable debate has raged over the extent, if any, of YHWH's subjection to an external order, whether, in Klaus Koch's words, YHWH did midwife service for the principle of deed/consequence or was thought to rule in majestic indifference to the concept. Walter Brueggemann, *Genesis* (Atlanta: John Knox, 1982), 171, recognizes the centrality of divine character in this argument.

8. The biblical deity often engages in dubious practices, at least from the modern perspective—a point that draws provocative comments from Jack Miles, *God: A Biography* (New York: Knopf, 1995), esp. 308–28, which deals with God as fiend.

9. Abraham is not always so quick to intercede. Not a word of protest escapes his lips in Genesis 22, where we would most expect it, and the patriarch proceeds to sacrifice his son on an altar without once asking why. The narrative locates the only hint of protest within the ranks of heavenly hosts, placing a jealous deity and a compassionate angel at odds. Yet when far less is at stake—two cities occupied, for the most part, by strangers—Abraham boldly questions the deity's good judgment. This silence that peals like thunder in Genesis 22 resembles the silence in the earlier story of the flood. Noah's righteousness caught God's eye but never moved the good man to implore the deity to reconsider his plan.

10. Claus Westermann, *Genesis 12–36* (Minneapolis: Augsburg, 1985), 292. Other possibilities, however, come to mind: Abraham is reluctant to become too precise; he recognizes that the smallest military units consist of ten; Abraham has made his point and to press it further would be useless. Nathan Macdonald, "Listening to Abraham—Listening to YHWH: Divine Justice and Mercy in Gen 18:16–33," *Catholic Biblical Quarterly* 66 (2004): 25–43, argues that YHWH was eager to spare and Abraham failed to press the point. Macdonald rejects the idea of "haggling" and urges readers to listen to God, not Abraham.

11. The Apocalypse of Sedrach resembles Genesis 18 in that the hero persuades God by degrees to be merciful toward repentant sinners. Initially, God specifies three years of penance, which strike Sedrach as too many. God then lowers the required time to one year, which still fails to satisfy. The deity responds by shortening the penance to forty days, but Sedrach insists that even so short a span may exclude some people from divine mercy. Whereupon God says, "My beloved Sedrach, I promise to have compassion even less than forty days, as far as twenty." At this point Sedrach, who has steadfastly refused to relinquish his soul to paradise, says, "Now, Master, take my soul." Apocalypse of Sedrach 16:3, 5 in *Old Testament Pseudepigrapha*, ed. J. H. Charlesworth, 2 vols. (New York: Doubleday, 1983), 1:613.

12. The narrator assiduously avoids any specific identification of Lot as righteous. For that matter, Abraham never appeals to his kinship with Lot as a bargaining chip. Further, the story offers no hint that Lot will be a salvific influence over the inhabitants of Zoar, the village for which Lot intercedes so that he might have a place to flee.

13. The story reckons with randomness, an ignoring of human merit—or lack thereof—that allows the wicked to escape, for nothing suggests that the people of Zoar are blameless.

14. Ronald J. Williams, "Theodicy in the Ancient Near East" *Canadian Journal of Theology* 2 (1956): 14–26; Wolfram von Soden, "Das Fragen nach der Gerechtigkeit Gottes im alten Orient," in *Bibel und Alter Orient* (Berlin: de Gruyter, 1985), 57–75; Johann Jakob Stamm, *Das Leiden des Unschuldigen in Babylon und Israel* (Zurich: Zwingli, 1946); Rainer Albertz, "Der sozialgeschichtliche Hintergrund des Hiobbuches und der 'Babylonischen Theodizee,' " in *Die Botschaft und die Boten: Festschrift für Hans Walter Wolff zum 70. Geburtstag*, ed. Jörg Jeremias and Lothar Perlitt (Neukirchen-Vluyn: Neukirchener, 1981), 349–72; Moshe Weinfeld, "Job and Its Mesopotamian Parallels: A Typological Analysis," in *Text and Context: Old Testament and*

Semitic Studies for F. C. Fensham, ed. Walter Claassen (Sheffield: JSOT Press, 1988), 217–26; Gerald L. Mattingly, "The Pious Sufferer: Mesopotamia's Traditional Theodicy and Job's Counselors," in *The Bible in the Light of Cuneiform Literature: Scripture in Context III*, ed. William Hallo, B. Jones, and Gerald Mattingly (Lewiston, N.Y.: Edwin Mellen, 1990), 305–48.

15. The Admonitions of Ipuwer, in M. Lichtheim, ed., *Ancient Egyptian Literature*, 3 vols. (Berkeley: University of California Press, 1971–80), 1:149–63, one of three surviving literary expressions of social distress from ancient Egypt, describes the turmoil of a topsy-turvy world and expresses puzzlement over the sun god's failure to set things right. A brief section of this interesting text—often believed to be intrusive—alludes to the creator as a missing pilot and, by implication, a careless herdsman. Why, the author asks, did the fashioner of humans not blot them out once he perceived their essentially violent nature? If only he would bring calm, people would say, "He is the herdsman of all; there is no evil in his heart. His herds are few, but he spends the day herding them." But because the punisher of crimes also commits them, people see no evidence of deity: "There is no Pilot in their hour. Where is he today? Is he asleep? Lo, his power is not seen!"

16. The Poem of the Righteous Sufferer [Ludlul], in W. G. Lambert, *Babylonian Wisdom Literature* (Oxford: Clarendon, 1960), 21–62; Benjamin R. Foster, *From Distant Days: Myths, Tales, and Poetry of Ancient Mesopotamia* (Bethesda, Md.: CDL, 1995), 298–313; and William M. Moran, *The Most Magic Word* (Washington, D.C.: Catholic Biblical Association, 2002), 182–200. The inability to ascertain the will of the gods by any means appears to have been a literary topos in the ancient world, despite various priestly and prophetic approaches to divine secrets. The Poem of the Righteous Sufferer has the suffering individual remark about the futility of religious observance toward that end:

> I wish I knew that these things would be pleasing to one's god!
> What is good for oneself may be offense to one's god,
> What in one's own heart seems despicable may be proper to one's god.
> Who can understand the plans of the underworld gods?
> Where have humans learned the way of a god?

Foster calls this familiar Akkadian text "one of the finest literary monuments of Mesopotamian antiquity" (299) and contrasts it with the biblical book of Job. He writes: "There is none of the defiance and bitterness of Job. In short, this text sees suffering and redemption as signs of divine power, while Job sees them as tests of human strength." Moran thinks the real purpose of the text is to proclaim the god Marduk and the reality of a new personal religion over against the inadequacy of conventional belief. He writes: "It declares that, despite what we may call the evidence, the world makes sense. Behind suffering is a plan. We may not understand the plan. No one can. Not even the other gods. But there is a plan, there is meaning, behind what can only seem not just mysterious but even willful and capricious" (192).

17. The Babylonian Theodicy, in *Babylonian Wisdom Literature*, ed. Lambert, 63–91, and Foster, *From Distant Days*, 316–23:

Narru, king of the gods, who created mankind,
And majestic Zulummar, who pinched off the clay for them,
And goddess Mami, the queen who fashioned them,
Gave twisted speech to the human race.
With lies, and not truth, endowed them forever.

A dialogue between a sufferer and his friend, only partially preserved, this text too emphasizes the near impossibility of discovering the will of the gods:

You are as stable as the earth, but the plan of the gods is remote. . . .
The mind of the god, like the center of the heavens, is remote;
Knowledge of it is very difficult; people cannot know it. . . .
Though it is possible to find out what the will of the god is,
   people do not know how to do it.

18. Donald E. Gowan, *The Triumph of Faith in Habakkuk* (Atlanta: John Knox, 1976), 20–50.

19. James L. Crenshaw, *A Whirlpool of Torment: Israelite Traditions of God as an Oppressive Presence* (Philadelphia: Fortress, 1984), 31–56.

20. Crenshaw, *Whirlpool of Torment*, 31–56, explores the depth of this rift between prophet and deity as expressed in the so-called confessions. The move from literary text to biography is far too complex for these laments to be used for determining personal information about Jeremiah, but they do give voice to the author's sentiments and reveal something about the audience's religious tolerances.

21. The language is that of the judiciary, with *tsaddiq* functioning as a declaration of innocence equivalent to the modern "Not guilty."

22. The commentary by Jack M. Sasson, *Jonah* (New York: Doubleday, 1990), is unsurpassed, but see also Phyllis Trible's elegant *Rhetorical Criticism: Context, Method, and the Book of Jonah* (Minneapolis: Fortress, 1994); Kenneth M. Craig, *A Poetics of Jonah: Art in the Service of Ideology* (Columbia: University of South Carolina Press, 1993); and Jonathan Magonet, *Form and Meaning: Studies in Literary Techniques in the Book of Jonah* (Bern: Herbert Lang, 1976).

23. Sasson, *Jonah*, 234–37, reads the crucial word *nehpaket* (overturned) as intentionally ambiguous, meaning "destroyed" or "overturned" as a function of the response of the city's residents.

24. The ancient *ger* came under royal protection, at least in ideology (Norbert Lohfink, "Poverty in the Laws of the Ancient Near East and the Bible," *Theological Studies* 52 [1991]: 34–50, and Leonidas Kalugila, *The Wise King* [Lund: Gleerup, 1980]). According to the sapiential tradition, one type of sojourner, the foreign woman (*nokriyyah; 'ishah zarah*), flaunted her outsider status for seductive advantage.

25. Consider the rather humorous example from the story of the anointing of Israel's second king: the statement that YHWH looks not at the outward appearance but at the heart—followed immediately by a report that David, whom the deity chose, was handsome (1 Sam 16:7, 12).

26. The reputation of prophecy itself was thrown into jeopardy by earlier efforts

to establish criteria that would enable citizens to distinguish between true and false prophets; see James L. Crenshaw, *Prophetic Conflict: Its Effect upon Israelite Religion* (Berlin: de Gruyter, 1971). This struggle and its influence on the understanding of prophecy is evident in Zech 13:1–9. The fact that the author of the story of Jonah presents the prophet in an ambiguous light suggests that the issue of authentic versus false intermediaries of YHWH had not yet been resolved.

27. James L. Crenshaw, *Joel* (New York: Doubleday, 1995).

28. The different Hebrew words for this witness suggest that the author is depicting Job as struggling to define the exact role of the elusive figure: here the word is *'edi*; in 9:33–35 it is *mokiakh* (mediator), and in 19:23–29 it is *go'el* (vindicator).

29. Adele Berlin, *Poetics and Interpretation of Biblical Narrative* (Sheffield: Almond, 1983). Point of view is also treated in Robert Alter, *The Art of Biblical Narrative* (New York: Basic, 1981); Meir Sternberg, *The Poetics of Biblical Narrative* (Bloomington: Indiana University Press, 1985); and Herbert Chanan Brichto, *Toward a Grammar of Biblical Poetics: Tales of the Prophets* (New York: Oxford University Press, 1992).

30. The rarity of the oracular formula in Joel calls attention to its context. There is only one other use of this kind in the book ("for YHWH has spoken," 4:8b).

31. Some interpreters would challenge this understanding of fiction in favor of the omniscient narrator as supreme authority. On this concept, see Sternberg, *Poetics of Biblical Narrative*, who emphasizes YHWH's omniscience as the essential difference between the creator and humans in the Bible.

32. What if Judah, like Job, is innocent of wrongdoing? In my view, modern interpreters have joined the ranks of Job's friends in associating calamity with guilt in the case of Joel's compatriots. Rather than blaming the sufferers, perhaps we should recognize the true source of the difficulty as the divine character and the human perception of ambiguity therein. See James L. Crenshaw, "Joel's Silence and Interpreters' Readiness to Indict the Innocent," in *"Lasset uns Brücken bauen . . . ,"* ed. Klaus-Dietrich Schunck and Matthias Augustin (Frankfurt am Main: Peter Lang, 1998), 255–59.

33. G. W. Ahlström, *Joel and the Temple Cult of Jerusalem* (Leiden: Brill, 1971), 26, argues from Joel's use of the stronger preposition *'aday* rather than *'elay* that the people have turned to worshiping other gods.

34. Hans Walter Wolff, *Joel and Amos*, ed. S. Dean McBride, trans. Waldemar Janzen et al. (Philadelphia: Fortress, 1977), 48–53, locates the fault in the people's reliance on the fact that they were YHWH's inheritance, which seemed in their minds to guarantee divine favor. In Wolff's view, the issue is God's freedom, which Joel zealously guards.

35. G. Wanke, "Prophecy and Psalms in the Persian Period," in *Cambridge History of Judaism*, ed. W. D. Davies and Louis Finkelstein (Cambridge: Clarendon Press, 1984), 1:177. Wanke writes that "the only suggestion of a criticism of the people of Jerusalem may be contained in 2:12f, where too intensive an orientation toward external ritual can dimly be perceived as a cause for lament."

36. Paul L. Redditt, "The Book of Joel and Peripheral Prophecy," *Catholic Biblical Quarterly* 48 (1986): 225–40, claims that Joel's accusations against cultic leaders even-

tually pushed him and his followers to the periphery of society, thus appreciably limiting his effectiveness.

37. Leslie C. Allen, *The Books of Joel, Obadiah, Jonah, and Micah* (Grand Rapids, Mich.: Eerdmans, 1976), 77–84. Although he observes that the covenant people have "evidently strayed from their Shepherd, turning to their own way," Allen also writes that "it is evidently left to the people and priests to search their own hearts and habits for evidence of the sin that God's reaction proved to be there" (78–79). In Allen's view, Joel's interpretation of the locust plague presupposes serious sin, although the prophet fails to use the normal place in the rhetoric of verse 12 to mention the people's sin.

38. Ronald Simkins, *Yahweh's Activity in History and Nature in the Book of Joel* (Lewiston, N.Y.: Edwin Mellen, 1991), 181–90.

39. On this book, see Michael V. Fox, *Character and Ideology in the Book of Esther* (Columbia: University of South Carolina Press, 1991). Marjo C. A. Korpel, "Theodicy in the Book of Esther," in *Theodicy in the World of the Bible*, ed. Antti Laato and Johannes C. de Moor (Leiden: Brill, 2003), 351–74, thinks the book of Esther criticizes those who take matters into their own hands, refusing to trust in God and thus becoming murderers. She calls such critique an ingenious theodicy.

40. See Crenshaw, *Whirlpool of Torment*, 50–56.

41. The four attributes in Exod 34:6 are in apposition to the divine name. In Joel 2:13 they appear as predicate adjectives in a nominal clause introduced by the adverbial particle *ki* (for).

42. An intriguing addition of "righteous" within Ps 112:4 to the usual attributes found in Exod 34:6–7 reveals the significance of balancing mercy with justice, for later usage was heavily weighted in the direction of compassion. The only instance of a vindictive application of an attribute from the covenant formulary occurs in Nah 1:3 and involves divine patience. This reference, however, pertains to Nineveh, whereas the other uses relate to Israel and Judah (cf. Pss 86:15, 103:8, 111:4, 112:4, 145:8; Neh 9:17, 31). The struggle between those who emphasized divine compassion and those who stressed YHWH's justice demonstrates both the tenacity of tradition and the powerful influence of communal experience.

43. James L. Crenshaw, "The Expression *mî yôdē'a* in the Hebrew Bible," *Vetus Testamentum* 36 (1986): 274–88 (= Crenshaw, *Urgent Advice and Probing Questions*, 279–91).

44. William L. Holladay, *The Root šûbh in the Old Testament* (Leiden: Brill, 1958) and J. A. Soggin, "*šûb* to return," in *Theological Lexicon of The Old Testament*, ed. E. Jenni with assistance from C. Westermann, trans. M. E. Biddle, 3 vols. (Peabody, Mass.: Hendrickson, 1997), 3:1312–17.

45. This interrelationship between the well-being of the people and their deity energizes the language of a short version of the formulary, Num 14:18.

46. Simkins, *Yahweh's Activity in History and Nature.*

47. Bertil Albrektson, *History and the Gods* (Lund: Gleerup, 1967), and Leo G. Perdue, *The Collapse of History: Reconstructing Old Testament Theology* (Minneapolis: Fortress, 1994).

48. The same nations could be depicted by the prophets as Israel's hated ene-mies and as equals on the world scene: "In that day Israel will be a third partner with Egypt and Assyria, as a blessing in the midst of the earth, whom YHWH of hosts blessed, thus 'Blessed be my people Egypt and Assyria the work of my hands and Israel my heritage' " (Isa 19:24–25). Logic compelled rigorous thinkers to recognize the universal implications of monotheism and its accompanying high view of the cre-ator, despite particularistic notions that did not fit into that scheme.

49. On the basis of Egyptian scholarship, in particular the work of Jan Assmann, *Ägypten: Theologie und Frommigkeit einer frühen Hochkultur* (Stuttgart: Kohlhammer, 1984), recent biblical interpreters have emphasized personal piety, which would seem to be less affected by socioeconomic circumstances than more communal types of be-lief. Such judgments are difficult to prove, given the nature of biblical evidence. See Ranier Albertz, *Persönliche Frömmigkeit und offizielle Religion: Religionsinterner Pluralis-mus in Israel und Babylon* (Stuttgart: Calwer, 1978).

50. The quotation from *Faust* is given a radical twist in Hermann Hesse's *De-mian*, where one reads "A thousand souls reside within my breast." For this tor-mented author, World War I and its atrocities seemed to confirm such a multiplica-tion of demons in the human soul.

CHAPTER 6

1. Biblical images of YHWH use only these two categories of the three dominant metaphors for deity that Thorkild Jacobsen, *The Treasures of Darkness* (New Haven: Yale University Press, 1976), 20–21, attributes to ancient Mesopotamia: élan vital, ruler, and parent.

2. The original Hebrew behind the phrase "in my house of instruction" (51:23) is uncertain. Manuscript B has *bebet midrashi*, but the Greek and Syriac suggest *bebet musar*. The former reading emphasizes the exegetical task; the latter, discipline. Some critics understand the expression metaphorically. On this reading, the house of in-struction is Ben Sira's scroll; see Oda Wischmeyer, *Die Kultur des Buches Jesus Sirach* (Berlin: de Gruyter, 1995).

3. In some ways Ben Sira was a conservative, as Alexander A. DiLella, "Conser-vative and Progressive Theology: Sirach and Wisdom," *Catholic Biblical Quarterly* 28 (1966): 139–54, has argued, but he also held many innovative views associated with Hellenism. He endorsed the medicine of his day, participated in Greek banquets, sub-scribed to Stoic teachings about opposites, accepted Greek concepts of friendship, and adapted Hellenistic debate formulas to his own use (James L. Crenshaw, "The Book of Sirach," *New Interpreter's Bible* 5:603–867).

4. The extent to which Ben Sira broke with tradition has not always been appre-ciated. His introduction of sacred narrative into wisdom literature—the use of figures from Israel's past to inspire youth who could not fail to be impressed by Greek he-roes—was indeed significant, as was his effort to elevate truth as revealed to Moses over philosophical ideas from Hellenistic authors. For the book of Sirach in context, see Patrick W. Skehan and Alexander A. DiLella, *The Wisdom of Ben Sira* (New York:

Doubleday, 1987), and Johan Marböck, *Weisheit im Wandel: Untersuchungen zur Weisheitstheologie bei Ben Sira* (Bonn: Hanstein, 1971).

5. James L. Crenshaw, "The Problem of Theodicy in Sirach: On Human Bondage," *Journal of Biblical Literature* 94 (1975): 49–64 (= Crenshaw, *Urgent Advice and Probing Questions*, 155–74), and Pancratius C. Beentjes, "Theodicy in the Wisdom of Ben Sira," in *Theodicy in the World of the Bible*, ed. Antti Laato and Johannes C. de Moor (Leiden: Brill, 2003), 509–24, who treats 15:11–20, 33:7–15, 40:10a, and 5:4–8. See also John J. Collins, *Jewish Wisdom in the Hellenistic Age* (Louisville: Westminster John Knox, 1997), 80–96, and Gian Luigi Prato, *Il problema della teodicea in Ben Sira: Composizione dei contrari e richiamo alle origini* (Rome: Pontifical Biblical Institute, 1975).

6. James K. Aitken, "Divine Will and Providence," in *Ben Sira's God*, ed. Renate Egger-Wenzel (Berlin: de Gruyter, 2002), 282–301, emphasizes reciprocity between God and humans, analogous to that between ruler and citizenry in the Hellenistic period.

7. Only about 65 percent of Sirach has survived in Hebrew. Text-critical study of the book must therefore draw also on the Greek (of which two manuscripts exist) and the Syriac.

8. Cf. Prov 8:17.

9. Hebrew has wisdom speak in the first person from v 15 through v 19.

10. Hebrew *'emet* (faithfully).

11. Hebrew omits this verse.

12. Hebrew omits this line.

13. The sequence of the cola in this verse is unclear.

14. Silvia Schroer, *Wisdom Has Built Her House: Studies on the Figure of Sophia in the Bible* (Collegeville, Minn.: Liturgical Press, 2000); Judith E. McKinlay, *Gendering Wisdom the Host: Biblical Invitations to Eat and Drink* (Sheffield: Sheffield Academic Press, 1996); Claudia V. Camp, *Wisdom and the Feminine in the Book of Proverbs* (Sheffield: Almond, 1985); and Christl M. Maier, *Die "fremde Frau" in Proverbien 1–9* (Freiburg: Universitätsverlag; Göttingen: Vandenhoeck & Ruprecht, 1995).

15. Skehan and DiLella, *Wisdom of Ben Sira*, use these poems to structure their discussion of the biblical book. Beentjes, "Theodicy in the Wisdom of Ben Sira," 511 n 12, lists the introductory hymns as 1:1–2:18, 4:11–19, 6:18–37, 14:20–15:10, 24:1–29, 32:14–33:15, and 38:34–39:11.

16. This domestication of wisdom posed a problem, the localizing of a universal concept. That is why an alternative voice was raised, an insistence that wisdom surveyed the whole scene on earth and returned to heaven, having found no suitable dwelling place: "Wisdom could not find a place in which she could dwell; but a place was found for her in the heavens. Then wisdom went out to dwell with the children of the people, but she found no dwelling place. So wisdom returned to her place and she settled permanently among the angels. Then iniquity went out of her rooms, and found whom she did not expect. And she dwelt with them, like rain in a desert, like dew on a thirsty land" (1 Enoch 42:1–3).

17. R. W. L. Moberly, *The Bible, Theology, and Faith: A Study of Abraham and Jesus* (Cambridge: Cambridge University Press, 2000), argues for the positive role of divine

230 NOTES TO PAGES 103–106

testing in the life of faith, but he does not give sufficient attention to the destructive aspects of this pedagogy, whether emotional (as seen in rabbinic reflections about Eve's response to the story about Isaac's ordeal), physical (as exemplified by Job's ten slain children), or mental (as experienced by countless individuals broken by trials too difficult to bear). Moberly perceives the potential for both good and ill in the process of testing: "The paradox, with the potential for both glory and tragedy, is that the very process which can develop and deepen human life [divine testing] is the one which can stunt, corrupt, and destroy human life [satanic temptation]" (240). Yet this perception does not compel him to question YHWH's actions when, from a human standpoint, they are immoral.

18. William P. Brown, *Character in Crisis: A Fresh Approach to the Wisdom Literature of the Old Testament* (Grand Rapids, Mich.: Eerdmans, 1996), and Charles F. Melchert, *Wise Teaching: Biblical Wisdom and Educational Ministry* (Harrisburg: Trinity, 1998).

19. McKinlay, *Gendering Wisdom the Host*, emphasizes the invitation to eat and drink as a religious theme in the ancient Near East, one that continues in New Testament times.

20. Jean Noël Aletti, "Séduction et parole en Proverbes I–IX," *Vetus Testamentum* 27 (1977): 129–44.

21. James L. Crenshaw, "The Primacy of Listening in Ben Sira's Pedagogy," in *Wisdom, You Are My Sister: Studies in Honor of Roland E. Murphy, O. Carm., on the Occasion of His Eightieth Birthday*, ed. Michael L. Barré (Washington, D.C.: Catholic Biblical Association, 1997), 172–87; Crenshaw, "Qoheleth's Understanding of Intellectual Inquiry," in *Qohelet in the Context of Wisdom*, ed. Antoon Schoors (Leuven: Leuven University Press, 1998), 205–24; and Crenshaw, *Education in Ancient Israel: Across the Deadening Silence* (New York: Doubleday, 1998).

22. The Canaanite Baal cycle, discovered at Ugarit in modern Syria in the third decade of the twentieth century, has demonstrated the extent of belief in a dying god in the immediate environs of the Israelites.

23. "One thing are the words which men say, another is that which the god does" (Amenemope 19.16–17); "Homo proposuit sed Deus disponit" (Thomas à Kempis).

24. Contrary to William P. Brown's claim in *Seeing the Psalms: A Theology of Metaphor* (Louisville: Westminster John Knox, 2002), 257 n 61. Not one of his examples from the Psalms refers to God's love for humans, and two of the four refer to love of the divine name.

25. M. Lichtheim, ed., *Ancient Egyptian Literature*, 3 vols. (Berkeley: University of California Press, 1971–80), 1:61–80, esp. 73–76, and Nili Shupak, *Where Can Wisdom Be Found? The Sage's Language in the Bible and in Ancient Egyptian Literature* (Göttingen: Vandenhoeck & Ruprecht, 1993).

26. Skehan and DiLella, *Wisdom of Ben Sira*, 169 (following Smend).

27. The text is in considerable disarray here, as evidenced by the inconsistent verse length. Verse 17 comprises three bicola; the other verses in the passage have only one.

28. The same literary device occurs in the story of the resurrected Jesus' appearance to disciples on the road to Emmaus (Luke 24:13–32).

29. Joseph Blenkinsopp, "The Social Context of the 'Outsider Woman' in Proverbs 1–9," *Biblica* 71 (1991): 457–73, and Harold C. Washington, "The Strange Woman of Proverbs 1–9 and Post-Exilic Judean Society," in *Second Temple Studies 2* (Sheffield: JSOT Press, 1994), 217–42.

30. Crenshaw, *Education in Ancient Israel*, 139–85.

31. This reading is not accepted by Antoon Schoors, "Theodicy in Qohelet," in *Theodicy in the World of the Bible*, ed. Laato and de Moor, 382. He bases his interpretation on all the other uses of *'olam* in the book, which have a temporal sense. In my view, "hidden" fits the context better than "duration," and Qoheleth certainly uses novel ideas and one word with different meanings.

32. David Winston, *The Wisdom of Solomon* (New York: Doubleday, 1979).

33. Collins, *Jewish Wisdom in the Hellenistic Age*, 135–232.

34. Michael Kolarcik, *The Ambiguity of Death in Wisdom Chapters 1–6: A Study of Literary Structure and Interpretation* (Rome: Editrice Pontificio Istituto Biblico, 1991).

35. Moyna McGlynn, *Divine Judgment and Divine Benevolence in the Book of Wisdom* (Tübingen: Mohr Siebeck, 2001), 25–53.

36. Such ridicule continues in the Apocalypse of Abraham (c. 100 CE), where a wooden image that Abraham has instructed to watch over the fire on which Terah's food is cooking ignites and burns, convincing Terah that the god Barisat has sacrificed itself for its devotee. This mocking reference to a god's self-immolation for another's benefit shares the stage with tales of other easily destroyed images, as well as man-made replacements that, when thrown in the river, cannot save themselves or, when sold to foreigners, cannot control their own destiny.

37. Maurice Gilbert, *La Critique des dieux dans le livre de la Sagesse* (Rome: Pontifical Biblical Institute, 1973), and Gerhard von Rad, *Wisdom in Israel* (Nashville, Tenn.: Abingdon, 1972), 177–85.

38. In the context of this discussion, the specific assertion in the Mercy Dialogue that the world was created from preexistent matter suggests that the author understood the grammatically ambiguous Gen 1:1 as temporal: "When God began to create the heavens and the earth, the earth was waste and void." Not until 2 Macc 7:28 do we find an explicit claim that the creative act was a true beginning—that is, creation from nothing. On the philosophical background and ambiguity of this terminology, see Jonathan A. Goldstein, *II Maccabees* (Garden City, N.Y.: Doubleday, 1983), 307–11. Greek philosophical speculation about the material world as opposed to the spiritual soon infiltrated Jewish and Christian thinking, with divisive consequences.

39. David Winston, "Theodicy in the Wisdom of Solomon," in *Theodicy in the World of the Bible*, ed. Laato and de Moor, 535–45. Winston notes that the author is virtually obsessed with the problem of theodicy (525). Death in general, and suffering brought on righteous individuals by childlessness and premature death in particular, serves to focus the problem for the author. Winston remarks that the persecution in the time of Caligula made it difficult for the author to resist the apocalyptic solution to the problem of evil (545).

40. For excellent commentaries on Amos from the perspective of form criticism and ancient Near Eastern parallels, respectively, see Jörg Jeremias, *The Book of Amos* (Louisville: Westminster John Knox, 1995), and Shalom M. Paul, *Amos* (Minneapolis: Fortress, 1991).

41. Hans Walter Wolff, *Hosea: A Commentary on the Book of the Prophet Hosea*, ed. Paul D. Hanson, trans. Gary Stansell (Philadelphia: Fortress, 1974).

42. James L. Crenshaw, *Hymnic Affirmation of Divine Justice: The Doxologies of Amos and Related Texts in the Old Testament* (Missoula, Mont.: Scholars Press, 1975).

43. James L. Crenshaw, "A Liturgy of Wasted Opportunity: Am 4:6–12; Isa 9:7–10:4," *Semitics* 1 (1971): 27–37.

44. "Their faces."

45. Hebrew "his."

46. Ben Sira applies the image of a yoke to the educative process, urging students to submit to wisdom's yoke (Sir 51:26). Compare the similar use attributed to Jesus in Matt 11:29–30, on which see M. Jack Suggs, *Wisdom, Christology, and Law in Matthew's Gospel* (Cambridge, Mass.: Harvard University Press, 1970). The yoke also has negative connotations in Ben Sira's teaching, specifically, the iron yoke of slander and the burden laid on mortals from birth (Sir 28:20, 40:1).

47. Johannes C. de Moor, "Theodicy in the Texts of Ugarit," in *Theodicy in the World of the Bible*, ed. Laato and de Moor, 108–40, provides an illuminating discussion of theodicy as education as it is developed in the three mythic texts from Ugarit (Baal, Keret, and Danel, to use the language of J. B. Pritchard, ed., *Ancient Near Eastern Texts Relating to the Old Testament*, 3rd ed. [Princeton, N.J.: Princeton University Press, 1969]). Ilimalku, the author of these texts, views the gods as capricious and human suffering as tragic. The protagonists' life and death are equally matched, which produces a power vacuum. In the end, Ilimalku becomes a skeptic. The progression to this intellectual position is evident in the myths, which describe a disintegrating pantheon. The city of Ugarit followed the fate of the Canaanite pantheon, falling to invading soldiers between 1190 and 1185 BCE.

CHAPTER 7

1. The Easter proclamation, "He is risen," functions in the same way as the ancient myths in the establishing of order. The forces of chaos have been overcome for now, the myths announced, and life can continue. For the ancients, the annual commemoration of the conflict between good and evil served as a permanent reminder that chaos would be no more. For Christians, that positive message is summed up in the affirmation that Good Friday has given way to Easter Sunday, bringing hope in the place of despair.

2. Although chaos was believed to have been overcome, the memory of its awesome power lingered, surfacing during unstable times. In the face of calamitous defeat, Jeremiah entertained the horrendous possibility of a return to the original chaotic state recorded in Genesis 1:

I saw the earth—waste and void,
  the heavens—devoid of light;
I saw the mountains—quaking,
  every hill—rocking;
I saw—no human,
  and every bird—vanished. . . . (Jer 4:23–25)

Robert P. Carroll, *Jeremiah* (Philadelphia: Westminster, 1986), 168–70, may be correct in finding apocalyptic themes in this poem, which he considers non-Jeremianic. Carroll relates the imagery to the Holocaust, quoting Elie Wiesel, *Five Biblical Portraits* (Notre Dame: University of Notre Dame Press, 1981), 126. The connections with Genesis 1, although real, are less extensive than thought by Michael Fishbane, "Jeremiah IV 23–26 and Job III 3–13: A Recovered Use of the Creation Pattern," *Vetus Testamentum* 21 (1971): 151–67.

3. René Girard, *Violence and the Sacred* (Baltimore: Johns Hopkins University Press, 1977), and Girard, *Things Hidden since the Foundation of the World* (Stanford, Calif.: Stanford University Press, 1987), explains the human tendency toward tit-for-tat in terms of mimesis, rivalry, and collective violence, the last of which is brought under control through sacrifice. He believes that the biblical deity is beyond the differences established by the victimization mechanism and that YHWH demonstrated this truth by allowing himself to be driven out by violence. See James G. Williams, *The Bible, Violence, and the Sacred: Liberation from the Myth of Sanctioned Violence* (San Francisco: HarperSanFrancisco, 1991).

4. Similarly, the eighteen Psalms of Solomon—the product of a community of devout Jews in the first century BCE, probably in Jerusalem—reflect a determined confidence in the midst of bewildering crisis. Barred from the desecrated temple and beset by Jew and Gentile alike, the authors frequently raise the issue of theodicy. Hostile treatment from fellow Jews defies explanation, for both belong to the covenanted people. Still, the justice of God is manifest in that sinners are punished to expose their wickedness; in this way God uses suffering to distinguish between the good and the wicked. These authors accept sin as universal but argue that "devout" sinners deserve God's favor, since they try to keep the Torah. What role does suffering play in their own lives? It proves their faithfulness, atoning for sin, just like prayer and fasting. Until vindication comes, they will await a militant Messiah. On these psalms, see Kenneth Atkinson, "Theodicy in the Psalms of Solomon," in *Theodicy in the World of the Bible*, ed. Antti Laato and Johannes C. de Moor (Leiden: Brill, 2003), 546–75; George W. E. Nickelsburg, *Jewish Literature between the Bible and Mishnah: A Historical and Literary Introduction* (Philadelphia: Fortress, 1981), 202–12; and Herbert Braun, "Vom Erbarmen Gottes über den Gerechten: Zur Theologie der Psalmen Salomos," *Zeitschrift für die neutestamentliche Wissenschaft und die Kunde der älteren Kirche* 43 (1950/51): 32–42.

5. The idea of justice after death is strongly affirmed in a collection of verses included (in differing forms) in several patristic sources, variously attributed to the fourth- and fifth-century poets Diphilus, Philemon, and Euripides:

234 NOTES TO PAGE 120

Justice has an eye, which looks upon all things.
And we believe there are two paths in Hades,
one for the just, the other for the impious,
even if the earth forever covers both.
For if just and unjust will have one end,
go off and rob, steal, plunder, act in rage.
Make no mistake. There is, even in Hades, judgment,
which God, the Lord of all, will execute,
whose name is awesome, and I would not utter it. . . .
He gives to sinners a long life.
And if some mortal thinks he has escaped
the notice of the gods while doing evil all day long,
he reckons ill, and in his reckoning will be seized,
when Justice at her leisure comes upon him.
Give heed, you who think there is no God,
erring twice without careful thought,
for there is, there is indeed, and if someone prospers,
while really being wicked, let him take advantage of the present time,
for in time to come he will pay the penalty.

Quotation from J. H. Charlesworth, ed., *Old Testament Pseudepigrapha*, 2 vols. (New York: Doubleday, 1983), 2:828–29.

6. Patrick D. Miller, *Sin and Judgment in the Prophets* (Chico, Calif.: Scholars Press, 1982), examines Klaus Koch's theory about an automatic nexus between an act and its consequence and finds it wanting ("Is There a Doctrine of Retribution in the Old Testament?" in Crenshaw, ed. *Theodicy in the Old Testament*, 42–56).

7. Hans Heinrich Schmid, *Wesen und Geschichte der Weisheit* (Berlin: Töpelmann, 1966), and Schmid, *Gerechtigkeit als Weltordnung* (Tübingen: Mohr Siebeck, 1968).

8. The Mesha Stela attributes defeat to Chemosh's anger toward the Moabites and victory to his good will; see J. B. Pritchard, ed., *Ancient Near Eastern Texts Relating to the Old Testament*, 3rd ed. (Princeton, N.J.: Princeton University Press, 1969), 320–21. On the similarities between biblical narrative and the stories of neighboring cultures, see Simon B. Parker, *Stories in Scripture and Inscriptions: Comparative Studies on Northwest Semitic Inscriptions and the Hebrew Bible* (New York: Oxford University Press, 1997).

9. Philippe Nemo, *Job and the Excess of Evil* (Pittsburgh, Pa.: Duquesne University Press, 1998), writes: "The transition from speculative aloofness to anguished situatedness is a transition from a simple judgment—life passes, death comes—to a judgment of value: life passes *too quickly*, death comes *too soon*" (24). Moreover, "all human certainty, all knowledge, all power, all technique is perverted, inexorably, by the one whom the friends [of Job] call 'God' " (87). Finally, "God is currently as if in hell—until we free God from hell by surrendering to God. . . . God knows dereliction,

indecision. God burns to encounter us, we who are His *go'el*, rising up on the earth for Him. We are God's dream, just as God is our dream. God, like us, must traverse the *nada*" (160–61).

10. For the most part, the conclusions reached by the sages are based on personal observation, unlike Torah and prophecy, which purport to derive from the deity. The author of Ecclesiastes carries this claim to an extreme, frequently calling attention to the act of attentive observation. Even his claims about divine work are deductions from observable reality.

11. David Kraemer, *Responses to Suffering in Classical Rabbinic Literature* (New York: Oxford University Press, 1995); Oliver Leaman, *Evil and Suffering in Jewish Philosophy* (Cambridge: Cambridge University Press, 1995); Wendy Farley, *Tragic Vision and Divine Compassion: A Contemporary Theodicy* (Louisville: Westminster John Knox, 1990); Dorothee Sölle, *Suffering* (Philadelphia: Fortress, 1975); Arthur A. McGill, *Suffering: A Test of Theological Method* (Philadelphia: Fortress, 1982); E. D. Klemke, ed., *The Meaning of Life,* 2nd ed. (New York: Oxford University Press, 2000); Erhard S. Gerstenberger and Wolfgang Schrage, *Suffering* (Nashville: Abingdon, 1980).

12. James L. Crenshaw, "Wisdom and Authority: Sapiential Rhetoric and Its Warrants," in *Congress Volume: Vienna, 1980* ed. John A. Emerton (Leiden: Brill, 1982), 10–29 (= Crenshaw, *Urgent Advice and Probing Questions*, 326–43).

13. The context favors a reading of *me'eloah* that emphasizes the impossible, either "more than" Eloah or "as against." I prefer the former translation and understand the point to be that the spirit was describing the contested issue in terms of a wholly innocent mortal who claimed to be more just than the deity who had permitted his undeserved suffering. Older translations such as the King James render the Hebrew in this way, but most translators have shown a reluctance to take this route. The New English Bible is a welcome exception.

14. For an interesting perspective on theophany, see Emmanuel Levinas, "Postface: Transcendence and Evil," in *Job and the Excess of Evil*, ed. Nemo, 178–82: "The face puts into question the adequacy and complacency of my identity as I, it constrains to an infinite responsibility with respect to the other" (181). Levinas goes on to say that another person's suffering touches me, "putting into question my *relying upon myself* and my *connatus essendi*, as if before my lamenting over my woes here below, I have to answer for the other—*is it not this that is a breach of the Good into evil, into the 'intention' that targets me so exclusively in my woe?* Theophany. Revelation." For another perspective, see Seyyed Hossein Nasr, "The Cosmos as Theophany," in *Knowledge and the Sacred* (Albany: State University of New York Press, 1989), 189–220.

15. On this literary device, see James L. Crenshaw, "Impossible Questions, Sayings, and Tasks," in *Gnomic Wisdom*, ed. J. D. Crossan (Chico, Calif.: Scholars Press, 1980), 19–34 (= Crenshaw, *Urgent Advice and Probing Questions*, 265–78).

16. J. Edward Wright, *The Early History of Heaven* (Oxford: Oxford University Press, 2000), describes ancient cosmologies and illustrates them with iconography from Egypt, Syria-Palestine, and Mesopotamia.

17. Some interpreters have viewed the abrupt ending of the third round of debate between Job and his three friends as the authorial signal that they have run out of anything worthwhile to say to Job.

18. This expression occurs also in Egyptian wisdom literature. Its exact meaning is unclear—that is, beyond an indication of rarity. Qoheleth uses the phrase in this sense (Eccl 7:28) after a reference to having added one to one to find the sum, without success.

19. A *mosquito*, as it settled on an elephant,
> Said, "Brother, did I press your side? I will make [off] at the watering-place."
> The elephant replied to the *mosquito*,
> "I do not care whether you get on—what is it to have you?—
> Nor do I care whether you get off."

Quotation from W. G. Lambert, *Babylonian Wisdom Literature* (Oxford: Clarendon, 1960), 217, 219.

20. F. A. Munch, "Das Problem des Reichtums in den Psalmen 37; 49; 73," *Zeitschrift für die alttestamentliche Wissenschaft* 55 (1937): 36–45, and K. J. Torjesen, "Interpretation of the Psalms: Study of the Exegesis of Ps 37," *Augustinianum* 22 (1982): 349–55.

21. Sara Japhet, "Theodicy in Ezra-Nehemiah and Chronicles," in *Theodicy in the World of the Bible*, ed. Laato and de Moor, 429–69 notes the "cleaner" position of Chronicles, a systematic application to all of history. For the Chronicler, justice includes the many good gifts bestowed on Israel and not just the punishment of the wicked.

22. Judith H. Newman, *Praying by the Book: The Scripturalization of Prayer in Second Temple Judaism* (Atlanta: Scholars Press, 1999), and Moshe Greenberg, "On the Refinement of the Conception of Prayer in Hebrew Scriptures," in *Studies in the Bible and Jewish Thought*, ed. Moshe Greenberg (Philadelphia: Jewish Publication Society, 1995), 75–108.

23. John J. Collins, *Daniel* (Minneapolis: Fortress, 1993); Louis F. Hartman and Alexander A. DiLella, *The Book of Daniel* (New York: Doubleday, 1978); Maurice Gilbert, "La Prière de Daniel, Dn 9,4–19," *Revue théologique de Louvain* 3 (1972): 284–310; and B. W. Jones, "The Prayer in Daniel IX," *Vetus Testamentum* 18 (1968): 488–93. A similar prayer occurs in Bar 1:15–3:8, on which see B. N. Wambacq, "Les Prieres de Baruch 1:15–2:19 et de Daniel 9:5–19," *Biblica* 40 (1950): 463–75.

24. Leviticus 26:24, however, articulates a principle at great variance with a strict understanding of retributive punishment, unless it is meant to be understood as rhetorical emphasis: "I myself will strike you sevenfold for your sins." At any rate, the text leaves open the possibility of pardon after the harsh sentence has fallen and therefore a restoration of the covenantal relationship (vv 41–42). Jacob Milgrom, *Leviticus 17–22* (New York: Doubleday, 2000).

CHAPTER 8

1. To some extent the following discussion is indebted to the brilliant analysis by Maurice Gilbert, "God, Sin, and Mercy: Sirach 15:11–18:14," in *Ben Sira's God: Proceedings of the International Ben Sira Conference, Durham, Ushaw College 2001*, ed. Renate Egger-Wenzel (Berlin: de Gruyter, 2002), 118–35, although I have a different view of the literary structure (see James L. Crenshaw, "The Book of Sirach," *New Interpreter's Bible* 4:721–31). In my judgment, the section contains two independent units, 15:11–16:23 and 16:24–18:14. The summary judgment in 16:23 closes the first, and the direct address in 18:15, which forms an inclusio with 16:24, delineates the second and signals the beginning of a new section.

2. Cited from Ephraim E. Urbach, *The Sages: Their Concepts and Beliefs* (Jerusalem: Magnes, 1975), 481 and 900 n 66. Courtesy of my colleague Kalman Bland.

3. Jacob Neusner, "Theodicy in Judaism," in *Theodicy in the World of the Bible*, ed. Antti Laato and Johannes C. de Moor (Leiden: Brill, 2003), 685–727.

4. Wisdom of Solomon makes the same point (4:11).

5. Paul Ricoeur, *The Symbolism of Evil*, trans. Emerson Buchanan (Boston: Beacon, 1967), examines the explanations for evil that have been proposed over the millennia. In essence, they place the responsibility on humans (the fall), the gods (tragic blinding), and the cosmos (dualism).

6. J. A. Scurlock, "Magic," in D. N. Freedman, ed., *Anchor Bible Dictionary*, 6 vols. (New York: Doubleday, 1992), 4:464–68. Much of this magic was medicinal or associated with fertility. Both formulaic expressions and imitative ritual were used freely, often by priests but also by specialists, among whom were old women. For similar practices of magic in ancient Israel, see Joanne K. Kuemmerlin-McLean, "Magic. Old Testament," in *Anchor Bible Dictionary*, ed. Freedman, 4:468–71.

7. Robin C. Cover, "Sin, Sinners," in *Anchor Bible Dictionary*, ed. Freedman, 6:31–40, and Rolf Knierim, *Die Hauptbegriffe für Sünde im Alten Testament* (Gütersloh: Gütersloher Verlagshaus, 1965).

8. Pamela Tamarkin Reis, *Reading the Lines: A Fresh Look at the Hebrew Bible* (Peabody, Mass.: Hendrickson, 2002), 105–30, considers the young girl a spoiled child whom the father wisely steered into a life of abstinence. For this reading, she must understand *'olah* and the cognate verb in Judg 11:31 as metaphor.

9. Gary A. Anderson, "Sacrifice and Sacrificial Offerings," in *Anchor Bible Dictionary*, ed. Freedman, 5:870–86.

10. This ritual was a part of the Day of Atonement, a holy day on which special provision was made to wipe the slate clean of all unatoned sins of the past year. In the course of time, this occasion came to mark the year's sole enunciation of the Tetragrammaton, the sacred name of YHWH. On that day the high priest proclaimed the name that had become so numinous that a substitute word, Adonai, or Lord, was always read aloud in the synagogue when the name YHWH appeared in the biblical text.

11. On this ritual, see Jacob Milgrom, *Leviticus 1–16* (New York: Doubleday, 1991), 1071–79. Impurity was nullified in one of three ways: curse, destruction, or banish-

238 NOTES TO PAGES 140–146

ment. In the ancient Near East, the third practice was used often, as Milgrom demonstrates in detail.

12. John F. Kutsko, *Between Heaven and Earth: Divine Presence and Absence in the Book of Ezekiel* (Winona Lake, Ind.: Eisenbrauns, 2000), 101–49.

13. Antti Laato, *The Servant of YHWH and Cyrus: A Reinterpretation of the Exilic Messianic Programme in Isaiah 40–55* (Stockholm: Almqvist & Wiksell, 1992); Henning Graf Reventlow, "Basic Issues in the Interpretation of Isaiah 53," in *Jesus and the Suffering Servant: Isaiah 53 and Christian Origins*, ed. W. H. Bellinger and William R. Farmer (Harrisburg: Trinity, 1998), 23–38; Bernd Janowski and Peter Stuhlmacher, eds., *Der leidende Gottesknecht* (Tübingen: Mohr Siebeck, 1996); R. Norman Whybray, *Thanksgiving for a Liberated Prophet: An Interpretation of Isaiah Chapter 53* (Sheffield: JSOT Press, 1978); and Philip E. Satterthwaite, Richard S. Hess, and Gordon J. Wenham, eds., *The Lord's Anointed: Interpretation of Old Testament Messianic Texts* (Carlisle, U.K.: Paternoster, 1995).

14. Linguistic affinities between the servant poems and the ritual of the scapegoat are noted by Tryggve N. D. Mettinger, *A Farewell to the Servant Songs: A Critical Examination of an Exegetical Axiom* (Lund: Gleerup, 1983).

15. Here alone in the Hebrew Bible is the word *meshiakh* applied to a foreigner. The text implies the king's ignorance of his mission in YHWH's service. First Isaiah had earlier used the notion of an Assyrian king functioning as YHWH's agent of punishment in Israel. Marvin A. Sweeney, "Isaiah and Theodicy after the Shoah," in *Strange Fire: Reading the Bible after the Holocaust*, ed. Tod Linafelt (New York: New York University Press, 2000), 208–19, faults YHWH on three counts: (1) his identification with the conqueror, (2) his decree of judgment against Israel, and (3) his failure to establish world peace.

16. Hedwig Jahnow, *Das hebräische Leichenlied im Rahmen der Völkerdichtung* (Giessen: Töpelmann, 1923), 262–65.

17. Henry M. Orlinsky, "The So-Called 'Servant of the Lord' and 'Suffering Servant' in Second Isaiah," in *Studies on the Second Part of the Book of Isaiah* (1967): 1–333, esp. 51–56, and J. A. Soggin, "Tod und Auferstehung des leidenden Gottesknechtes Jesaja 53, 8–10," *Zeitschrift für die alttestamentliche Wissenschaft* 87 (1975): 346–55.

18. Antti Laato and Johannes C. de Moor, introduction to *Theodicy in the World of the Bible* (Leiden: Brill, 2003), xlix–liii.

19. Hugh Anderson, "4 Maccabees," in *Old Testament Pseudepigrapha*, ed. J. H. Charlesworth, 2 vols. (New York: Doubleday, 1983), 2:531–64, esp. 551–53.

20. The crucifixion of Jesus was a fundamental problem for early Christians, although certainty in his resurrection led them to transform the scandal into a cause for boasting. Far from indicating infamy, Jesus' death revealed the profound depth of God's love. In that way the burden of suffering became a sign of what the Christian mission was all about.

CHAPTER 9

1. Among the many books and articles on the subject of life after death in the thought of ancient Israel, a few have been particularly useful. Robert Martin-Achard, "Resurrection (OT)," in *Anchor Bible Dictionary*, ed. D. N. Freedman, 6 vols. (New York: Doubleday, 1992), 4:680–84, and earlier Martin-Achard, *From Death to Life* (Edinburgh: Oliver & Boyd, 1960); G. Johannes Botterweck, "Marginalien zum alten Auferstehungsglaubens," *Wiener Zeitschrift für die Kunde des Morgenlandes* 53 (1957): 1–8; Victor Maag, "Tod und Jenseits nach dem Alten Testament," in *Kultur, Kulturkontakt, und Religion* (Göttingen: Vandenhoeck & Ruprecht, 1980), 181–202; Leonhard Rost, "Alttestamentliche Wurzeln der ersten Auferstehung," in *In Memoriam Ernst Lohmeyer*, ed. Werner Schmauch (Stuttgart: Evangelisches Verlagswerk, 1961), 67–72; Otto Kaiser, "Die Zukunft der Toten nach den Zeugnissen der alttestamentlich-frühjüdischen Religion," in *Der Mensch unter dem Schicksal* (Berlin: de Gruyter, 1985), 182–95; Horst Dietrich Preuss, " 'Auferstehung' in Texten Alttestamentlicher Apokalyptik (Jes 26, 7–19; Dan 12, 1–4)," in *"Linguistische" Theologie*, ed. Uwe Gerber and Erhardt Güttgemanns (Bonn: Linguistica Biblica, 1972), 103–333; Ernst Haenchen, *Die Bibel und Wir* (Tübingen: Mohr Siebeck, 1968), 2:73–90; Gerhard F. Hasel, "Resurrection in the Theology of Old Testament Apocalyptic," *Zeitschrift für die alttestamentliche Wissenschaft* 92 (1980): 267–83; John J. Collins, "The Root of Immortality: Death in the Context of Jewish Wisdom," *Harvard Theological Review* 71 (1978): 177–92, and Collins "Apocalyptic Eschatology as the Transcendence of Death," *Catholic Biblical Quarterly* 36 (1974): 21–43.

2. John Barton, *Oracles of God: Perceptions of Ancient Prophecy in Israel after the Exile* (New York: Oxford University Press, 1986), discusses the shift to understanding prophecy as twice-removed from its divine source, a late phenomenon that elevated earlier prophets above postexilic exemplars. In Barton's view, this loss of immediacy, with a sacred text replacing a sense of having received the divine word directly, was accompanied by increased emphasis on prophetic miracles. We can already see this principle at work in Numbers 12. Perhaps it represents a heightened sense of awe that certain groups always nurtured with respect to prophetic figures, some of whom inevitably towered over their peers.

3. Neil Gillman, *The Death of Death: Resurrection and Immortality in Jewish Thought* (Woodstock, Vt.: Jewish Lights, 1997), examines Jewish views about the afterlife from biblical times to the present and identifies two competing concepts: resurrection and immortality. Gillman beautifully illuminates this tension within modern liturgical prayers.

4. Kaiser, "Zukunft der Toten," 186. The persistence of these concepts can be observed in later understandings of life after death. The funerary cult of the dead was concerned with providing the necessities of the living dead, particularly fluids; see Charles A. Kennedy, "Dead, Cult of the," in *Anchor Bible Dictionary*, ed. Freedman, 2:105–8.

5. The confidence with which interpreters during the first half of the twentieth century envisioned seminomadic existence in Israel's remote ancestry has

diminished considerably as a result of competing theories about its origins. Critics nowadays question the older assumption that seminomadism preceded cultivation of land.

6. On Qoheleth's views about the finality of death as a powerful force in shaping conduct, see James L. Crenshaw, "The Shadow of Death in Qoheleth," in *Israelite Wisdom: Theological and Literary Essays in Honor of Samuel Terrien*, ed. John G. Gammie et al. (Missoula, Mont.: Scholars Press, 1978), 205–16 (= Crenshaw, *Urgent Advice and Probing Questions*, 573–85). This oppressive shadow prefigured (or foreshadowed) the kind of existence everyone was destined to endure in the next life.

7. Biblical authors were reluctant to depict the underworld, but Egyptian and Mesopotamian writers offered graphic accounts. Besides these descriptions, Egyptian literature includes books that lead the dead through various gates and caverns, while Mesopotamian texts detail Ishtar's descent into the netherworld. The name "Sheol" seems to derive from *sha'al* (to ask, inquire) and to reflect the practice of necromancy. On this hypothesis, see Theodore J. Lewis, "Dead, Abode of the," in *Anchor Bible Dictionary*, ed. Freedman, 2:101–5. Nicholas J. Tromp, *Primitive Conceptions of Death and the Nether World in the Old Testament* (Rome: Pontifical Biblical Institute, 1969), draws on Ugaritic literature to provide a comprehensive examination of biblical views about Sheol and the denizens of that world, the Rephaim.

8. Although most apparent in the book of Psalms (6:6; 30:10, 88:6, 11), this belief is found as well in the book of Isaiah, in the prayer attributed to King Hezekiah (38:11, 18–19), and it even surfaces in a wisdom setting (Sir 17:27–28). Hermann Gunkel, *Genesis* (Göttingen: Vandenhoeck & Ruprecht, 1965), explains the rationale for this view: "Das Licht ist der erste Schöpfung; ohne Licht kein Leben und keine Ordnung. Vor dem Licht war die Welt dunkel, leblos, wirr; Finsternis und Chaos sind grauenvoll; grauenvoll ist auch die Sheol, die kein Licht hat; das Licht ist gut und heilsam." [Light is the first creation; without light, no life and no order. Before light the world was dark, lifeless, confused; darkness and chaos are horrible; Sheol, which has no light, is also horrible; light is good and salutary.]

9. Wisdom of Solomon, the fullest representative in biblical literature of such disparaging of the material world, reflects the Platonic concept of heavenly ideas, together with their pale reflection on earth, and Pythagorean teachings. Similarly, 1 Esd 4:33–41 contrasts everything earthly with eternal truth. All things of this world are *adikoi* (unrighteous).

10. The citation derives from Martin-Achard, "Resurrection (OT)," 683. The question of theodicy lies at the heart of this revolutionary development. On a passage with similar import, Isa 26:19, Horst Dietrich Preuss writes: " 'Auferstehung' ist aber in diesem Text nicht Ziel oder Zweck als solche, sondern sie steht im Dienst der Theodizeefrage." [But in this text "resurrection" is not the goal or purpose as such, but it stands in service of the question of theodicy.] And, on Dan 12:1–4: " 'Auferstehung' begegnet auch hier als gewagter Glaube, als Glaubenspostulat . . . , als Heilszusage, als Sprache des Glaubens, als Trost. . . . Das Theodizeeproblem ist folglich auch hier (vgl. Dan 9,24) für das Enstehen der Zusage 'Auferstehung' konstitutiv." ["Resurrection" also occurs here as risked faith, as a postulate of belief . . . , as salvific

promise, as language of faith, as trust. . . . Therefore the problem of theodicy is also here (cf. Dan 9:24) constitutive for the origin of the promise of "resurrection."]
Preuss, " 'Auferstehung' in Texten Alttestamentlicher Apokalyptik (Jes 26, 7–19; Dan 12, 1–4)," *"Linguistic" Theologie*, ed. Uwe Gerber and Erhardt Güttgemanns (Bonn: Linguistica Biblica, 1972) 103–33, especially 122, 130.

11. Gisela Fuchs, *Mythos und Hiobdichtung* (Stuttgart: Kohlhammer, 1993); Jon D. Levenson, *Creation and the Persistence of Evil: The Jewish Drama of Divine Omnipotence* (San Francisco: Harper & Row, 1988); and Michael Fishbane, *Biblical Myth and Rabbinic Mythmaking* (Oxford: Oxford University Press, 2003).

12. Leo G. Perdue, "The Riddles of Psalm 49," *Journal of Biblical Literature* 93 (1974): 533–42, detects hidden meaning beneath the surface of the language, a weighty endeavor to intensify the gloomy aspects of the human situation. In v 5 the psalmist uses *khidati* (my riddle) in parallel with *mashal* (proverbial saying). This psalm incorporates rival understandings of the realm of the dead: that place is the Pit; corpses remain in graves forever; the dead waste away in Sheol with Death as shepherd; they go to the ancestors, dwelling in darkness. On the characteristics of wisdom literature and wisdom psalms in particular, see James L. Crenshaw, *Old Testament Wisdom: An Introduction*, revised and enlarged (Louisville: Westminster John Knox, 1998), and Crenshaw, *The Psalms: An Introduction* (Grand Rapids, Mich.: Eerdmans, 2001), 87–95.

13. The commentaries (International Critical Commentary, Biblischer Kommentar, Altes Testament, Word Biblical Commentary, Old Testament Library [e.g., Briggs, Krauss, Craigie, Weiser]) generally favor this change, supported by a few manuscripts, although Dahood in the Anchor Bible defends the Masoretic Text *'akh*, translating "alas" on the theory that terms of intimacy occasionally express dismay.

14. For analysis of the theological struggle charted in Psalm 73, see Martin Buber, "The Heart Determines: Psalm 73," in *On the Bible* (New York: Schocken, 1968), 199–210 and James L. Crenshaw, "Standing Near the Flame: Psalm 73," in Crenshaw, ed., *A Whirlpool of Torment: Israelite Traditions of God as an Oppressive Presence* (Philadelphia: Fortress, 1984), 93–109.

15. The alternative view, that Job refers to the preservation of a permanent witness on progressively more enduring surfaces, highlights his growing frustration over unfair treatment on both fronts, heavenly and earthly. On the larger problem of literacy, see James L. Crenshaw, *Education in Ancient Israel: Across the Deadening Silence* (New York: Doubleday, 1998).

16. Perhaps the example from Proverbs should be omitted, for it belongs to the section strongly influenced by the Egyptian Instruction of Amenemope and does not identify the divine(?) redeemer who takes up (adjudicates) the cause of the widow (reading *'almanah*) and orphans. The text from the book of Jeremiah uses a stereotypical formula, *YHWH tseba'ot shemo*, in identifying this powerful litigator. On this refrain, see James L. Crenshaw, *"YHWH tsebā'ôt šemô*: A Form Critical Analysis," *Zeitschrift für die alttestamentliche Wissenschaft* 83 (1969): 156–75, and Crenshaw, *Hymnic Affirmation of Divine Justice: The Doxologies of Amos and Related Texts in the Old Testament* (Missoula, Mont.: Scholars Press, 1975).

17. David J. A. Clines, *Job 1–20* (Dallas: Word, 1989), 457–58, 461–62, and Carol A. Newsom, "The Book of Job," *New Interpreter's Bible* 4:479.

18. The monumental step from believing in the resurrection of exceptional victims of malevolence to a general raising of all the dead suggests an easing of theodicy as the driving force. Nevertheless, divine character continues to be central, inasmuch as the destiny of mortals reflects on the deity's power and benevolence.

19. For modern readers, personal time marches inevitably onward to the beat of the heart's muffled drum until it comes to the last measure, a decisive end. Prior to the final drumbeat, an individual is alive; after that instant, he or she is dead. The Israelites did not think this way. Individuals frequently descended into the realm of the dead, transported by adversity of some sort, then emerged on the wings of divine deliverance to fully restored life. Poets employed vivid images to portray this perilous state of existence, often choosing extreme language of distress, perhaps to improve the chance of being heard by the deity.

20. Donald Charles Polaski, *Authorizing an End: The Isaiah Apocalypse and Intertextuality* (Leiden: Brill, 2001), 238–63, views this text as similar to Ezekiel 37, the restoration of a nation. He thinks Isa 26:19 functions to contain social tensions by creating a present moment that blends both ineffectiveness and effectiveness. In short, even in their apparent ineffectuality, the righteous are far more powerful than they think, and both wicked and righteous will ultimately receive their due (vv 14 and 19).

21. Jewish weavers of fantasy played with this idea of an eschatological banquet and came up with intriguing scenarios (cf. Isa 25:6, 8; Isa 55:1–5; Prov 9:1–6; Slav En 2:5; Bar Apoc 29; and Pss Sol 17:40). The final consumption of Leviathan (chaos personified) at this feast is the supreme irony, because Death was notorious for swallowing its victims (cf. 1 Cor 15:54). In a Hellenistic context, banquets assumed enormous social significance, even receiving favorable comments from Ben Sira (Sir 31:12–32: 13).

22. On the prominence of this theological problem in wisdom literature, see James L. Crenshaw, *Urgent Advice and Probing Questions: Collected Writings on Old Testament Wisdom* (Macon, Ga.: Mercer University Press, 1995), 141–221. I address this issue more broadly in Crenshaw, "The Sojourner Has Come to Play the Judge: Theodicy on Trial," in *God in the Fray: A Tribute to Walter Brueggemann*, ed. Tod Linafelt and Timothy K. Beal (Minneapolis: Fortress, 1998), 83–92.

23. F. J. Helfmeyer, " 'Deine Toten—Meine Leichen': Heilszusage und Annahme in Jes 26.19," in *Bausteine biblischer Theologie: Festgabe für G. Johannes Botterweck zum 60. Geburtstag dargebr. von seinen Schülern*, ed. B. G. Weiss and J. Welch (Bonn: Hanstein, 1977), 254–57. The dew of heaven figures prominently in rabbinic legend about the resuscitation of Isaac in the garden of Eden, to which he has been transported following Abraham's actual sacrifice of his son. On this speculation, see Shalom Spiegel, *The Last Trial* (New York: Schocken, 1969), and Jürgen Ebach, *Gott im Wort: Drei Studien zur biblischen Exegese und Hermeneutik* (Neukirchen-Vluyn: Neukirchener, 1997), 1–25.

24. Note the depiction of a pugilistic YHWH in Isa 27:1–5, a text in counterpoint

with the earlier song of the vineyard in 5:1–7. The eschatological reference in 27:2 ("in that day") is unmistakable; here YHWH finally slays Leviathan, the coiling serpent that lurks in the sea. Ugaritic texts also stand in the background, for they feature the twisting serpent and hostile Yam.

25. Shalom M. Paul, "Heavenly Tablets and the Book of Life," *Journal of the Ancient Near Eastern Society of Columbia University* 5 (1973): 345–53, demonstrates the scope of this belief in the existence of celestial scribal activity, which has grave consequences for mortals.

26. The religio-historical significance of radiant souls is attested by its presence in Zoroastrianism, where the dead pass through a fiery stream and are purified; in Qumran eschatology; in various Hellenistic depictions of heavenly sparks that become trapped in human bodies until their liberation through *gnosis*; and in Jewish mysticism generally. Does the biblical author know the concept of stars as personal beings? (Cf. Isaiah 14 [Lucifer, son of the Day Star] and a similar tradition in Ugaritic literature.)

27. John J. Collins, "Apocalyptic Eschatology as the Transcendence of Death," *Catholic Biblical Quarterly* 36 (1974): 33–35, thinks that the resurrected ones are elevated to the ranks of angels. George W. E. Nickelsburg Jr., *Resurrection, Immortality, and Eternal Life in Intertestamental Judaism* (Cambridge: Harvard University Press, 1972), 19, observes a difference between Isa 26:19, where resurrection is itself the vindication of righteousness, and Dan 12:1–3, where "resurrection is a *means* by which both the righteous and the wicked dead are enabled to receive their respective vindication or condemnation."

28. "Instructing a woman is like having a sack of sand whose side is split open" (The Instruction of Ankhsheshonq 13.20). A single example of such nonsense is one too many.

29. Nickelsburg, *Resurrection, Immortality, and Eternal Life*, 93–109, thinks that the original form of this genre referred to a father and his seven sons, to which were added traditions of apocalyptic catastrophe and Isaianic exaltation. The figure of the mother, in Nickelsburg's view, derived from another contemporary tradition, which has been enriched from the language of the Isaianic servant. For an exhaustive discussion of this story about a mother and her seven sons, see Jonathan A. Goldstein, *II Maccabees* (Garden City, N.Y.: Doubleday, 1983), 289–317.

30. On the diaspora setting of Wisdom of Solomon, see John J. Collins, *Jewish Wisdom in the Hellenistic Age* (Louisville: Westminster John Knox, 1997), 135–57.

31. Michael Kolarcik, *The Ambiguity of Death in the Book of Wisdom 1–6* (Rome: Pontifical Biblical Institute, 1991), thinks the author works with quite different concepts of death, specifically, actual death and spiritual death. Kolarcik tries to show that the Christian notion of transcending physical death is philosophically valid.

32. The quest for immortality is the theme of the Gilgamesh Epic. Neither Gilgamesh nor his friend Enkidu succeeds in overcoming the threat of death, which manifests itself gruesomely in Enkidu's decaying corpse. See J. B. Pritchard, ed., *Ancient Near Eastern Texts Relating to the Old Testament*, 3rd ed. (Princeton, N.J.: Princeton University Press, 1969), 72–99, 503–7.

33. The Tale of Aqhat, in *Ancient Near Eastern Texts Relating to The Old Testament*, ed. Pritchard, 151.

34. For further discussion of Job 14:13–17 in its larger context, see James L. Crenshaw, "Flirting with the Language of Prayer (Job 14:13–17)," in *Worship and the Hebrew Bible: Essays in Honor of John T. Willis*, ed. M. Patrick Graham, Rick R. Marrs, and Steven L. McKenzie (Sheffield: Sheffield Academic Press, 1999), 110–23.

35. See James L. Crenshaw, "The Expression *mî yôdēʿa* in the Hebrew Bible," *Vetus Testamentum* 36 (1986): 274–88 (= Crenshaw, *Urgent Advice and Probing Questions*, 279–91).

36. For my understanding of Ben Sira, see James L. Crenshaw, "Sirach," *New Interpreter's Bible* 5:601–867.

37. The facile liturgy in Hos 6:1–3, with its explicit imagery from nature, looks to national restoration after three days, a symbolic number in mythic texts of the ancient Near East used to signal a decisive event. The text has nothing to do with life after death.

CHAPTER 10

1. Jack Miles, *God: A Biography* (New York: Knopf, 1995), develops this theme in magisterial fashion. He focuses on the images of the deity as creator, destroyer, friend of the family, liberator, lawgiver, conqueror, father, arbiter, executioner, holy one, wife, counselor, guarantor, friend, sleeper, bystander, recluse, puzzle, absence, ancient of days, scroll, and perpetual round. His final question, "Does God lose interest?" is sobering. Miles writes: "Silent as the Ancient of Days may be, *he knows*. As the Lord God's knowledge has grown, we must ask, 'What has he learned that has reduced him to silence?' " (402).

2. Two distinct approaches to the theology of ancient Israel that have had enormous influence on later scholarship are Walther Eichrodt, *Theology of the Old Testament*, 2 vols. (Philadelphia: Westminster, 1961, 1967), and Gerhard von Rad, *Old Testament Theology*, 2 vols. (New York: Harper & Row, 1965). A recent study by Walter Brueggemann, *Theology of the Old Testament* (Minneapolis: Fortress, 1997), largely continues the approach of von Rad, although with current emphases. James Barr, *The Concept of Biblical Theology* (Minneapolis: Fortress, 1999), examines the various approaches to writing biblical theologies.

3. Moshe Weinfeld, *Deuteronomy and the Deuteronomic School* (New York: Oxford University Press, 1972), remains an indispensable repository for information about this biblical book; see also Weinfeld, "Deuteronomy, Book of," in *Anchor Bible Dictionary*, ed. D. N. Freedman, 6 vols. (New York: Doubleday, 1992), 2:168–83.

4. Stephen A. Geller, " 'Where Is Wisdom?' A Literary Study of Job 28 in Its Settings," in *Judaic Perspectives on Ancient Israel*, ed. Jacob Neusner, Baruch A. Levine, and Ernest S. Frerichs (Philadelphia: Fortress, 1987), 169–75, Jürgen Van Oorschot, "Hiob 28: Die verborgene Weisheit und die Furcht Gottes als Überwindung einer generalisierten hokmâ," in *The Book of Job*, ed. W. A. M. Beuken (Leuven: Leuven Uni-

versity Press, 1994), 183–202, and *Job 28: Cognition in Context*, ed. Ellen van Wolde (Leiden: Brill, 2003).

5. For a stimulating discussion of conflicting epistemologies, see Seyyed Hossein Nasr, *Knowledge and the Sacred* (Albany: State University of New York Press, 1989).

6. Antoon Schoors, "Theodicy in Qohelet," in *Theodicy in the World of the Bible*, ed. Antti Laato and Johannes C. de Moor (Leiden: Brill, 2003), 375–409; Thomas Krüger, *Kohelet (Prediger)* (Neukirchen-Vluyn: Neukirchener, 2000); Tilmann Zimmer, *Zwischen Tod und Lebensglück: Eine Untersuchung zur Anthropoligie Kohelets* (Berlin: de Gruyter, 1999); Alexander A. Fischer, *Skepsis oder Furcht Gottes? Studien zur Komposition und Theologie des Buches Kohelet* (Berlin: de Gruyter, 1997); and Eric S. Christianson, *A Time to Tell: Narrative Strategies in Ecclesiastes* (Sheffield: Sheffield Academic Press, 1998), represent recent fascination with this intriguing book.

7. Other authors as well recognize the limits to human knowledge. On divine mystery in Sirach, see Núria Calduch-Benages, "God, Creator of All (Sir 43:27–33)," in *Ben Sira's God: Proceedings of the International Ben Sira Conference, Durham, Ushaw College 2001*, ed. Renate Egger-Wenzel, BZAW 321 (Berlin: de Gruyter, 2002), 93–95. Pancratius C. Beentjes, "God's Mercy: 'Racham' (pi), 'Rachum,' and 'Rachamim' in the Book of Ben Sira," in *Ben Sira's God*, ed. Egger-Wenzel, 114 n 59, writes that "a special investigation into the use and function of *sôd* [divine counsel], together with terms like *mstr* [the hidden] (4:18), *kruptein/kruptós*, and *mustérion* [mystery] would be welcomed."

8. Hartmut Gese, *Lehre und Wirklichkeit in der alten Weisheit* (Tübingen: Mohr, 1958), and Frank Crüsemann, "The Unchangeable World: The 'Crisis of Wisdom' in Koheleth," in *The God of the Lowly: Socio-historical Interpretations of the Bible*, ed. Willy Schottroff and Wolfgang Stegemann, trans. Matthew J. O'Connell (Maryknoll, N.Y.: Orbis, 1984), 57–77.

9. This idea has been developed from a Barthian perspective by Kornelis H. Miskotte, *When the Gods Are Silent*, trans. John W. Doberstein (New York: Harper & Row, 1967).

10. Schoors, "Theodicy in Qohelet," 376–403.

11. Egon Pfeiffer, "Die Gottesfurcht im Buche Kohelet," in *Gottes Wort und Gottes Land: Festschrift für Hans Wilhelm Hertzberg*, ed. Henning Graf Reventlow (Göttingen: Vandenhoeck & Ruprecht, 1965), 133–58. Fear of God is not just devotion and adoration but has an element of awe before the numinous.

12. Schoors, "Theodicy in Qohelet," 377–80. I argue for the second alternative, darkness, in James L. Crenshaw, "The Eternal Gospel (Ecclesiastes 3:11)," in *Essays in Old Testament Ethics: J. Philip Hyatt, In Memoriam*, ed. James L. Crenshaw and John T. Willis (New York: Ktav, 1974), 23–55 (= Crenshaw, *Urgent Advice and Probing Questions*, 548–72).

13. This sexual understanding of "casting stones," held among some ancient rabbis, is based on the recognition that an important aspect of life is not otherwise covered in this literary unit and on the association of menstruation with throwing off "stones."

14. Joseph Blenkinsopp, "Ecclesiastes 3:1–15: Another Interpretation," *Journal for the Study of the Old Testament* 66 (1995): 55–64, thinks of 3:1–8 as embedded Stoic philosophy (or a product of a Stoicizing Jewish sage) and 3:9–22 as commentary on it, but R. N. Whybray, " 'A Time to Be Born and a Time to Die': Some Observations on Ecclesiastes 3:2–8," in *Near Eastern Studies Dedicated to H. I. H. Prince Takahito Mikasa*, ed. M. Mori et al. (Wiesbaden: Harrassowitz, 1991), 469–83, adheres to earlier views.

15. Michael V. Fox, *A Time to Tear Down and a Time to Build Up: A Re-reading of Ecclesiastes* (Grand Rapids, Mich.: Eerdmans, 1999), emphasizes the empirical nature of Qoheleth's inquiry (but see James L. Crenshaw, "Qoheleth's Understanding of Intellectual Inquiry," in *Qohelet in the Context of Wisdom*, ed. Antoon Schoors [Leuven: Leuven University Press, 1998], 205–24). A rigid empiricism permeates the Book of Creation, on which see A. Peter Hayman, "Qohelet and the Book of Creation," *Journal for the Study of the Old Testament* 50 (1991): 93–111.

16. James L. Crenshaw, "The Shadow of Death in Qoheleth," in *Israelite Wisdom: Theological and Literary Essays in Honor of Samuel Terrien*, ed. John G. Gammie et al. (Missoula, Mont.: Scholars Press, 1978), 205–16 (= Crenshaw, *Urgent Advice and Probing Questions*, 573–85), and Shannon Burkes, *Death in Qoheleth and Egyptian Biographies of the Late Period* (Atlanta: Society of Biblical Literature, 1999).

17. C. L. Seow, *Ecclesiastes* (New York: Doubleday, 1964), stresses the influence of apocalyptic thinking, especially in the final description of old age and death in 11:7–12:7.

18. Schoors, "Theodicy in Qohelet," 409 writes: "In his view, the solution of the theodicy problem is concealed in the unfathomable mystery of God. He is the maker of a problematic world, a *Deus absconditus*. He makes what is the way it is, but he is no factor in human knowledge about the world." See also Pin'has Carny, "Theodicy in the Book of Qohelet," in *Justice and Righteousness: Biblical Themes and Their Influence*, ed. Henning Graf Reventlow and Yair Hoffman (Sheffield: Sheffield Academic Press, 1992), 71–81.

19. Michael E. Stone, *Fourth Ezra: A Commentary on the Book of Fourth Ezra* (Minneapolis: Fortress, 1990), and Stone, "The Way of the Most High and the Injustice of God in 4 Ezra," in *Knowledge of God in the Graeco-Roman World*, ed. R. van der Broek and J. Mansfield (Leiden: Brill, 1988), 132–42. For the larger Jewish context, see P. W. van Boxel, "Man's Behaviour and God's Justice in Early Jewish Tradition: Some Observations," in *Knowledge of God in the Graeco-Roman World*, ed. van der Broek and Mansfield, 143–59. Van Boxel stresses the incompatibility of the divine attributes of justice and mercy and notes that rabbinic thought held to both but was dominated by the idea of God's love rather than his justice (144–47). He discusses the well-known story about Honi's drawing a circle and vowing to stay inside it until God has mercy on Israel and sends rain. The basis for Honi's appeal, van Boxel asserts, is divine mercy, not justice (151–53).

20. Of the many studies that deal with apocalyptic, I wish to call attention to John J. Collins, *The Apocalyptic Imagination: An Introduction to the Jewish Matrix of Christianity* (New York: Crossroad, 1984). See also Collins, "Apocalypses and Apoca-

lypticism," in *Anchor Bible Dictionary*, ed. Freedman 1:279–88, and Paul L. Redditt, "The Vitality of the Apocalyptic Vision," in *Passion, Vitality, and Foment: The Dynamics of Second Temple Judaism* ed. Lamontte M. Luker (Harrisburg: Trinity, 2001), 77–118.

21. J. H. Charlesworth, ed., *Old Testament Pseudepigrapha*, 2 vols. (New York: Doubleday, 1983), provides convenient translations of these significant texts (except, of course, for the biblical Daniel).

22. Anssi Simojoki, "The Book of Revelation," in *Theodicy in the World of the Bible*, ed. Laato and de Moor, 652–84.

23. Except where otherwise noted, quotations of 4 Ezra are from Charlesworth, *Old Testament Pseudepigrapha*.

24. Ancient fascination with the impossible is reflected in stories of the famous Ahiqar in which he is challenged to produce a rope from sand and to build a castle in the sky, both of which he accomplishes to the satisfaction of a curious audience.

25. The moment of Faust's spontaneous outburst, "Stay, thou art so fair!" involves a comparable quest—to construct a habitation for others, despite the sea's encroachment on the land.

26. "Spittle" (*sielos*; Hebrew *raq*) appears in the Septuagint version of Isa 40:15, replacing the Hebrew *daq* (specks of dust). Michael A. Knibb, *2 Esdras*, in *The First and Second Books of Esdras: Commentary on 1 Esdras by R. J. Coggins and Commentary on 2 Esdras by M. A. Knibb* (Cambridge: Cambridge University Press, 1979), 159–60.

27. D. Simonson, "Ein Midrasch im IV. Buch Esra," in *Festschrift zu Israel Lewy's siebzigstem Geburtstag*, ed. M. Brann and J. Elbogen (Breslau: M. & H. Marcus, 1911), 270–78.

28. Stone, *Fourth Ezra*, uses conversion as an interpretive clue to the book, but Philip F. Esler, "The Social Function of 4 Ezra," *Journal for the Study of the New Testament* 53 (1994): 99–123, esp. 110, rejects that hypothesis on three grounds: (l) the failure to take into account the tensions that inevitably attend dissonance and its reduction, (2) the tying of explanations of a text to an authorial personality that is utterly unknown, and (3) the ignoring of the textual difficulties of such a reading.

29. The hidden books are clearly seen as divine wisdom, esoteric lore available to only a few. See Michael A. Knibb, "Apocalyptic and Wisdom in 4 Ezra," *Journal for the Study of Judaism in the Persian, Hellenistic, and Roman Periods* 13 (1982): 56–74, who argues that Fourth Ezra was written for a learned group and resembles later pesharim. Knibb cautions against identifying the book with wisdom or late prophecy and points to the depiction of Ezra as a second Moses (72). On pesharim, see Maurya P. Horgan, *Pesharim: Qumran Interpretations of Biblical Books* (Washington, D.C.: Catholic Biblical Association, 1979).

30. The social context of Fourth Ezra has been seen as Jabneh. Bruce W. Longenecker, "Locating 4 Ezra: A Consideration of Its Social Setting and Functions," *Journal for the Study of Judaism in the Persian, Hellenistic, and Roman Periods* 28 (1997): 271–93.

31. Charlesworth, *Old Testament Pseudepigrapha*, 1:615–52; J. Edward Wright, *Baruch Ben Neriah: From Biblical Scribe to Apocalyptic Seer* (Columbia: University of South Carolina Press, 2003); and A. F. J. Klijn, "Recent Developments in the Study of

the Syriac Apocalypse of Baruch," *Journal for the Study of the Pseudepigrapha* 4 (1989): 3–17.

32. Quotations of 2 Baruch are from Charlesworth, *Old Testament Pseudepigrapha*.

33. Nevertheless, this figure has moved a long way from the companion of Jeremiah, as Wright, *Baruch Ben Neriah*, demonstrates admirably. The fidelity to the sacred story in the two apocalypses extends to complete silence about the devil, a figure who barely appears in the Hebrew Bible. This convenient explanation for evil is not seized by either author, for both of whom an evil heart plays the role of villain—although one could argue that the mythical Behemoth and Leviathan approximate the devil's function. The contrast with early Christian literature in this regard could scarcely be greater.

CHAPTER II

1. Pioneer research into ancient iconography has been done by Othmar Keel, *The Symbolism of the Biblical World: Ancient Near Eastern Iconography and the Book of Psalms*, trans. Timothy J. Hallett (Winona Lake, Ind.: Eisenbrauns, 1997).

2. YHWH's overriding of the pharaoh's repentant attitude is paralleled in other stories—for example, that of the prophets in Ahab's court (1 Kgs 22:19–23). The articulation of a principle concerning this matter in Isa 6:9–13 and Mark 4:12 suggests that consequence was understood as intention: if something occurred, YHWH must have desired it.

3. On the tragic results of the biblical condemnation of witches, see Hedwig Meyer-Wilmes, "Persecuting Witches in the Name of Reason: An Analysis of Western Rationality," in *The Fascination of Evil*, ed. David Tracy and Hermann Häring, *Concilium* 1998/1 (London: Student Christian Movement; Maryknoll, N.Y.: Orbis, 1998), 11–17.

4. I use this language in James L. Crenshaw, *A Whirlpool of Torment: Israelite Traditions of God as an Oppressive Presence* (Philadelphia: Fortress, 1984). For discussion in the present volume, see chapters 3 and 5.

5. Edward L. Greenstein, "Deconstruction and Biblical Narrative," *Prooftexts. A Journal of Jewish Literary History* 9 (1989): 63.

6. The metaphor of divine shepherd, widely employed in the ancient Near East, labored under obvious difficulty, for its human analogy embraced both virtuous and wicked people (cf. Zech 11:4–17).

7. Jack Miles, *God: A Biography* (New York: Knopf, 1995), 308–28; R. N. Whybray, "Shall Not the Judge of All the Earth Do What Is Just? God's Oppression of the Innocent in the Old Testament," in *Shall Not the Judge of All the Earth Do What Is Right? Studies on the Nature of God in Tribute to James L. Crenshaw*, ed. David Penchansky and Paul L. Redditt (Winona Lake, Ind.: Eisenbrauns, 2000), 1–20; David Penchansky, *What Rough Beast? Images of God in the Hebrew Bible* (Louisville: Westminster John Knox, 1999); and Otto Kaiser, "*Deus Absconditus* and *Deus Revelatus*: Three Difficult Narratives in the Pentateuch," in *Shall Not the Judge of All the Earth Do*

What Is Right? ed. Penchansky and Redditt, 73–88. Virtually every article in this volume relates to the issue under discussion here.

8. Although such hostile conduct makes up only a small portion of the Bible, YHWH's insatiable appetite for punishment and revenge, together with his pride and constant complaining about Israel's complaints, strikes readers as less than godlike.

9. James L. Crenshaw, *Prophetic Conflict: Its Effect upon Israelite Religion* (Berlin: de Gruyter, 1971).

10. The distinction between the actual religion of ancient Israelites and the authorized account has assumed considerable significance as our knowledge of that world increases, thanks to inscriptions and more sophisticated models for studying the ancient Near East.

11. Even if every instance of divine testing produced desirable results, we could question the pedagogy. Søren Kierkegaard's reflections on the offering of Isaac highlight this issue (*Fear and Trembling* [Garden City, N.Y.: Doubleday, 1941]).

12. The Anselmic theory of the atonement carries a connotation of payment for sin, which raises the question, To whom? Moreover, it assumes the validity of vicarious sacrifice, as well as a high Christology that was alien to the earliest disciples.

13. The exquisite text in Joel 3:1–2, cited in Acts 2:17–18, breaks the shackles of gender, class, and age without overcoming ethnic limitations. See James L. Crenshaw, *Joel* (New York: Doubleday, 1995), 163–72.

14. As Peter Berger and Thomas Luckman, *The Social Construction of Reality: A Treatise in the Social Construction of Knowledge* (Garden City, N.Y.: Doubleday, 1966), perceived with great clarity, humans construct a worldview, which then exercises remarkable power over them. Whereas theological analyses like that of Friedrich Schleiermacher openly acknowledge the anthropological base, Karl Barth's approach substitutes a human story of divine revelation for a feeling of absolute dependence.

15. Ludwig Feuerbach, *The Essence of Christianity* (New York: Harper, 1957), recognized an intimate connection between human desire and the imaging of deity.

16. The exact meaning of the Hebrew phrase *'ehyeh 'asher 'ehyeh* is much disputed, although scholars suggest several possibilities, implying essence, causality, presence, sufficiency, and a force of nature.

17. Samuel E. Balentine, *The Hidden God: The Hiding of the Face of God in the Old Testament* (Oxford: Oxford University Press, 1983).

18. A modicum of comfort can be found in that the Bible has no equivalent of the ancient Mesopotamian myth about drunken gods competing to create the most hideous monster or of King Lear's cynical observation "As flies to wanton boys are we. The gods have created us for sport."

19. Certain affinities between this depiction of YHWH and process theology readily come to mind, for the biblical God learns from interaction with humans and responds to their decisions.

20. The name Job may be translated "inveterate foe."

21. A variant of this story involves a vision of an angel by Teresa of Avila, but the point is the same.

22. Johannes Hempel, "The Contents of the Literature," in *Record and Revelation:*

Essays on the Old Testament by the Members of the Society for Old Testament Study, ed H. Wheeler Robinson (Oxford: Clarendon, 1938), 73.

23. Ellen van Wolde, *Mr. and Mrs. Job*, trans. John Bowden (London: SCM, 1997), 25–26.

24. Nahum Glatzer, "The Book of Job and Its Interpreters," in *Biblical Motifs*, ed. Alexander Altmann (Cambridge, Mass.: Harvard University Press, 1966), 197–220.

25. Gabrielle Oberhänsli-Widmer, *Hiob in jüdischer Antike und Moderne: Die Wirkungsgeschichte Hiobs in der jüdischen Literatur* (Neukirchen-Vluyn: Neukirchener, 2003), and Adelheid Hausen, *Hiob in der französischen Literatur* (Bern: Herbert Lang; Frankfurt am Main: Peter Lang, 1972).

26. Such openness is in direct contrast to the present liturgical silencing of Job's dissent, church readings that entirely omit the questioning dimension of the book. Philippe Rouillard, "The Figure of Job in the Liturgy: Indignation, Resignation, or Silence?" in *Job and the Silence of God*, ed. Christian Duquoc and Casiano Floristán (New York: Concilium, 1983), 8–12.

27. For further detail, see James L. Crenshaw, *Urgent Advice and Probing Questions: Collected Writings on Old Testament Wisdom* (Macon, Ga.: Mercer University Press, 1995), 426–98; Crenshaw, *Old Testament Wisdom: An Introduction*, revised and enlarged (Louisville: Westminster John Knox, 1998), 89–115; and Crenshaw, "Job," in *The Oxford Bible Commentary*, ed. John Barton and John Muddiman (Oxford: Oxford University Press, 2001), 331–55.

28. This remarkable assertion resembles that in Ps 50:10–12, which concludes with the words "for the world, and everything in it, belongs to me."

29. Carol A. Newsom, "The Book of Job," *New Interpreter's Bible* 4:627–29.

30. The first systematic philosopher of Judaism, Saadia ben Joseph (882–942), known—as head of one of the two ancient Talmudic academies of Babylon—as Saadia Gaon, argued that because creation was an act of pure grace there could be no question of God's "shortchanging" mortals. In short, Saadia believed that God gave being where none was needed, then enabled all creatures to pursue their own good within an environment that was so constituted to make that possible. The basis of Saadia's argument was nature. His theodicy is thus universal, for nature has no favorites, nor is it moral. Because the grace that is manifest in creation extends universally, God is just. See Saadia ben Joseph, *The Book of Theodicy: Translation and Commentary on the Book of Job*, trans. L. E. Goodman (New Haven, Conn.: Yale University Press, 1988).

Select Bibliography

Ackerman, James. "An Exegetical Study of Psalm 82." Ph.D. diss., Harvard University, 1966.

Adams, Marilyn McCord, and Robert Merrihew Adams, eds. *The Problem of Evil*. Oxford: Oxford University Press, 1990.

Aitken, James K. "Divine Will and Providence." In *Ben Sira's God*, ed. Renate Egger-Wenzel. Berlin: de Gruyter, 2002, 282–301.

Albertz, Rainer. *A History of Israelite Religion in the Old Testament Period*. 2 vols. Louisville: Westminster John Knox, 1994.

———. *Persönliche Frömmigkeit und offizielle Religion: Religionsinterner Pluralismus in Israel und Babylon*. Stuttgart: Calwer, 1978.

———. "Der sozialgeschichtliche Hintergrund des Hiobbuches und der 'Babylonischen Theodizee.'" In *Die Botschaft und die Boten: Festschrift für Hans Walter Wolff zum 70. Geburtstag*, ed. Jörg Jeremias and Lothar Perlitt, 349–72. Neukirchen-Vluyn: Neukirchener, 1981.

Anderson, Gary A. *The Genesis of Perfection: Adam and Eve in Jewish and Christian Imagination*. Louisville: Westminster John Knox, 2001.

Anshen, Ruth Nanda. *The Reality of the Devil: Evil in Man*. New York: Harper & Row, 1988.

Assmann, Jan. *Ägypten: Theologie und Frömmigkeit einer frühen Hochkultur*. Stuttgart: Kohlhammer, 1984.

Atkinson, Kenneth. "Theodicy in the Psalms of Solomon." In *Theodicy in the World of the Bible*, ed. Laato and de Moor, 546–75.

Auerbach, Erich. *Mimesis*. Princeton, N.J.: Princeton University Press, 1953.

Balentine, Samuel E. *The Hidden God: The Hiding of the Face of God in the Old Testament*. Oxford: Oxford University Press, 1983.

———. *Prayer in the Hebrew Bible*. Minneapolis: Fortress, 1993.

———. "Prayer in the Wilderness Traditions: In Pursuit of Divine Justice." *Hebrew Annual Review* 9 (1985): 53–74.

———. "Prayers for Justice in the Old Testament: Theodicy and Theology." *Catholic Biblical Quarterly* 51 (2001): 597–616.

———. "Who Will Be Job's Redeemer?" *Perspectives in Religious Studies* 26 (1999): 269–89.

Barr, James. *The Concept of Biblical Theology.* Minneapolis: Fortress, 1999.

Barton, John. *Oracles of God: Perceptions of Ancient Prophecy in Israel after the Exile.* New York: Oxford University Press, 1986.

———. *Understanding Old Testament Ethics: Approaches and Explorations.* Louisville: Westminster John Knox, 2003.

Batto, Bernard F. *Slaying the Dragon: Mythmaking in the Biblical Tradition.* Louisville: Westminster John Knox, 1992.

Becker, Ernest. *The Denial of Death.* New York: Free Press, 1973.

Beentjes, Pancratius C. "Theodicy in the Wisdom of Ben Sira." In *Theodicy in the World of the Bible,* ed. Laato and de Moor, 509–24.

Bellinger, W. H., and William R. Farmer, eds. *Jesus and the Suffering Servant: Isaiah 53 and Christian Origins.* Harrisburg: Trinity, 1998.

Berger, Peter. *The Sacred Canopy.* Garden City, N.Y.: Doubleday, 1967.

Berkovits, Eliezer. *Faith after the Holocaust.* New York: Ktav, 1973.

Berlin, Adele. *Zephaniah.* New York: Doubleday, 1994.

Bernhardt, Reinhold. "Die Erfahrung des Tragischen als Herausforderung für die Theologie: Versuch zur Theodizee." *Theologische Zeitschrift* 59 (2003): 248–70.

Berquist, Jon L. *Judaism in Persia's Shadow: A Social and Historical Approach.* Minneapolis: Fortress, 1995.

Beuken, W. A. M., ed. *The Book of Job.* Leuven: Leuven University Press, 1994.

Birnbaum, David. *God and Evil.* Hoboken, N.J.: Ktav, 1989.

Blumenthal, David R. "Confronting the Character of God: Text and Praxis." In *God in the Fray: A Tribute to Walter Brueggemann,* ed. Tod Linafelt and Timothy K. Beal, 38–51. Minneapolis: Fortress, 1998.

———. *Facing the Abusing God: A Theology of Protest.* Louisville: Westminster John Knox, 1993.

Boxel, P. W. van. "Man's Behaviour and God's Justice in early Jewish Traditions: Some Observations." In *Knowledge of God in the Graeco-Roman World,* ed. R. van der Broek and J. Mansfield. Leiden: Brill, 1988.

Boyd, Gregory A. *Satan and the Problem of Evil: Constructing a Trinitarian Warfare Theodicy.* Downers Grove, Ill.: InterVarsity, 2001.

Bricker, Daniel P. "Innocent Suffering in Mesopotamia." *Tyndale Bulletin* 51 (2000): 193–214.

Brown, William P. *Character in Crisis: A Fresh Approach to the Wisdom Literature of the Old Testament.* Grand Rapids, Mich.: Eerdmans, 1996.

———. *Seeing the Psalms: A Theology of Metaphor.* Louisville: Westminster John Knox, 2002.

Brueggemann, Walter. "Some Aspects of Theodicy in Old Testament Faith." *Perspectives in Religious Studies* 26 (1999): 253–68.

———. "Theodicy in a Social Dimension." *Journal for the Study of the Old Testament* 33 (1985): 3–25.

Buber, Martin. "The Heart Determines: Psalm 73." In *Theodicy in the Old Testament,* ed. Crenshaw, 109–18.

Bucellati, Giorgio. "Wisdom and Not: The Case of Mesopotamia." *Journal of the American Oriental Society* 101 (1981): 35–47.

Burkes, Shannon. *Death in Qoheleth and Egyptian Biographies of the Late Period.* Atlanta: Society of Biblical Literature, 1999.

Carny, Pin'has. "Theodicy in the Book of Qohelet." In *Justice and Righteousness: Biblical Themes and their influence,* ed. H. G. Reventlow and Y. Hoffman. Sheffield: Sheffield Academic Press, 1992.

Caspi, Mishael Maswari, and Sascha Benjamin Cohen. *The Binding [Aqedah] and Its Transformations in Judaism and Islam.* Lewiston, N.Y. Mellen Biblical Press, 1995.

Charlesworth, J. H., ed. *Old Testament Pseudepigrapha.* 2 vols. New York: Doubleday, 1983.

Chilton, Bruce. "Theodicy in the Targumim." In *Theodicy in the World of the Bible,* ed. Laato and de Moor, 728–52.

Chin, Catherine. "Job and the Injustice of God: Implicit Arguments in Job." *Journal for the Study of the Old Testament* 64 (1994): 91–101.

Collins, John J. "Apocalyptic Eschatology as the Transcendence of Death." *Catholic Biblical Quarterly* 36 (1974): 33–35.

———. *The Apocalyptic Imagination: An Introduction to the Jewish Matrix of Christianity.* New York: Crossroad, 1984.

———. *Does the Bible Justify Violence?* Minneapolis: Fortress, 2004.

———. *Jewish Wisdom in the Hellenistic Age.* Louisville: Westminster John Knox, 1997.

Cooper, Alan. "In Praise of Divine Caprice: The Significance of the Book of Jonah." In *Among the Prophets: Language, Image, and Structure in the Prophetic Writings,* ed. Philip R. Davies and David J. A. Clines, 144–63. Sheffield: Journal for the Study of the Old Testament Press, 1993.

———. "Reading and Misreading the Prologue of Job." *Journal for the Study of the Old Testament* 46 (1990): 67–79.

Cover, Robin C. "Sin, Sinners." *Anchor Bible Dictionary* 6: 31–40.

Crenshaw, James L. "The Book of Sirach." *New Interpreters Bible* 5: 601–867.

———. "The Concept of God in Old Testament Wisdom." In *In Search of Wisdom,* ed. Leo G. Perdue, B. B. Scott, and W. J. Wiseman, 1–18. Louisville: Westminster John Knox, 1993 (= *Urgent Advice and Probing Questions,* 191–205).

———. *Ecclesiastes.* Philadelphia: Westminster, 1987.

———. *Education in Ancient Israel: Across the Deadening Silence.* New York: Doubleday, 1998.

———. "The Expression *mî yôdē'a* in the Hebrew Bible." *Vetus Testamentum* 36 (1986): 274–88 (= *Urgent Advice and Probing Questions,* 279–91).

————. "Flirting with the Language of Prayer (Job 14: 13–17)." In *Worship and the Hebrew Bible: Essays in Honor of John T. Willis,* ed. M. P. Graham, R. R. Marrs, and S. L. McKenzie. Sheffield: Sheffield Academic Press, 1999.

————. *Hymnic Affirmation of Divine Justice: The Doxologies of Amos and Related Texts in the Old Testament.* Missoula, Mont.: Scholars Press, 1975.

————. "Impossible Questions, Sayings, and Tasks." In *Gnomic Wisdom,* ed. Crossan (= *Urgent Advice and Probing Questions,* 265–78).

————. "Introduction: The Shift from Theodicy to Anthropodicy." In *Theodicy in the Old Testament,* 1–16 (= *Urgent Advice and Probing Questions,* 141–54).

————. "Job." In *The Oxford Bible Commentary,* ed. J. Barton and J. Muddiman. Oxford: Oxford University Press, 2001.

————. "Job, Book of." *Urgent Advice and Probing Questions,* 426–48.

————. *Joel.* New York: Doubleday, 1995.

————. "A Liturgy of Wasted Opportunity: Am 4:6–12; Isa 9:7–10: 4." *Semitics* 1 (1971): 27–37.

————. *Old Testament Wisdom: An Introduction.* Revised and enlarged. Louisville: Westminster John Knox, 1998.

————. *The Psalms: An Introduction.* Grand Rapids, Mich.: Eerdmans, 2001.

————. "Popular Questioning of the Justice of God in Ancient Israel." *Zeitschrift für die alttestamentliche Wissenschaft* 82: (1970): 380–95 (= *Urgent Advice and Probing Questions,* 175–90).

————. "The Problem of Theodicy in Sirach: On Human Bondage." *Journal of Biblical Literature* 94 (1975): 47–64 (= *Urgent Advice and Probing Questions,* 155–74).

————. *Prophetic Conflict: Its Effect upon Israelite Religion.* Berlin: de Gruyter, 1971.

————. "Qoheleth's Understanding of Intellectual Inquiry." In *Qohelet in the Context of Wisdom,* ed. Antoon Schoors. Leuven: Leuven University Press, 1998, 205–24.

————. "The Restraint of Reason, the Humility of Prayer." In *The Echoes of Many Texts: Reflections on Jewish and Christian Traditions. Essays in Honor of Lou H. Silberman,* ed. William G. Dever and J. Edward Wright, 81–97. Atlanta: Scholars Press, 1997 (= *Urgent Advice and Probing Questions,* 206–21).

————. "The Shadow of Death in Qoheleth." In *Israelite* Wisdom: Theological and Literary Essays in Honor of Samuel Terrien, ed. J. G. Gammie et al. Missoula, Mont.: Scholars Press, 1978 (= *Urgent Advice and Probing Questions,* 573–85).

————. "The Sojourner Has Come to Play the Judge: Theodicy on Trial." In *God in the Fray: A Tribute to Walter Brueggemann,* ed. Tod Linafelt and Timothy K. Beal, 83–92. Minneapolis: Fortress, 1998.

————. "Suffering." In *The Oxford Companion to the Bible,* ed. Bruce M. Metzger and Michael D. Coogan, 718–19. Oxford: Oxford University Press, 1993.

————. "Theodicy." In *Anchor Bible Dictionary.* Edited by D. N. Freedman. 6:444–47. 6 vols. New York: Anchor, 1992.

————. "Theodicy and Prophetic Literature." In *Theodicy in the World of the Bible,* ed. Laato and de Moor, 236–55.

————. "Theodicy in the Book of the Twelve." In *Thematic Threads in the Book of the Twelve,* ed. Paul L. Redditt and Aaron Schart, 175–91. Berlin: de Gruyter, 2003.

———. ed. *Theodicy in the Old Testament*. Philadelphia: Fortress; London: Society for the Propagation of Christian Knowledge, 1983.

———. "Theodicy, Theology, and Philosophy: Early Israel and Judaism." In *Religions of the Ancient World: A Guide*, ed. Sarah Iles Johnston, 537–39. Cambridge: Harvard University Press, 2004.

———. *Urgent Advice and Probing Questions: Collected Writings on Old Testament Wisdom*. Macon, Ga.: Mercer University Press, 1995.

———. *A Whirlpool of Torment: Israelite Traditions of God as an Oppressive Presence*. Philadelphia: Fortress, 1984.

———. "Who Knows What YHWH Will Do? The Character of God in the Book of Joel," In *Fortunate the Eyes That See: Essays in Honor of David Noel Freedman*, ed. Astrid Beck et al., 185–96. Grand Rapids, Mich.: Eerdmans, 1995.

Crüsemann, Frank. "The Unchangeable World: The 'Crisis of Wisdom' in Koheleth." In *The God of the Lowly: Socio-historical Interpretations of the Bible*, ed. Willy Schottroff and Wolfgang Stegemann, trans. Matthew J. O'Connell. Maryknoll, N.Y.: Orbis, 1984.

Davies, W. D., and Louis Finkelstein, eds. *Cambridge History of Judaism*, vol. 1. Cambridge: Clarendon 1984.

Davis, Ellen F. *Getting Involved with God: Rediscovering the Old Testament*. Cambridge, Mass.: Cowley, 2001.

———. "Self-consciousness and Conversation: Reading Genesis 22." *Bulletin for Biblical Research* (1991): 27–40.

Day, John. *God's Conflict with the Dragon and the Sea*. Cambridge: Cambridge University Press, 1985.

Day, Peggy L. *An Adversary in Heaven: Satan in the Hebrew Bible*. Atlanta: Scholars Press, 1988.

Dietrich, W., and C. Link. *Die dunklen Seiten Gottes*. Neukirchen-Vluyn: Neukirchener, 2000.

Duke, David Nelson. "Theodicy at the Turn of Another Century: An Introduction." *Perspectives in Religious Studies* 26 (1999): 241–48.

Eagleton, Terry. *Literary Theory: An Introduction*, 2nd ed. Oxford: Blackwell, 1996.

Ebach, Jürgen. *Gott im Wort: Drei Studien zur biblischen Exegese und Hermeneutik*. Neukirchen-Vluyn: Neukirchener, 1997.

———. *Hiobs Post: Gesammelte Aufsätze zum Hiobbuch zu Themen biblischer Theologie und zur Methodik der Exegese*. Neukirchen-Vluyn: Neukirchener, 1995.

Eichrodt, Walther. "Faith in Providence and Theodicy in the Old Testament." In *Theodicy in the Old Testament*, ed. Crenshaw, 17–41.

———. *Theology of the Old Testament*, 2 vols. Philadelphia: Westminster, 1961, 1967.

Eliade, M., ed. *The Encyclopedia of Religion*. 16 vols. New York, 1987.

Farley, Wendy. *Tragic Vision and Divine Compassion: A Contemporary Theodicy*. Louisville: Westminster John Knox, 1990.

Feininger, Bernd. " 'Denk ich an Gott, muss ich seufzen' Ps 77, 4: Schwierigkeiten und Hoffnungen in unserem Umgang mit den dunklen Seiten des Alttestamentlichen Gottesbildes." *Bibel und Kirche* 46 (1991): 152–58.

Fiddes, Paul. *The Creative Suffering of God*. Oxford: Clarendon, 1988.

Fischer, Alexander A. *Skepsis oder Furcht Gottes? Studien zur Komposition und Theologie des Buches Kohelet*. Berlin: de Gruyter, 1997.

Fishbane, Michael. *Biblical Faith and Rabbinic Mythmaking*. Oxford: Oxford University Press, 2003.

———. *The Garments of Torah: Essays in Biblical Hermeneutics*. Bloomington: University of Indiana Press, 1989.

———. *Text and Texture: Close Readings of Selected Biblical Texts*. New York: Schocken, 1979.

———. *Biblical Intepretation in Ancient Israel*. Oxford: Clarendon, 1985.

Foster, Benjamin R. *From Distant Days: Myths, Tales, and Poetry of Ancient Mesopotamia*. Bethesda, Md.: CDL, 1995.

Fox, Michael V. *A Time to Tear Down and a Time to Build Up: A Re-reading of Ecclesiastes*. Grand Rapids, Mich.: Eerdmans, 1999.

Franklyn, Paul. "The Sayings of Agur in Proverbs 30: Piety or Skepticism?" *Zeitschrift für die alttestamentliche Wissenschaft* 95 (1983): 238–52.

Freedman, D. N., ed. *Anchor Bible Dictionary*. 6 vols. New York: Doubleday, 1992.

Fretheim, Terence E. "Jonah and Theodicy." *Zeitschrift für de alttestamentliche Wissenschaft* 90 (1978): 227–37.

———. *The Suffering of God*. Philadelphia: Fortress, 1984.

Fretheim, Terence E., and Curtis L. Thompson, eds. *God, Evil, and Suffering: Essays in Honor of Paul R. Sponheim*. St. Paul, Minn.: Luther Seminary, 2000.

Frost, Stanley Brice. "The Death of Josiah: A Conspiracy of Silence." *Journal of Biblical Literature* 87 (1968): 369–82.

Garrison, Roman. *Why Are You Silent, Lord?* Sheffield: Sheffield Academic Press, 2000.

Geller, Stephen A. " 'Where Is Wisdom?' A Literary Study of Job 28 in Its Settings." In *Judaic Perspectives on Ancient Israel*, ed. J. Neusner, B. A. Levine, and E. S. Frerichs. Philadelphia: Fortress, 1987.

Gerstenberger, Erhard S., and Wolfgang Schrage. *Suffering*. Nashville: Abingdon, 1980.

Gese, Hartmut. "The Crisis of Wisdom in Koheleth." In *Theodicy in the Old Testament*, ed. Crenshaw, 141–53.

Gilbert, Maurice. *La Critique des dieux dans le livre de la Sagesse*. Rome: Pontifical Biblical Institute, 1973.

———. "God, Sin, and Mercy: Sirach 15:11–18:14." In *Ben Sira's God: Proceedings of the International Ben Sira Conference, Durham, Ushaw College, 2001*, ed. Renate Egger-Wenzel, 118–35.

Glatzer, Nahum. "The Book of Job and Its Interpreters." In *Biblical Motifs*, ed. A. Altmann. Cambridge, Mass.: Harvard University Press, 1966.

Gillman, Neil. *The Death of Death: Resurrection and Immortality in Jewish Thought*. Woodstock, Vt.: Jewish Lights, 1997.

Girard, René. *Job: The Victim of His People*. Stanford, Calif.: Stanford University Press, 1987.

———. *Violence and the Sacred*. Baltimore: Johns Hopkins University Press, 1977.

Gnuse, Robert. *Heilsgeschichte as a Model for Biblical Theology.* Lanham, Md.: University Press of America, 1989.

Goldstein, Jonathan A. *11 Maccabees.* Garden City, N.Y.: Doubleday, 1983.

Good, Edwin M. *In Turns of Tempest: A Reading of Job with a Translation.* Stanford: Stanford University Press, 1990.

Goodman, L. E. *The Book of Theodicy: Translation and Commentary on the Book of Job by Saadiah Ben Joseph Al-Fayyūmī.* New Haven, Conn.: Yale University Press, 1988.

Gowan, Donald E. *The Triumph of Faith in Habakkuk.* Atlanta: John Knox, 1976.

Green, R. M. "Theodicy." In *The Encyclopedia of Religion,* ed. M. Eliade, 14:430–31. 16 vols. New York: Macmillan, 1987.

Greenberg, Moshe, ed. *Studies in the Bible and Jewish Thought.* Philadelphia: Jewish Publication Society, 1995.

Griffin, David Ray. *Evil Revisited: Responses and Reconsiderations.* Albany: State University of New York Press, 1991.

Gross, Walter, and Karl-Josef Kuschel. *"Ich schaffe Finsternis und Unheil!" Ist Gott verantwortlich für das Übel?* Mainz: M. Grünewald, 1992.

Habel, Norman C. *The Book of Job.* Philadelphia: Fortress, 1984.

Hayman, A. Peter. "Qohelet and the Book of Creation." *Journal for the Study of the Old Testament.* 50 (1991): 93–111.

Hempel, Johannes. "Das theologische Problem des Hiob." *Zeitschrift für sytematische Theologie* 6 (1929); reprinted in Johannes Hempel, *Apoxysmata.* Berlin: de Gruyter, 1961.

Heschel, Abraham Joshua. *The Prophets.* New York: Harper & Row, 1962.

Höffken, Peter. "Genesis 22 als religions pädagogisches Problem." In *Frömmigkeit und Freiheit: theologische, ethische, und seelsorgerliche Anfragen,* ed. Friedrich Wintzer, Henning Schröer, and Johannes Heide. Rheinbach-Merzbach: CMZ, 1995.

———. "Werden und Vergehen der Götter." *Theologische Zeitschrift* 39 (1983): 129–37.

Hoffman, Yair. *A Blemished Perfection: The Book of Job in Context.* Sheffield: Sheffield Academic Press, 1996.

———. "The Creativity of Theodicy." In *Justice and Righteousness: Biblical Themes and Their Influence,* ed. Reventlow and Hoffman, 115–30.

Holmén, Tom. "Theodicean Motifs in the New Testament." In *Theodicy in the World of the Bible,* ed. Laato and de Moor, 605–51.

Houtman, Cornelis. "Theodicy in the Pentateuch." In *Theodicy in the World of the Bible,* ed. Laato and de Moor, 151–82.

Hunter, Cornelius. *Darwin's God: Evolution and the Problem of Evil.* Grand Rapids, Mich.: Brazos, 2002.

Huxley, Julian. "The Creed of a Scientific Humanist." In *The Meaning of Life,* ed. E. D. Klemke, 2nd ed., 78–83. New York: Oxford University Press, 2001.

Illman, Karl-Johan. "Theodicy in Job." In *Theodicy in the World of the Bible,* ed. Laato and de Moor, 304–33.

Janowski, Bernd, and Peter Stuhlmacher, eds. *Der leidende Gottesknecht.* Tübingen: Mohr Siebeck, 1996.

Japhet, Sara. "Theodicy in Ezra-Nehemiah and Chronicles." In *Theodicy in the World of the Bible*, ed. Laato and de Moor, 429–69.

Jenni, Ernst, ed., with assistance from C. Westermann. *Theological Lexicon of the Old Testament*. Trans. M. E. Biddle. 3 vols. Peabody, Mass.: Hendrickson, 1997.

Jeremias, Jörg. *The Book of Amos*. Louisville: Westminster John Knox, 1995.

Jüngling, Hans-Winfried. *Der Tod der Götter: Eine Untersuchung zu Psalm 82*. Stuttgart: Kathölisches Bibelwerk, 1969.

Kaiser, Otto. "*Deus Absconditus* and *Deus Revelatus*: Three Difficult Narratives in the Pentateuch." In *Shall Not the Judge of All the Earth do What Is Right?* ed. Penchansky and Redditt, 73–88.

Katz, S. T. "Holocaust, Judaic Theology, and Theodicy." In *The Encyclopedia of Judaism*, ed. Jacob Neusner, A. J. Avery-Peck, and W. Scott Green, 1: 406–20. Leiden: Brill, 2000.

Kautzsch, E., ed. *Gesenius' Hebrew Grammar*. Trans. A. E. Cowley. 2nd ed. Oxford: Clarendon 1910.

Kepnes, Stephen. "Job and Post-Holocaust Theodicy." In *Strange Fire: Reading the Bible after the Holocaust*, ed. Tod Linafelt, 252–66. New York: New York University Press, 2000.

Kierkegaard, Søren. Fear and Trembling. Garden City, N.Y.: Doubleday, 1941.

Klemke, E. D., ed. *The Meaning of Life*. 2nd ed. New York: Oxford University Press, 2000.

Kluger, Rivkah Schärf. *Satan in the Old Testament*. Translated by Hildegard Nagel. Evanston, Ill.: Northwestern University Press, 1967.

Knierim, Rolf. *Die Hauptbegriffe für Sünde im Alten Testament*. Gütersloh: Gütersloher, 1965.

Koch, Klaus. "Is There a Doctrine of Retribution in the Old Testament?" In *Theodicy in the Old Testament*, ed. Crenshaw, 57–87.

Kolarcik, Michael. *The Ambiguity of Death in Wisdom Chapters 1–6: A Study of Literary Structure and Interpretation*. Rome: Editrice Pontificio Instituto Biblico, 1991.

Korpel, Marjo C. A. "Theodicy in the Book of Esther." In *Theodicy and the World of the Bible*, ed. Laato and de Moor, 351–74.

Kraemer, David. *Responses to Suffering in Classical Rabbinic Literature*. New York: Oxford University Press, 1995.

Kuschke, A. "Altbabylonische Texte zum Thema 'Der leidende Gerechte.' " *Theologische Literaturzeitung* 81 (1956): 69–76.

Kushner, Harold S. *When Bad Things Happen to Good People*. New York: Schocken, 1981.

Kutsko, John F. *Between Heaven and Earth: Divine Presence and Absence in the Book of Ezekiel*. Winona Lake, Ind.: Eisenbrauns, 2000.

Laato, Antti. *The Servant of YHWH and Cyrus: A Reinterpretation of the Exilic Messianic Programme in Isaiah 40–55*. Stockholm: Almqvist & Wiksell, 1992.

———. "Theodicy in the Deuteronomistic History." In *Theodicy in the World of the Bible*, ed. Laato and de Moor, 183–235.

Laato, Antti, and Johannes C. de Moor, eds. *Theodicy in the World of the Bible*. Leiden: Brill, 2003.

Lambert, W. G. *Babylonian Wisdom Literature*. Oxford: Clarendon, 1960.

Leaman, Oliver. *Evil and Suffering in Jewish Philosophy*. Cambridge: Cambridge University Press, 1995.

Leibniz, G. W. *Theodicy: Essays on the Goodness of God, the Freedom of Man, and the Origin of Evil*, trans. E. M. Huggard. New Haven: Yale University Press, 1952.

Levenson, Jon D. *Creation and the Persistence of Evil: The Jewish Drama of Divine Omnipotence*. San Francisco: Harper & Row, 1988.

————. *The Death and Resurrection of the Beloved Son: The Transformation of Child Sacrifice in Judaism and Christianity*. New Haven, Conn.: Yale University Press, 1993.

————. "The Sources of Torah: Psalm 119 and the Modes of Revelation in Second Temple Judaism." In *Ancient Israelite Religion*, ed. Patrick D. Miller, Paul D. Hanson, and S. Dean McBride. Philadelphia: Fortress, 1987.

Levinas, Emmanuel. "Postface: Transcendence and Evil." In *Job and the Excess of Evil*, ed. Nemo, 178–82.

Lichtheim, Miriam. *Ancient Egyptian Literature*, 3 vols. Berkeley: University of California Press, 1976.

Lindström, Fredrik. *God and the Origin of Evil: A Contextual Analysis of Alleged Monistic Evidence in the Old Testament*. Lund: Gleerup, 1983.

————. "Theodicy in the Psalms." In *Theodicy in the World of the Bible*, ed. Laato and de Moor, 256–303.

Loprieno, Antonio. "Theodicy in Ancient Egyptian Texts." In *Theodicy in the World of the Bible*, ed. Laato and de Moor, 27–56.

Mandry, Stephen A. *There Is No God! A Study of the Fool in the Old Testament, Particularly in Proverbs and Qoheleth*. Rome: Catholic Book Agency, 1972.

Marböck, Johan. *Weisheit im Wandel: Untersuchungen zur Weisheitstheologie bei Ben Sira*. Bonn: Hanstein, 1971.

Marcus, Joel. *Jesus and the Holocaust: Reflections on Suffering and Hope*. New York: Doubleday, 1997.

Mattingly, Gerald L. "The Pious Sufferer: Mesopotamia's Traditional Theodicy and Job's Counselors." In *The Bible in the Light of Cuneiform Literature: Scripture in Context III*, ed. William Hallo, B. Jones, and Gerald Mattingly, 305–48. Lewiston, N.Y.: Edwin Mellen, 1990.

McGill, Arthur A. *Suffering: A Test of Theological Method*. Philadelphia: Fortress, 1982.

McGlynn, Moyna. *Divine Judgment and Divine Benevolence in the Book of Wisdom*. Tübingen: Mohr Siebeck, 2001.

Mettinger, Tryggve N. *A Farewell to the Servant Songs: A Critical Examination of an Exegetical Axiom*. Lund: Gleerup, 1983.

Meyer-Wilmes, Hedwig. "Persecuting Witches in the Name of Reason: An Analysis of Western Rationality." In *The Fascination of Evil*, ed. D. Tracy and H. Häring, 11–17. London: Student Christian Movement, 1998.

Michel, Andreas. "Ijob und Abraham: Zur Rezeption von Gen 22 in Ijob 1–2 und 42, 7–17." In *Gott, Mensch, Sprache: Schülerfestschrift für Walter Gross zum 60. Geburtstag*, ed. Andreas Michel and Herman-Josef Stipp. St. Ottilien: EOS, 2001.

Miles, Jack. *God: A Biography*. New York: Knopf, 1995.

Miller, Patrick D. *The Religion of Ancient Israel*. London: Society for the Propagation of Christian Knowledge; Louisville: Westminster John Knox, 2000.

Miskotte, Kornelis H. *When the Gods Are Silent*, trans. J. W. Doberstein. New York: Harper & Row, 1967.

Moberly, R. W. L. *The Bible, Theology, and Faith: A Study of Abraham and Jesus*. Cambridge: Cambridge University Press, 2000.

———. "Christ as the Key to Scripture: Genesis 22 Reconsidered." In *He Swore an Oath: Biblical Themes from Genesis 12–50*, ed. R. S. Hess. Grand Rapids, Mich.: Eerdmans, 1994.

———. "The Earliest Commentary on the Akedah." *Vetus Testamentum* 38 (1988): 302–23.

Moor, Johannes C. de. "Theodicy in the Texts of Ugarit." In *Theodicy in the World of the Bible*, ed. Laato and de Moor, 108–50.

Moran, William M. *The Most Magic Word*. Washington, D.C.: Catholic Biblical Association, 2002.

Müller, Hans-Peter. "Die Theodizee und das Buch Hiob." *Neue Zeitschrift für systematische Theologie* 39 (1997): 140–56.

Nasr, Sayyed Hossein. *Knowledge and the Sacred*. Albany: State University of New York Press, 1989.

Nemo, Philippe. *Job and the Excess of Evil*. Pittsburgh, Pa.: Duquesne University Press, 1998.

Neusner, Jacob. "Theodicy in Judaism." In *Theodicy in the World of the Bible*, ed. Laato and de Moor, 685–727.

Newman, Judith H. *Praying by the Book: The Scripturalization of Prayer in Second Temple Judaism*. Atlanta: Scholars Press, 1999.

Newsom, Carol A. "The Book of Job." *New Interpreter's Bible* 4: 317–637.

———. *The Book of Job: A Contest of Moral Imaginations*. Oxford: Oxford University Press, 2003.

———. "The Book of Job." *New Interpreters Bible* 4: 627–29.

Nickelsburg, George W. E. *Jewish Literature between the Bible and Mishnah: A Historical and Literary Introduction*. Philadelphia: Fortress, 1981.

Nicholson, Ernest W. "The Limits of Theodicy as a Theme of the Book of Job." In *Wisdom in Ancient Israel: Essays in Honour of J. A. Emerton*, ed. John Day, Robert P. Gordon, and H. G. M. Williamson, 71–82. Cambridge: Cambridge University Press, 1995.

Pagels, Elaine. *The Origin of Satan*. New York: Oxford University Press, 1995.

Paul, Shalom M. *Amos*. Minneapolis: Fortress, 1991.

———. "Heavenly Tablets and the Book of Life." *Journal of the Ancient Near East of Columbia University* 5 (1973): 345–53.

Penchansky, David. *What Rough Beast? Images of God in the Hebrew Bible*. Louisville: Westminster John Knox, 1999.

Penchansky, David, and Paul L. Redditt, eds. *Shall Not the Judge of All the Earth Do What Is Right? Studies on the Nature of God in Tribute to James L. Crenshaw*. Winona Lake, Ind.: Eisenbrauns, 2000.

Perdue, Leo G. *The Collapse of History: Deconstructing Old Testament Theology*. Minneapolis: Fortress, 1994.

Prato, Gian Luigi. *Il problema della teodicea in Ben Sira: Composizione dei contrari e richiamo alle origini*. Rome: Biblical Institute Press, 1975.

Preuss, Horst Dietrich. " 'Auferstehung' in Texten Alttestamentlicher Apokalyptik (Jes 26, 7–19; Dan 12, 1–4)." In *"Linguistic" Theologie*, ed. Uwe Gerber and Erhardt Güttgemanns. Bonn: Linguistica Biblica, 1972, 103–33.

Price, Reynolds. *Letter to a Man in the Fire: Does God Exist and Does He Care?* New York: Scribner, 1999.

Pritchard, J. B., ed. *Ancient Near Eastern Texts Relating to the Old Testament*. 3rd ed. Princeton, N.J.: Princeton University Press, 1969.

Rad, Gerhard von. *Das Opfer des Abraham*. Munich: Kaiser, 1971.

———. *Old Testament Theology*, 2 vols. New York: Harper & Row, 1965.

———. *Wisdom in Israel*. Nashville, Tenn.: Abingdon, 1972.

Renkema, Johan. "Theodicy in Lamentations." In *Theodicy in the World of the Bible*, ed. Laato and de Moor, 410–28.

Reventlow, Henning Graf. "Righteousness as Order of the World: Some Remarks Towards a Programme." In *Justice and Righteousness*, ed. Reventlow and Hoffman, 163–72.

———. "Basic Issues in the Interpretation of Isaiah 53." In *Jesus and the Suffering Servant: Isaiah 53 and Christian Origins*, ed. W. H. Bellinger and William R. Farmer. Harrisburg: Trinity, 1998.

Reventlow, Henning Graf, and Yair Hoffman, eds. *Justice and Righteousness: Biblical Themes and Their Influence*. Sheffield: Sheffield Academic Press, 1992.

Ricoeur, Paul. *The Symbolism of Evil*. Translated by Emerson Buchanan. Boston: Beacon, 1967.

Rouillard, Philippe. "The Figure of Job in the Liturgy: Indignation, Resignation, or Silence?" In *Job and the Silence of God*, ed. C. Duquoc and C. Floristán, 7–12. New York: Concilium, 1983.

Schmidt, Ludwig. *"De Deo": Studien zur Literaturkritik und Theologie des Buches Jona, des Gesprächs zwischen Abraham und Jahwe in Gen. 18,22ff. und von Hi 1*. Berlin: de Gruyter, 1976.

Sanders, J. A. *Suffering as Divine Discipline in the Old Testament and Post-biblical Judaism*. Rochester, N.Y.: Colgate Rochester Divinity School, 1955.

Schmid, Hans Heinrich. *Gerechtigkeit als Weltordnung.*. Tübingen: Mohr Siebeck, 1968.

———. *Wesen und Geschichte der Weisheit*. Berlin: Töpelmann, 1966.

Schoors, Antoon. "Theodicy in Qohelet." In *Theodicy in the World of the Bible*, ed. Laato and de Moor, 375–409.

Schulweis, Harold M. *Evil and the Morality of God*. Cincinnati: Hebrew Union College Press, 1984.

Schwartz, Regina. *The Book and the Text: The Bible and Literary Theory*. Oxford: Blackwell, 1990.

Schwarz, Hans. *Evil: A Historical and Theological Perspective*. Translated by Mark W. Worthing. Minneapolis: Fortress, 1995.

Scoralick, Ruth. *Gottes Güte und Gottes Zorn: Die Gottesprädikationen in Exodus 34,6f. und ihre intertextuellen Beziehungen zum Zwölfprophetenbuch*. Freiburg: Herder, 2002.

Shupak, Nili. *Where Can Wisdom Be Found? The Sage's Language in the Bible and in Ancient Egyptian Literature*. Göttingen: Vandenhoeck & Ruprecht, 1993.

Simojoki, Anssi. "The Book of Revelation." In *Theodicy in the World of the Bible*, ed. Laato and de Moor, 652–84.

Sitzler, Dorothea. *"Vorwurf gegen Gott": Ein religiöses Motiv im alten Orient (Ägypten und Mesopotamien)*. Wiesbaden: Harrassowitz, 1995.

Smith, Mark S. *The Early History of God: Yahweh and the Other Deities in Ancient Israel*, 2nd ed. San Francisco: Harper & Row, 2002.

Soden, Wolfram von. "Das Fragen nach der Gerechtigkeit Gottes im alten Orient." In *Bibel und Alter Orient*. Berlin: de Gruyter, 1985.

Sölle, Dorothee. *Suffering*. Philadelphia: Fortress, 1975.

Spiegel, Shalom. *The Last Trial*. New York: Schocken, 1967.

Stackhouse, Max. *Can God Be Trusted? Faith and the Challenge of Evil*. New York: Oxford University Press, 1998.

Stamm, Jakob Josef. *Das Leiden des Undschuldigen in Babylon und Israel*. Zurich: Zwingli, 1946.

———. "Die Theodizee im Babylon und Israel." *Jaarbericht van het Vooraziatisch-Egyptisch Gezalschap (Genootscnap) ex oriente lux* 9 (1944): 99–107.

Steins, Georg. *Die "Bindung Isaaks im Kanon" (Gen 22): Grundlagen und Programm einer kanonisch-intertextuellen Lektüre*. Freiburg: Herder, 1999.

Stone, Michael E. *Fourth Ezra: A Commentary on the Book of Fourth Ezra*. Minneapolis: Fortress, 1990.

———. "The Way of the Most High and the Injustice of God in 4 Ezra." In *Knowledge of God in the Graeco-Roman World*, ed. R. van der Broeck and J. Mansfield. Leiden: Brill, 1988.

Strauss, Hans. *Hiob, Kapitel 19, 1–42, 17*. Neukirchen-Vluyn: Neukirchener, 1963.

Sutherland, Robert. *Putting God on Trial: The Biblical Book of Job*. Victoria, B.C.: Trafford, 2004.

Sweeney, Marvin A. "Isaiah and Theodicy after the Shoah." In *Strange Fire: Reading the Bible after the Holocaust*, ed. Tod Linafelt, 208–19. New York: New York University Press, 2000.

Swinburne, Richard. *Providence and the Problem of Evil*. Oxford: Clarendon, 1998.

Terrien, Samuel. *The Elusive Presence: Toward a New Biblical Theology*. New York: Harper & Row, 1978.

———. *The Psalms: Strophic Structure and Theological Commentary.* Grand Rapids, Mich.: Eerdmans, 2003.

Thompson, A. L. *Responsibility for Evil in the Theodicy of IV Ezra.* Missoula, Mont.: Scholars Press, 1977.

Tilley, Terrence W. *The Evils of Theodicy.* Eugene, Ore.: Wipf & Stock, 2000.

Toorn, Karel van der, Bob Becking, and Pieter W. van der Horst, eds. *Dictionary of Deities and Demons in the Bible.* 2d ed. Leiden: Brill, 1999.

Towner, W. Sibley. *How God Deals with Evil.* Philadelphia: Westminster, 1976.

Tracy, David, and Hermann Häring, eds. *The Fascination of Evil. Concilium.* 1998/1. London: SCM; Maryknoll, N.Y.: Orbis, 1998.

Turner, Denys. *The Darkness of God.* Cambridge: Cambridge University Press, 1995.

Urbach, Ephraim. *The Sages: Their Concepts and Beliefs.* Jerusalem: Magnes, 1975.

Volgger, David. "Es geht um das Ganze: Gott prüft Abraham (Gen 22, 1–19)." *Biblische Zeitschrift* 45 (2001): 1–19.

Volz, Paul. *Das Dämonische in Jahwe.* Tübingen: Mohr, 1924.

Wahl, Harald-Martin. *Der gerechte Schöpfer: Eine redaktions- und theologiegeschichtliche Untersuchung der Elihureden-Hiob 32–37.* Berlin: de Gruyter, 1993.

Waltke B. K., and O'Connor, M. *An Introduction to Biblical Hebrew Syntax.* Winona Lake Ind., Eisenbrauns 1990.

Weil, Eric. "What Is a Breakthrough in History?" *Daedalus* (Spring 1975): 21–36.

Weinfeld, Moshe. "Job and Its Mesopotamian Parallels: A Typological Analysis." In *Text and Context: Old Testament and Semitic Studies for F. C. Fensham,* ed. Walter Claassen. Sheffield: JSOT Press, 1988.

Weiss, Meir. *The Story of Job's Beginning.* Jerusalem: Magnes, 1983.

Westermann, Claus. *Roots of Wisdom: The Oldest Proverbs of Israel and Other Peoples.* Louisville: Westminster John Knox, 1995.

Wettstein, Howard. "Against Theodicy." *Judaism* 50 (2001): 341–50.

Whybray, R. N. "Shall Not the Judge of All the Earth Do What Is Just? God's Oppression of the Innocent in the Old Testament." In *Shall Not the Judge of All the Earth Do What Is Right? Studies on the Nature of God in Tribute to James L. Crenshaw,* ed. D. Penchansky and P. Redditt, 1–19.

———. " 'A Time to Be Born and a Time to Die': Some Observations on Ecclesiastes 3:2–8." In *Near Eastern Studies Dedicated to H. I. H. Prince Takahito Mikasa,* ed. M. Mori et al. Wiesbaden: Harrassowitz, 1991.

———. *Thanksgiving for a Liberated Prophet: An Interpretation of Isaiah Chapter 53.* Sheffield: JSOT Press, 1978.

Williams, Ronald J. "Theodicy in the Ancient Near East." *Canadian Journal of Theology* 2 (1956): 14–26.

Winston, David. "Theodicy in Ben Sira and Stoic Philosophy." In *Of Scholars, Savants, and Their Texts,* ed. Ruth Link-Salinger, 239–49. New York: Lang, 1989.

———. *The Wisdom of Solomon.* New York: Doubleday, 1979.

Wolde, Ellen J. van. *Mr. and Mrs. Job,* trans. J. Bowden. London: SCM, 1997.

Wright, J. Edward. *Baruch Ben Neriah: From Biblical Scribe to Apocalyptic Seer.* Columbia: University of South Carolina Press, 2003.

————. *The Early History of Heaven.* Oxford: Oxford University Press, 2000.

Zimmer, Tilmann. *Zwischen Tod und Legensgluck: Eine Untersuchung zur Anthropologie Kohelets.* Berlin: de Gruyter, 1999.

Scripture Index

Person Index

Subject Index